The Political Philosophy of Benjamin Franklin

THE POLITICAL PHILOSOPHY OF THE AMERICAN FOUNDERS

Garrett Ward Sheldon, Series Editor

THE POLITICAL PHILOSOPHY OF *Benjamin Franklin*

LORRAINE SMITH PANGLE

The Johns Hopkins University Press
Baltimore

This book was brought to publication with the generous assistance
of a University Co-operative Society Subvention Grant
awarded by the University of Texas at Austin.

Printed in the United States of America on acid-free paper
2 4 6 8 9 7 5 3 1

The Johns Hopkins University Press
2715 North Charles Street
Baltimore, Maryland 21218-4363
www.press.jhu.edu

Library of Congress Cataloging-in-Publication Data

Pangle, Lorraine Smith.
The political philosophy of Benjamin Franklin / Lorraine Smith Pangle.
p. cm. — (The political philosophy of the American founders)
Includes bibliographical references and index.
ISBN-13: 978-0-8018-7931-9 (hardcover : alk. paper)
ISBN-13: 978-0-8018-8666-9 (pbk. : alk. paper)
ISBN-10: 0-8018-7931-0 (hardcover : alk. paper)
ISBN-10: 0-8018-8666-X (pbk. : alk. paper)
1. Franklin, Benjamin, 1706–1790. I. Title.
JC211.F73P36 2007
320.092—dc22
2006101684

A catalog record for this book
is available from the British Library.

FOR

Linda Rabieh

CONTENTS

NOTE ON SOURCES

All references to Franklin's *Autobiography* are to the Leonard Labaree edition (New Haven: Yale University Press, 1964). Unless otherwise noted, all other citations from Franklin's writings are to *The Papers of Benjamin Franklin,* edited by Leonard W. Labaree et al. The digital edition, sponsored by the American Philosophical Society and Yale University and produced by the Packard Humanities Institute, is available online at www.franklinpapers.org. It is searchable by name, date, word, and phrase. Although the online edition reaches to the end of Franklin's life, it is not yet complete for the final years. The print edition, with thirty-seven volumes to date (New Haven: Yale University Press, 1959–), contains material from the almanacs and useful notes and relevant documents not available online. The editors of the *Papers* have been very conservative in attributing to Franklin early unsigned essays from the *Pennsylvania Gazette.* I have followed J. A. Leo Lemay in accepting as authentic some essays that the *Papers* do not include. These are published in Lemay's collection, Franklin, *Writings* (New York: Library of America, 1987), and his attributions are defended in Lemay, *The Canon of Benjamin Franklin, 1722–1776: New Attributions and Reconsiderations* (Newark: University of Delaware Press, 1986).

ACKNOWLEDGMENTS

I had the good fortune to be introduced to Ben Franklin in a fine seminar given many years ago at the University of Chicago by Ralph Lerner and Amy Kass. The idea for this book arose from a Liberty Fund conference on Franklin organized more recently by Michael Zuckert. For their stimulating observations and questions, I am grateful to the participants in that conference, the participants in a pair of workshops on Franklin for school teachers sponsored by the National Endowment for the Humanities, the participants in several workshops for judges sponsored by the George Mason Law School, and faculty who took part in colloquia on Franklin at Villanova University and Notre Dame University. For encouragement in pursuing the project, I am grateful to Henry Tom of the Johns Hopkins University Press. I am indebted to Thomas Pangle and an anonymous reader for the press for their thoughtful suggestions on the manuscript, and to the Earhart Foundation for funding to complete it. But for making this book such an enjoyable one to research, I can thank only Ben himself.

The Political Philosophy of Benjamin Franklin

INTRODUCTION

BENJAMIN FRANKLIN is and has always been the most American of Americans. He embodies the best of what we are and what we aspire to be. He is a wellspring of homespun wisdom, a self-made man, hopeful, clever, skeptical, and wry, a fierce lover of liberty and plain dealing, thoroughly independent, and forever inventing new projects for the common good. How could we not love the man who carries our virtues to such charming perfection? Franklin has been much commented upon, much praised and imitated, and sometimes fiercely reviled in every century since his birth; but seldom has there been such a flurry of fascination with this national icon as there is today, with the publication of a trove of recent volumes on the life he lived and the story he made of it.

All this attention is well deserved. The most famous man of his age, Franklin was influential in an amazing number of ways: as a founder of fire departments and libraries, sanitation projects, militias, hospitals, and a great university; as the inventor of wood-burning stoves, lightning rods, and matching grants; as the author of the popular *Poor Richard's Almanack* and of the runaway best seller *The Way to Wealth;* and as a scientist of almost the very first rank, who laid the foundation for the modern understanding of electricity. But it was in politics that Franklin made the greatest impact and to politics that he gave the lion's share of his energies. Thus, it is curious that while so much attention has been paid to Franklin's life, so little has hitherto been given to his political thought.

To begin to repair that neglect, this volume offers an introduction to Franklin's political philosophy, using his own inimitable words as much as possible but giving them an order and system that he did not. Order was never Franklin's strong point, as he will tell us himself. The work aims also both to illuminate important congruences and contrasts between Franklin and other political thinkers and to provide the best response we can make to Franklin's major critics.

But perhaps it would be well to confront at the outset the possibility that even Franklin himself did not regard his political thought as worth systematizing or defending. He says almost as much in a 1767 letter to his sister (although he also gives us ample reason to be skeptical of all Franklinian displays of modesty).

> You desire me to send you all the political Pieces I have been the Author of. I have never kept them. They were most of them written occasionally for transient Purposes, and having done their Business, they die and are forgotten. I could as easily make a Collection for you of all the past Parings of my Nails.[1]

The neglect of Franklin's political philosophy seems to stem from a general concurrence with this judgment, a belief that in political matters Franklin was a man of action and not of systematic or profound theorizing.[2] And there is something to be said for this view. On the plane of political action, Franklin's importance can scarcely be overrated. Once he came to support American independence from Britain, his influence was so weighty that the British suspected him of being the prime source of all their troubles in the colonies. His deft negotiations for French aid were vital to American success in the Revolutionary War, and his equally skillful handling of the peace treaty ensured, against the wishes of enemies and even European friends, that the new United States would have the territory and economic strength to become a great nation. But Franklin never wrote a political treatise or even devised an important political doctrine. Nor was he inclined, as Jefferson and Madison were, to speak and think in terms of universal human rights. Even among Franklin's practical proposals for political reform, most bore little direct fruit; this is true of his efforts to overturn proprietary government in Pennsylvania, his advocacy of a continental union loyal to the British crown, his unflagging efforts over many years to prevent the breach with Britain, and his long-avowed support for unicameral legislatures, plural executives, and prohibitions on salaries for elected officials.

Franklin's modesty and his failings notwithstanding, his writings on these matters are well worth reading; they are full of fascinating reflections on human nature, on the character of good leadership, and on why government is such a messy and problematic business. Franklin has much of interest to say about political institutions and constitutional arrangements as well. But at the heart of his political vision is a view of democratic citizenship, a rich and subtle understanding of the habits and qualities of heart and mind that need to be fostered in order to sustain liberty and, Franklin insists, to support the way of life best suited to human happiness altogether. Of the American Founders and perhaps of all Americans, Franklin has unrivaled insight into the individual human soul, both in its chaotic impulses and in its happiest fulfillment, both in its profound suitability for republican self-government and in the careful cultivation that is nevertheless necessary if that potential is to be realized.

In keeping with the priority he placed on citizenship and civic virtue, the one systematic book Franklin always intended to write was a treatise on virtue. In his *Autobiography* he explains:

> I purposed writing a little Comment on each Virtue, in which I would have shown the Advantages of possessing it, and the Mischiefs attending its opposite Vice; and I should have called my Book the ART *of Virtue,* because it would have shown the *Means* and *Manner* of obtaining Virtue, which would have distinguished it from the mere Exhortation to be good. . . . In this Piece it was my Design to explain and enforce this Doctrine, that vicious Actions are not hurtful because they are forbidden, but forbidden because they are hurtful, the Nature of Man alone consider'd: That it was therefore every one's Interest to be virtuous, who wish'd to be happy even in this World.[3]

But Franklin never wrote this treatise on virtue. Instead, the most fully developed and by far the most compelling account he left of his thought is contained in the *Autobiography,* although it too remained unfinished. No doubt his neglect of the first project in favor of the second has something to do with his disinclination for systematic work and his love of telling a good story, and also much to do with an old man's pleasure in speaking of himself, for which he makes no apologies. Recounting his reasons—public spirited, paternal, and personal—for taking up his pen to write his own life, he says:

> And lastly (I may as well confess it, since my Denial of it will be believ'd by no body) perhaps I shall a good deal gratify my own *Vanity.* Indeed I scarce ever heard or saw the introductory Words, *Without Vanity I may say,* &c. but some vain thing immediately follow'd. Most people dislike Vanity in others whatever Share they have of it themselves, but I give it fair quarter wherever I meet with it, being persuaded that it is often productive of Good to the Possessor and to others that are within his Sphere of Action: And therefore in many Cases it would not be quite absurd if a Man were to thank God for his Vanity among the other Comforts of Life.[4]

Franklin knew, in this case, the great public utility of his own vanity: he knew that in telling stories he was at his most charming and persuasive, and at some level he realized that his vision of happiness and of democratic citizenship could be advanced in no better way than by telling his own story, the story of the democratic citizen *par excellence.*

And so we come back to Franklin the man, who made his whole life into a study in the art of living, an art that, like all arts, he considered eminently subject to improvement through thoughtful experimentation and careful reporting of results. In every way the life he lived was a project to transform human life, to make it more rational, more humane, more dignified and happy and comfortable. Through writings, conversations, and associations small and large, he sought to bring others along the same path he had found himself. His unflagging energy, his contagious hopefulness, his capacity for self-deprecating humor, even his foibles make him the perfect model. Or so at least he paints himself. One who writes his own biography better than anyone else ever can will always, in a sense, have the first and last word, and Franklin is as masterful a storyteller as he is a man of action and as adept at concealing his true self and his true thoughts as he is at making himself unforgettable.

But setting aside for the moment the vexed question of his veracity, is Franklin according to Franklin a good model? Is he an attainable ideal for citizens at large or merely a happy accident of nature? And if the former, how do we move from our constricted, lazy, disorganized lives to something more like his? Is it still possible to create the meaningful webs of connection on a human scale that he so inspiringly portrays himself creating throughout the *Autobiography*? Does he offer wisdom that can be useful for us in face of the growing atomization, polarization, and intolerance of contemporary civil society? Does the fate of his thoughtful but failed attempt to forge a new kind of transatlantic unity hold lessons for present-day internationalism? And what would Franklin, our nation's most famous ambassador, have to say about America's embattled position in the world today, as we face charges of imperialism and insularity, pushy moralism and materialistic decadence, excessive religiosity and empty relativism—sometimes, to be sure, from opposite quarters, but often from the very same quarters? It will be the thesis of this book that Franklin does indeed have much to offer us and that his healthy democratic vision is uniquely suited as an antidote for some of our worst civic woes, and in particular for our tendency to go to extremes of cynical, world-weary withdrawal from public life on the one hand and zealous, intolerant moralism on the other.

The Earliest Franklin

To begin forming a better acquaintance with this extraordinary man and his democratic vision, we could do no better than to follow him in his first appearance on the American public stage, with his foray into journalistic opinion making as a sixteen-year-old apprentice printer, surreptitiously submitting letters to his brother's newspaper under the pseudonym Silence Dogood. Here, already, we are faced with the enigma of disentangling Franklin the man from his public persona and of determining the relation between the wry, detached observer who wishes to entertain and the earnest promoter of good works. Here also, to a surprising degree, are all the major themes of Franklin's life and thought, conveyed in their characteristic flavors and colors, yet now in the startling voice of a middle-aged woman.

Ironies abound in Franklin's adoption of this persona. A spirited boy, he drapes himself in widow's weeds. His invention calls herself Silence Dogood (an imitation and yet a twist on the Puritan Cotton Mather's "Silent Sufferer"), yet she confesses that she is in fact infamous for her acerbic tongue and has never done anything for her country. She is now determined to correct the latter fault if not the former, and hence she has launched a new career as a writer. But of course this remedy is all words. Throughout the Dogood letters Franklin exposes and even revels in the gap between human words and deeds, pious pretensions and earthy realities, high expectations and paltry results.

In the first installment Silence relates the unfortunate circumstances of her own birth, aboard a ship bound for America with all its promises of a new life:

> My Entrance into this troublesome World was attended with the Death of my Father, a Misfortune, which tho' I was not then capable of knowing, I shall never be able to forget; for as he, poor Man, stood upon the Deck rejoycing at my birth, a merciless Wave entered the Ship, and in one Moment carry'd him beyond Reprieve.[5]

This event is sad, of course, so why does it make us almost want to smile? Perhaps it is just the undignified way the father perishes at the hands of this freak wave. If we doubt whether any irreverence towards death is intended by Franklin's "merciless wave," the doubt is removed a few installments later, as Franklin devotes an entire letter to mocking the high-blown funeral elegies then popular in New England.

In the second letter, Franklin treats love with the same light irreverence with which he treats death in the first. Taken under the protection of a pastor, the young Silence finds herself the surprised object of her guardian's amorous advances. The impropriety of his behavior is quickly eclipsed by her own irrepressible amusement at the awkward figure he cuts: "There is certainly scarce any part of a man's life in which he appears more silly and ridiculous, than when he makes his first onset in courtship." But equally striking is the frankness of the widow's introspection. Once she overcomes her laughter, she promises to consider the offer and decides to accept, though she confesses she could not tell "whether it was love, or gratitude, or pride, or all three that made me consent."[6] Thus Franklin introduces one of his great themes, the obscure and mixed motives of human beings.[7]

Somewhere behind all these veils is our chuckling author, working the strings, but we cannot quite make him out. Is he wise beyond his years, or simply full of youthful irreverence, or some of both? Or, to put the question another way, what is the meaning of Franklin's laughter? To what extent is it a diversion from seriousness, and to what extent does it show a seriousness too deep to tolerate the sentimental hypocrisy usually served up with grave topics? When Franklin's laser vision cuts through all layers of pretense, what solid realities does it still see in the human soul? What principles does it still judge sound? What faith does it still have in humanity, and on what grounds? Where and how does Franklin's irrepressible optimism make contact with his enormous insight into the disproportion between our soaring claims and hopes for ourselves and the paltriness of what we usually in fact turn out to be?

One clue about the layers of lightness and seriousness in Franklin comes from the single Dogood letter that is by no means humorous, the only one that Franklin did not write himself. Silence quotes Thomas Gordon's famous letter of "Cato" on freedom of speech and the press, reprinted from the *London Journal.* The subject is of course of special concern to Franklin, as a young printer and contributor to a paper that would be one of the earliest critics of colonial government. Franklin embraces Cato's revolutionary teaching on the ends and prerogatives of government:

> "That Men ought to speak well of *their Governours* is true, while *their Governours* deserve to be well spoken of; but to do publick Mischief, without hearing of it, is only the Prerogative and Felicity of Tyranny: A free People will be shewing that they are *so,* by their Freedom of Speech.
>
> "The Administration of Government, is nothing else but the Attendance of the *Trustees of the People* upon the Interest and Affairs of the People: And as it is the Part and Business of the People, for whose Sake alone all publick Matters are, or ought to be transacted, to see whether they be well or ill transacted; so it is the Interest, and ought to be the Ambition, of all honest Magistrates, to have their Deeds openly examined, and publickly scann'd: Only the *wicked Governours* of Men dread what is said of them."[8]

Silence herself echoes this fierce love of liberty in a passage that is as earnest as we ever see her, as she sums up her character:

> *Know then,* That I am an Enemy to Vice, and a Friend to Vertue. I am one of an extensive Charity, and a great Forgiver of *private* Injuries: a hearty Lover of the Clergy and all good Men, and a mortal Enemy to arbitrary Government and unlimited Power. I am naturally very jealous for the Rights and Liberties of my Country; and the least appearance of an Incroachment on those invaluable Priviledges, is apt to make my Blood boil exceedingly.[9]

In these last words we see traces of Franklin's sly wit playing about Silence's eyes, even on what seems for him (or her) to be the most serious of topics. It is all well and good for the blood to boil at injustice, he seems to say, but perhaps a bit over the top for it to boil exceedingly.

Yet to put the case like this is again to raise the question of whether the wry wit we keep finding in Franklin reflects an inability to take anything seriously or merely a recognition of other important truths, such as the value of moderation in all things and the utility of humor in moral education. If man cannot ever be taken quite seriously, is it only because he invariably fails to live up to his highest claims or because there is a fundamental flaw in those claims, a flaw in all moralizing that makes it absurd from the highest perspective? Such was perhaps the final judgment of Aristophanes and Machiavelli, two of the most profound political thinkers who wrote comedies. Did Franklin share at all in this judgment? Tracing the threads of seriousness and humor in Franklin's political philosophy will be a major project of this book. Suffice it to say, for now, that the young Franklin somehow succeeded in weaving them together in a way that does seem to advance a coherent and constructive political program.

If the letters have one unifying theme, it is their assault on proud privilege and their deft, gentle defense of the rights and dignity of little folk and underdogs. Franklin, the youngest son of the youngest son for five generations, now apprenticed to his overbearing elder brother James, has a natural sympathy for the woman whose guise he adopts. No one expects great things from her, and she exults in displaying her resourceful pluck and defending her unjustly maligned sex. In the same spirit, Franklin lampoons with relish the temple of learning and privilege, Harvard College, which his former grammar school classmates are attending while he labors in his brother's print shop. He paints these scholars as a proud, lazy, ignorant mob, and goes so far as to portray the goddess "Learning" turning her back on them in order to write the *New-England Courant.* Implicit here is a plea for the education of the deserving poor; explicit in the next letter is a defense of female education as well. The love of equality that we see in these earliest writings would continue throughout Franklin's life. It is no accident that his first foray into public life was a campaign to reform the city watch, a citizen police force that was ineffective and unfair to poor widows. His first journey as ambassador to London in 1757 was to petition the king against the Pennsylvania proprietors' insistence on immunity from taxation on their vast land holdings in the province. In the same spirit, his subsequent diplomatic efforts were aimed first at setting English Americans on an equal footing with residents of the old country and subsequently at establishing America itself as a country among equals.

Another enduring theme in Franklin's thought that emerges in the Dogood letters is religion and its reform. In his lampoon of Harvard, Franklin castigates the clergy as a band of idle plagiarizers, motivated by greed. Franklin's quarrel with the clergy would persist, although his presentation of it would grow far more circumspect in later life. In an even more daring foray than the Harvard lampoon, he broaches in another Dogood letter the question "Whether a Commonwealth suffers more by hypocritical Pretenders to Religion, or by the openly Profane?" His answer is the former: everyone is on guard against the openly profane, but the church is taken in by hypocrites. By giving them its sanction of approval, it helps them deceive the public, to the detriment of liberty and good government.

> [T]he most dangerous Hypocrite in a Common-Wealth, is one who *leaves the Gospel for the sake of the Law:* A Man compounded of Law and Gospel, is able to cheat a whole Country with his Religion, and then destroy them under *Colour of Law:* And here the Clergy are in great Danger of being deceiv'd, and the People of being deceiv'd by the Clergy, until the Monster arrives to such Power and Wealth, that he is out of the reach of both, and can oppress the People without their own blind Assistance. And it is a sad Observation, that when the People too late see their Error, yet the Clergy still persist in their Encomiums on the Hypocrite.[10]

The problem is, at bottom, that religion, and especially the Christian religion, makes us credulous dupes instead of the sharp-witted, independent-thinking defenders of our liberties that we should be. The church is willing to forgive countless villainies if one does a single brave deed or endows a chapel or merely professes repentance, but the public that is to succeed in defending its liberties must be more wary. This charge reminds us of Machiavelli's radical critique of Christianity for making modern Europeans soft and naïve, at the cost of their liberties.[11] But where Machiavelli throws down the gauntlet to the church and sees between it and true clarity and freedom a titanic struggle, Franklin makes his peace with the church but erodes its authority through gentle ridicule. Silence's whole personal narrative is a quiet mockery of the clergy, more subtle and more effective for its perfect composure and decorum. For all her praise of her late husband, we remember him only for his ridiculous foray into courtship.[12] Though her years with him were years of contentment, it is only after his death that Silence is freed to take up her pen to expose the world's hypocrisy and defend its liberties. The attitude Franklin expresses towards Christianity is that it has mostly been very useful, but that now, in an age of freer thought, we can surely improve upon it, even if we will never be in a position to dispense with it altogether.

The last important theme of Franklin's thought that emerges in these earliest essays is connected with this turn away from traditional piety. This theme is his lifelong concern with democracy on the smallest scale, as exercised through voluntary organizations for mutual self-help. While this interest may have had its roots in the Puritanism Franklin grew up with, it also represents a fundamental departure from the otherworldly focus of genuine Puritanism. The self-help project he has the widow propose is, appropriately enough, an insurance program for wives against the eventuality of their husbands' deaths. Initial membership and continuing participation are to be entirely voluntary, Franklin stresses, but with the proviso that if subscribers "do not continue their Payments, they lose the Benefit of their past Contributions." The widow adds, "I am humbly of Opinion, that the Country is ripe for many such *Friendly Societies,* whereby every Man might help another, without any Disservice to himself."[13]

By launching his advocacy of self-help societies with a proposal so close to the widow's heart, Franklin acknowledges that our concerns begin with ourselves, even when we are at our most public spirited. Yet of course Silence could never benefit personally from such a scheme, being already a widow; and Franklin, the true proposer, has no special stake at all in the condition of widows. Franklin recognizes that the strength of mutual aid societies lies in the fact that people tend to work hardest when they are helping themselves rather than working selflessly for others, yet he will also argue that the impluse to be helpful cannot be wholly explained by self-interest, for man is a social being with a natural capacity for empathy. Narrow self-interest is a stronger motive than pure charity, but best of all is finding the abundant common ground between one's own good and that of others and enlisting both self-interest and fellow feeling in projects that make life better for everyone, both through the tangible benefits secured and through the rich, satisfying web of human connections created along the way.

But even saying this may go too far in the direction of a smug and tidy moralism for Franklin. Lest we take his life insurance program too seriously, he follows it in the next paper with a similar proposal for the relief of old maids, proposed, most appropriately, by one repentant Margaret Aftercast, who, "puff'd up in her younger Years with a numerous Train of Humble Servants, had the Vanity to think, that her extraordinary Wit and Beauty would continually recommend her to the Esteem of the Gallants," and that she could hence take her time in finding the perfect mate.[14] With his facetious proposal of old maid insurance, Franklin does not mean to deny that human beings *can* collectively make life better for themselves when they approach their problems reasonably, but he does suggest that anyone who thinks he has a perfect solution to any of life's problems is ripe fruit for the comedian's picking.

Franklin, Socrates, and Modern Rationalism

The ironic distance on life that Franklin displays in his earliest essays would prevail, with few exceptions, through a lifetime of public and private writings. In this as in many ways Franklin reminds us of Socrates. Nor is this any accident: Franklin relates that he read Xenophon's *Memorabilia of Socrates* with great interest in his youth, promptly modified his habitual mode of conversation in imitation of Socrates, and wrote several "Socratic" dialogues as a young man. He shows a remarkable affinity for the earthy practicality of Xenophon's Socrates and resembles him in his constant readiness to make his companions more sober, moderate, and useful members of their community.[15] As Franklin explains in the *Autobiography*, he adopted a Socratic method of discourse when he realized that his habitually aggressive mode of arguing was more apt to give offense and less apt to persuade his hearers than a more modest, questioning approach. But he also admits that with this new mode of discourse,

> I . . . grew very artful and expert in drawing People even of superior Knowledge into Concessions the Consequences of which they did not foresee, entangling them in Difficulties out of which they could not extricate themselves, and so obtaining Victories that neither my self nor my Cause always deserved.[16]

Over time Franklin stopped laying traps for people and retained "only the Habit of expressing my self in Terms of modest Diffidence," evidently because he came to place more value on real friendship and on teaching and learning from his conversations and less on merely winning victories. This change brought him a step further from the victory-loving spirit that Thrasymachus attributes to Socrates and closer to the true spirit of Socrates, though not to his outward style. If we follow the indications of Plato and Xenophon as to the meaning of Socratic dialectic, we find that this important difference remained, however: Franklin saw nothing deeply puzzling in justice and the other virtues that Socrates was forever asking about; it never occurred to him that wisdom was to be gained by listening carefully to and pondering the self-contradictions within ordinary moral opinion. But is it possible that Franklin saw almost instinctively the deeper lessons that Socrates labored to discover? There are hints, at least, that he did.

One hint lies in Franklin's critical stance towards ordinary views of moral responsibility. Already as a very young man he assailed the Christian notion of a free will, and for a time he entertained the hedonistic explanation of human motivation that Socrates floats in the *Protagoras.* Soon Franklin realized that he had gone much too far in denying any significant difference between virtue and vice, but his conclusion here, too, has a Socratic ring. Virtue is not good because God commands it, he then concluded, but is commanded because it is good for us. (Whether it is in fact commanded by God or only by men purporting to speak for God, Franklin does not quite say.)[17] He had come to see virtue as the essential foundation if not the substance of happiness, which implies that all vice is folly. As he declares in one essay, echoing Socrates, "Wisdom and Vertue are the same thing."[18] Most striking is the way Franklin seems to draw the Socratic corollary that anger is irrational. "A Man in a Passion rides a mad Horse," he warns, and "Anger is never without a Reason, but seldom with a good One."[19] As Socrates argues in Plato's *Apology,* such a crime as corrupting the youth is so foolishly self-destructive that it cannot be voluntary; hence, he insists that if he has done wrong, the correct remedy is to educate him and not to pile evil upon evil by subjecting him to retributive punishment. Franklin never explicitly makes this argument, but he does show a remarkable equanimity towards human failing, habitually characterizing the misdeeds of himself and others as "errata" (a word used for printing errors) rather than sins that merit damnation.

To be sure, Franklin seems at first sight to have been much more sensibly aware than Socrates of the weakness of reason in convincing the heart and governing behavior. He loved to laugh at this weakness, even in himself. Telling the story of how he once rationalized his way out of his vegetarianism when hunger conspired with the marvelous smell of freshly cooked cod to overwhelm principle, he observes, "So convenient a thing it is to be a *reasonable Creature,* since it enables one to find or make a Reason for every thing one has a mind to do."[20] But even this recognition (though not the easy-going spirit in which it is made) proves a certain affinity between Franklin and Socrates, for one of the subtexts of many Socratic dialogues is precisely this difficulty of bringing reason and passion into harmony, the multifarious, far-reaching sources of the difficulty, and the consequently paradoxical and complex nature of the true Socratic teaching that virtue is knowledge.

For all their resemblances, Franklin and Socrates do take significantly different views of human nature, human society, and justice; in many crucial respects Franklin is thoroughly modern in outlook. Tracing the convergences and disagreements between Franklin and Socrates will help lead us into the vital heart of Franklin's political philosophy. And just as Franklin stands as a uniquely revealing test of the possibility of putting some of Socrates' key insights into effect in a life that is active rather than contemplative, he also provides a wonderful test case for the modern hope that a different sort of rationalism might come to govern human life: the secular rationalism of the Enlightenment. This new form of rationalism expects far more from reason than ancient rationalism did, seeking to make us thoroughly at home in this world and attempting to explain all events and meet all basic human needs without recourse to divine revelation or miracles. It replaces faith in divine grace and eternal life with faith in experiment, method, and open-ended progress. Like its ancient precursor, modern rationalism teaches the reasonableness of virtue, but here again we see a crucial divergence as well as a resemblance. For while ancient thought stresses the importance of rare and difficult self-knowledge to a virtue that at its peak is more philosophic than political, Franklin's view lays emphasis on the accessibility of a bourgeois constellation of virtues that all embody the enlightened self-interest of citizens immersed in practical affairs. In tracing Franklin's thought we will elaborate and test his claims for this view of virtue, which lies at the heart of his thinking on economics, social relations, wise philanthropy, government, and even international relations.

CHAPTER 1

THE ECONOMIC BASIS OF LIBERTY

If Franklin stands in broad agreement with Socrates and other classical thinkers on the importance of virtue for happiness, the most arresting difference lies in the prominent place he gives to moneymaking. Classical proponents of republicanism looked askance at commerce and the profit motive. Many of them judged the best society to be a simple, austere, rural one on the model of Sparta, considering wealth and luxuries to be a corrupting source of inequalities and social divisions. Plato and Xenophon and Aristotle argued that those whose lives are absorbed in moneymaking bring to politics the wrong priorities by viewing not human excellence but wealth as the proper end of politics. Much better for republics than merchants, manufacturers, and moneylenders, they judged, are farmers, the most independent and moderate of working men, the group most respectful of ancestral virtues and least inclined to political tumult. But it was even a question for ancient friends of republicanism whether the work of farming was not already too much of a distraction from the higher pursuit of civic life and the cultivation of civic virtue. Citizenship, these theorists suggested, is properly a full-time commitment that needs a liberal education and continual thought and conversation to exercise well. Thus, the republican tradition contained an unresolved tension between the essentially democratic admiration for agrarian simplicity and the aristocratic thought that citizenship at its best requires leisure.[1] But that tradition was united in judging that a healthy republic will accord as little honor and attention to moneymaking as possible and will not make economic growth its goal.

Franklin, in contrast, regarded the class of hereditary leisure with deep suspicion and openly embraced moneymaking, treating it not as a necessary evil but as a positive good for the individual and society alike. The model he chose to hold up for emulation was not the simple, contented farmer but the successful Yankee merchant—shrewd, industrious, and thrifty, with his nose to the grindstone and his eye forever searching out new sources of profit. What is the meaning of this inversion of priorities? Was Franklin turning his back on the higher aspirations of the republican tradition, or did he have a new conception of citizenship that gave an equal place but a different interpretation to human excellence?

The Weber Critique

The strongest advocate for the first possibility is Max Weber, who, in *The Protestant Ethic and the Spirit of Capitalism,* takes the quintessentially Yankee Franklin as his prime example of the capitalist outlook. Weber's charge is that Franklin makes money into an end in itself and the acquisition of money into an all-consuming and irrational duty. His prime text is Franklin's "Advice to a Young Tradesman, Written by an Old One," which conveys powerfully the acquisitive spirit of Franklin's advice.

> Remember that TIME is Money. He that can earn Ten Shillings a Day by his Labour, and goes abroad, or sits idle one half of that Day, tho' he spends but Sixpence during his Diversion or Idleness, ought not to reckon That the only Expence; he has really spent or rather thrown away Five Shillings besides.
>
> Remember that CREDIT is Money. If a Man lets his Money lie in my Hands after it is due, he gives me the Interest, or so much as I can make of it during that Time. This amounts to a considerable Sum where a Man has good and large Credit, and makes good Use of it.
>
> Remember that Money is of a prolific generating Nature. Money can beget Money, and its Offspring can beget more, and so on. Five Shillings turn'd, is *Six:* Turn'd again, 'tis Seven and Three Pence; and so on 'til it becomes an Hundred Pound. The more there is of it, the more it produces every Turning, so that the Profits rise quicker and quicker. He that kills a breeding Sow,

> destroys all her Offspring to the thousandth Generation. He that murders a Crown, destroys all it might have produc'd, even Scores of Pounds.[2]

Weber's examination continues with a selection from *Poor Richard's Almanack.*

> For £6 a Year, you may have the Use of £100 if you are a Man of known Prudence and Honesty. He that spends a Groat a day idly, spends idly above £6 a year, which is the Price of using £100. He that wastes idly a Groat's worth of his Time per Day, one Day with another, wastes the Privilege of using £100 each Day. He that idly loses 5s. worth of time, loses 5s. and might as prudently throw 5s. in the River. He that loses 5s. not only loses that Sum, but all the Advantage that might be made by turning it in Dealing, which by the time that a young Man becomes old, amounts to a comfortable Bag of Money.[3]

Weber might have seized upon many other passages had his purpose been to show in general the narrow-eyed, closed-fisted practicality of Franklin's teaching, especially in the almanacs. Franklin advocates skepticism about friendship, with such sayings as "The favor of the great is no inheritance," "He that sells upon trust, loses many friends and always wants money," and "Distrust and caution are the parents of security."[4] He enjoins assiduous thrift, warning that "a small Leak will sink a great Ship" and that "[w]hat maintains one vice will bring up 2 children."[5] Above all he extols industry, proclaiming, "Diligence is the mother of Good-Luck" and "Industry need not wish."[6] But these sayings do not in themselves distinguish Franklin's practicality from that of a thousand others, ancient and modern. What fascinates Weber is the characteristically *moral* tone of Franklin's advocacy of acquisitiveness.

Weber acknowledges that "all Franklin's moral attitudes are colored with utilitarianism" and that Franklin prizes honesty, punctuality, industry, and frugality chiefly because they are essential for economic success.[7] But if this were the whole story, he observes, Franklin would be just as content with the *appearance* of virtue as with the thing itself, whenever the appearance served the same practical purpose. And indeed, Franklin does take such a view of humility, which he says he has failed to acquire but has successfully learned to feign: in this case he regards the appearance as good enough. "But in fact the matter is not by any means so simple," Weber continues; humility is the exception for Franklin because he does not truly regard it as a virtue at all. "Benjamin Franklin's own character, as it appears in the really unusual candidness of his autobiography, belies [the] suspicion" that he values virtue merely as a means to practical ends. Rather, Franklin finds in moneymaking the very highest duty, an almost sacred duty, maintains Weber: "In fact, the *summum bonum* of this ethic, the earning of more and more money, combined with the strict avoidance of all spontaneous enjoyment of life, is above all completely devoid of any eudaimonistic, not to say hedonistic, admixture. It is thought so purely as an end in itself, that from the point of view of the happiness of, or utility to, the single individual, it appear entirely transcendental and absolutely irrational." Or, as he says later, the "ideal type of the capitalistic entrepreneur," to whom Franklin's preaching points us, "gets nothing out of his wealth for himself, except the irrational sense of having done his job well."[8] Weber traces the irrational dutifulness he purports to find in Franklin and other capitalists to the Calvinist respect for diligence in one's calling that Franklin would have imbibed as a youth in Puritan New England, subsequently shorn of its religious meaning.[9]

The Value of Work

Weber does identify a crucial feature of Franklin's economic program when he observes that it has a distinctively moral cast and that Franklin's public praise of and personal dedication to the virtues of a good businessman go deeper than what would be required merely to make one's fortune. He sees correctly that Franklin extols hard work and the accumulation of money without treating money as merely a means to pleasure. But Weber goes astray when he assumes that therefore the diligent accumulation of wealth must, for Franklin, be a duty in the Kantian sense, an end in itself.[10] For all the early modern philosophers, the unleashing of acquisitive energies is a praiseworthy project because it contributes to the common good of society, generating employment, enhancing security, multiplying pleasures, and drawing energies away from deadly religious quarrels and military adventurism into more constructive channels. Franklin agrees with these judgments, and he adds to them a unique awareness of how the same qualities and habits that lead to wealth are also essential to our private happiness as beings who are much more than moneymakers, and equally essential for public liberty. Franklin sees a danger that men may become obsessed with property: "Wealth is not his that has it, but his that enjoys it," he observes, and he warns against being possessed by one's money rather than possessing it.[11] But while recognizing this danger, Franklin still finds many reasons, even many moral reasons, for his unprecedented advocacy of acquisitiveness.

Franklin's emphasis on the virtues of a good moneymaker in "Advice to a Young Tradesman" and *Poor Richard's Almanack* is in part a reflection of the particular audience of these pieces: beginners in trade and barely literate rural folk who will do best to set their farms and their personal finances in order before they attempt any greater efforts at self-improvement or public service. Franklin shows the same attention to putting first things first in his own program of self-improvement, which begins with the virtues of temperance, silence, and order, as the best foundations for acquiring all the others. Likewise, in proposing an academy for Philadelphia and a philosophic society for all the colonies, Franklin suggests that only after the "first drudgery" of providing for the necessities of life is it appropriate for a society to turn to the higher pursuits of science, literature, and inventions that benefit mankind.[12] In the *Autobiography* he explains his view of the almanac.

> [O]bserving that it was generally read, scarce any Neighborhood in the Province being without it, I consider'd it as a proper Vehicle for conveying Instruction among the common People, who bought scarce any other Books. I therefore filled all the little spaces that occurr'd between the Remarkable Days in the Calendar, with Proverbial Sentences, chiefly such as inculcated Industry and Frugality, as the Means of procuring Wealth and thereby securing Virtue, it being more difficult for a Man in Want to act always honestly, as (to use here one of those Proverbs) *it is hard for an empty Sack to stand upright.*[13]

Wealth in any form can forestall the temptation to theft, but wealth that one has earned oneself is by far the best kind, Franklin suggests, turning on its head the classical prejudice in favor of inherited wealth. The real value of earned wealth lies less in what one can do with it once one has it than in the qualities one necessarily acquires along the way if one pursues it rationally. At the simplest level, a person who works hard keeps out of trouble. "*Idleness* is the Dead Sea, that swallows all Virtues: Be active in Business, that *Temptation* may miss her Aim: The Bird that sits, is easily shot."[14] In the *Autobiography* Franklin returns to the same thought about idleness, in a passage that also brings out the positive side of the human need for work. He relates his experiences as leader of an expedition to the frontier to build fortifications, a project often interrupted by heavy rains.

> This gave me occasion to observe, that when Men are employ'd they are best contented. For on the Days they work'd they were good natur'd and chearful; and with the consciousness of having done a good Days work they spent the Evenings jollily; but on the idle Days they were mutinous and quarrelsome, finding fault with their Pork, the Bread, &c. and in continual ill-humour; which put me in mind of a Sea-Captain, whose Rule it was to keep his Men constantly at Work; and when his Mate once told him that they had done every thing, and there was nothing farther to employ them about; *O,* says he, *make them scour the Anchor.*[15]

Here again Franklin brings out the gulf between natural inclination and what is naturally good for us: we are happiest if we keep busy, but by nature we are inclined to be lazy and quarrelsome. Franklin is not as far from the view of Hobbes as he might at first appear. Indeed, he once chides a commentator for being "too severe upon Hobbes, whose Notion, I imagine, is somewhat nearer to the truth than that which makes the State of Nature a State of Love: But the Truth perhaps lies between both Extreams."[16]

Even intermittent work has a good effect on the spirits, giving one a good opinion of oneself for as long as one remains productive. Focusing one's mind on what one needs to do and what one has already accomplished well draws attention away from the things that are outside of one's own power, things that more often than not are sources of discontent. Even such a small matter as learning to shave oneself is nothing to be scorned:

> Human Felicity is produc'd not so much by great Pieces of good Fortune that seldom happen, as by little Advantages that occur every Day. Thus if you teach a poor young Man to shave himself and keep his Razor in order, you may contribute more to the Happiness of his Life than in giving him a 1000 Guineas. The Money may be soon spent, the Regret only remaining of having foolishly consum'd it. But in the other Case he escapes the frequent Vexation of waiting for Barbers, and of their some times, dirty Fingers, offensive Breaths and dull Razors. He shaves when most convenient to him, and enjoys daily the Pleasure of its being done with a good Instrument.[17]

Or as Poor Richard puts the same thought more pithily, "He that can travel well afoot, keeps a good horse."[18]

When industry becomes habitual, this focus upon one's own capacities and accomplishments likewise becomes habitual, resulting in a solid self-respect. For soldiers and sailors this may be as far as the benefits of hard work go, but for an independent farmer or artisan or merchant, the groundwork is laid for further benefits. "*He who has a Trade has an Office of Profit and Honour;* because he does not hold it during any other Man's Pleasure, and it affords him honest Subsistence with Independence."[19] These workers find that diligence and prudent management of small things begin to make a material difference in their circumstances. Little by little, they come to believe, in a way no book could persuade them, that they really are substantially in control of their own lives, that their own "little strokes" can indeed "fell great oaks."[20] Thus they become the opposite of the surly, passive, fatalistic Russian peasants about whom Tolstoy made such complaints, to whom communism added further habits of passive resentment, and who now provide such stony soil for democracy to take root in. By the same token, Franklin seeks to inoculate citizens against the fractious outlook so prevalent in troubled regions in all times, in which the purported injustices of enemies loom large in people's minds and violence seems the only dignified response.

Franklin shows abundant awareness that self-government and its requisite virtues do not come naturally to human beings, but he suggests that a spirit of liberty and the capacity for self-government can be taught. They begin with the simple elements of prudence, forethought, self-discipline, and pride in self-sufficiency that are within reach of the humblest worker. By learning to take responsibility for one's material well-being, one comes to cherish the liberty this provides and one gains the confidence to take on greater responsibilities. Learning the value for one's business of honesty, civility, and trustworthiness equips one for larger, cooperative ventures. Thus the bonds of trust and interdependence that arise in a merely economic context become the foundation for a richly interconnected society, in which self-interest is not sacrificed but rather is seen to be deeply intertwined with the common good. As Alexis de Tocqueville would later observe, this connection runs both ways. American political life benefits from the love of order, the good sense, and the practicality that citizens learn first in business; at the same time, "the people cannot meddle in public affairs without having the scope of their ideas extended and without having their minds be seen to go outside their ordinary routine." The citizen who is called upon to support "new improvements . . . to the common property . . . feels the desire being born to improve what is personal to him."[21]

It has always been the middling class of people, the respectable and self-respecting small farmer and small shopkeeper, who have learned these lessons the most readily. Thus, in political disputes Franklin was invariably their champion and the enemy both of mobs and of entrenched privilege, such as that enjoyed by the fabulously wealthy Pennsylvania proprietors. Unlike Thomas Jefferson, he made no excuses for the Boston Tea Party and never condoned the violence of the French Revolution.[22] In 1776 Franklin attempted to insert into the Pennsylvania constitution, along with a recognition of the right to acquire property, a statement of this right's natural limits: "That an enormous Proportion of Property vested in a few Individuals is dangerous to the Rights, and destructive of the Common Happiness, of Mankind; and therefore every free State hath a Right by its Laws to discourage the Possession of such Property."[23] And he made an active effort to dissuade European aristocrats from coming to America. Writing in Paris in 1784 to potential immigrants, he spoke with pride of the "happy mediocrity" of fortune that prevailed in America, which, by obliging everyone to follow some business for his livelihood, kept his countrymen industrious and virtuous.[24] Citizens schooled to such industry, self-control, and self-reliance are likely to put their trust in the democratic political process, but they will seek from it only what they cannot provide for themselves; they are not prone to the radical hope that political action will bring them everything. Thus, they are energetic defenders of their own liberty and rarely a danger to the liberty and property of others. As Franklin puts it in another letter from the same period, "only a virtuous people are capable of freedom. As nations become corrupt and vicious, they have more need of masters."[25]

Franklin knew, however, that if he held up the satisfactions of self-respect and liberty as the goal of self-improvement, no one would listen. So, with his unerring gift for persuasion, he promises his readers riches, and to induce them to swallow his prescriptions for wealth, he salts and peppers his advice with humor. In the 1739 preface to his almanac he explains candidly,

> In all the Dishes I have hitherto cook'd for thee, there is solid Meat enough for thy Money. There are Scraps from the Table of Wisdom, that will if well digested, yield strong Nourishment to thy Mind. But squeamish Stomachs cannot eat without Pickles; which, 'tis true are good for nothing else, but they provoke an Appetite. The Vain Youth that reads my Almanack for the sake of an idle Joke, will perhaps meet with a serious Reflection, that he may ever after be the better for.[26]

In consequence of Franklin's brilliant, multilayered packaging of his moral lessons, the almanac sold so well that it made Franklin himself rich, and the distillation of sayings from it that he published under the title *The Way to Wealth* was reproduced in hundreds of editions and many foreign languages. In taking this approach Franklin exercised a characteristic bit of benevolent duplicity, just as did the father in one of his stories, who, on his deathbed, tells his son that there is gold buried in their fields but that he must never dig deeper than plough deep to find it.[27] Find it he will, albeit in a form he does not quite expect, but how much he will gain besides for his happiness and his community he has at first no inkling.

Work, Acquisitiveness, and Nature

Alongside Franklin's hearty endorsement of hard work and material acquisition may be found elements of a different and more classical view of work, wealth, and leisure. One indication that Franklin does not view time as merely a commodity comes even in the almanac. "Dost thou love life?" he asks. "Then do not squander Time; for that's the Stuff Life is made of."[28] Another counterpoint to the modern liberal embrace of acquisitiveness is also prominent in the almanac, in Franklin's comments on the restlessness of desire and the unhappiness that comes of failing to curb it:

> The poor have little, beggars none, the rich too much, *enough* not one.
>
> Avarice and Happiness never saw each other, how then shou'd they become acquainted.
>
> A little House well fill'd, a little Field well till'd, and a little Wife well will'd, are great Riches.
>
> 'Tis easier to suppress the first Desire, than to satisfy all that follow it.[29]

These comments recall the oft-repeated advice of both Epicureans and Stoics in the ancient world: restrict your wants to their natural objects, which are few, simple, and easily obtained, and you will be free of turbulent passions that put you at the mercy of fortune and of others. Such sentiments were part of the common heritage of eighteenth-century colonists and Europeans, and Franklin readily adopted the traditional distinction between natural and artificial wants and recognized the problematic character of the latter. But in his hands the injunction to moderation takes on a new meaning, emphasizing less the hold that desires themselves have upon us than the hold that debts and creditors will have if we fail to practice economy. Poor Richard warns,

> Think what you do when you run into Debt; *You give to another Power over your Liberty.* If you cannot pay at the Time, you will be ashamed to see your Creditor; you will be in Fear when you speak to him; you will make poor pitiful sneaking Excuses, and by Degrees come to lose your Veracity, and sink into base downright

> lying. . . . [P]reserve your Freedom, and maintain your Independency: Be *industrious* and *free;* be *frugal* and *free.*[30]

In the same way, eschewing luxury became a way of establishing national independence. In 1769, after the colonies had adopted nonimportation resolutions to protest the injustice of British trade restrictions, Franklin wrote from London,

> It gives me great Pleasure to hear that our People are steady in their Resolutions of Non Importation, and in the Promoting of Industry among themselves. They will soon be sensible of the Benefit of such Conduct, tho' the Acts should never be repeal'd to their full Satisfaction. For their Earth and their Sea, the true Sources of Wealth and Plenty, will go on producing; and if they receive the annual Increase, and do not waste it as heretofore in the Gewgaws of this Country, but employ their spare time in manufacturing Necessaries for themselves, they must soon be out of debt, they must soon be easy and comfortable in their circumstances, and even wealthy. . . . And how can Freeman bear the thought of subjecting themselves to the hazard of being deprived of their personal liberty at the caprice of every petty trader, for the paltry vanity of tricking out himself and family in the flimsy manufactures of Britain, when they might by their own industry and ingenuity, appear in good substantial honourable homespun![31]

In a similar vein Franklin comments on the frugality of his household in the early days of his marriage.

> We kept no idle Servants, our Table was plain and simple, our Furniture of the cheapest. For instance my Breakfast was a long time Bread and Milk, (no Tea) and I ate it out of a twopenny earthen Porringer with a Pewter Spoon. But mark how Luxury will enter Families, and make a Progress, in Spite of Principle. Being call'd one Morning to Breakfast, I found it in a China Bowl with a Spoon of Silver. They had been bought for me without my Knowledge by my Wife, and had cost her the enormous Sum of three and twenty Shillings, for which she had no other Excuse or Apology to make, but that she thought *her* Husband deserv'd a Silver Spoon and China Bowl as well as any of his Neighbours. This was the first Appearance of Plate and China in our House, which afterwards in a Course of Years as our Wealth encreas'd augmented gradually to several Hundred Pounds in Value.[32]

Through both of these comments runs a rich vein of ambiguity. Is moderation, as the ancient moralists taught, a virtue for everyone at all times, conserving our energies for higher things? Or is it merely an important expedient for young entrepreneurs and young nations that need to build up their capital and independence? Franklin is not quite of one mind on the question. Luxury he certainly does not regard as intrinsically immoral, or wealth a danger that invariably takes over our lives, as Franklin's erstwhile hero Socrates argues in Xenophon's *Memorabilia*.[33] But how much luxury is too much Franklin never requires himself to determine.

Another counterpoint to Franklin's modern, commercial spirit comes in the qualifications that hedge his embrace of hard work. His reservations are connected to the fact that he holds the simplest, pre-agricultural life in higher regard than does John Locke. Franklin concedes, in fact, that the native American peoples lead the most natural and naturally satisfying way of life.

> The proneness of human Nature to a life of ease, of freedom from care and labour appears strongly in the little success that has hitherto attended every attempt to civilize our American Indians. . . . When an Indian Child has been brought up among us, taught our language and habituated to our Customs, yet if he goes to see his relations and make one Indian Ramble with them, there is no perswading him ever to return, and that this is not natural [to them] merely as Indians, but as men, is plain from this, that when white persons of either sex have been taken prisoners young by the Indians, and lived a while among them, tho' ransomed by their Friends, and treated with all imaginable tenderness to prevail with them to stay among the English, yet in a Short time they become disgusted with our manner of life, and the care and pains that are necessary to support it, and take the first good Opportunity of escaping again into the Woods, from whence there is no reclaiming them.[34]

Franklin has his own words of praise for the simple, leisured life of these people he says are called "savages" only because "their manners differ from ours": "The Indian Men when young are Hunters and Warriors; when old, Counsellors; for all their Government is by the Counsel or Advice of the Sages; there is no Force, there are no Prisons, no Officers to compel Obedience, or inflict Punishment. . . . Having few Artificial Wants, they have abundance of Leisure for Improvement by Conversation."[35]

This natural way of life defines for Franklin the extent of the natural right to property, which again he views very differently from Locke and his American followers James Madison and Alexander Hamilton. Franklin writes,

> All the Property that is necessary to a Man for the Conservation of the Individual & the Propagation of the Species, is his natural Right which none can justly deprive him of: But all Property superfluous to such purposes is the Property of the Publick, who, by their Laws have created it, and who may therefore by other Laws dispose of it, whenever the Welfare of the Publick shall demand such Disposition. He that does not like civil Society on these Terms, let him retire and live among Savages. He can have no right to the benefits of Society, who will not pay his Club towards the Support of it.[36]

But although the simple life of the savages is most natural, there is really no returning to it for civilized men and women.

> [W]ith us are infinite Artificial wants, no less craving than those of Nature, and much more difficult to satisfy; so that I am apt to imagine that close Societies subsisting by Labour and Arts, arose first not from choice, but from necessity. . . . However as matters [now] stand with us, care and industry seem absolutely necessary to our well being; they should therefore have every Encouragement we can invent.[37]

These remarks help make it clear that Franklin valued labor not for itself but for the good morals it preserves and the dignity and freedom for which it provides the foundation. But if these very advantages are available in a simple hunter-gatherer society without hard labor and without harsh laws, is civilization really an advance? At least once, shortly before the Revolution, Franklin suggested that for many or most human beings it may not be.

> I have lately made a Tour thro' Ireland and Scotland. In these Countries a small Part of the Society are Landlords, great Noblemen and Gentlemen, extreamly opulent, living in the highest Affluence and Magnificence: The Bulk of the People Tenants, extreamly poor, living in the most sordid Wretchedness in dirty Hovels of Mud and Straw, and cloathed only in Rags. . . . Had I never

been in the American Colonies, but was to form my Judgment of Civil Society by what I have lately seen, I should never advise a Nation of Savages to admit of Civilization: For I assure you, that in the Possession and Enjoyment of the various Comforts of Life, compar'd to these People every Indian is a Gentleman: And the Effect of this kind of Civil Society seems only to be, the depressing Multitudes below the Savage State that a few may be rais'd above it.[38]

We may contrast this observation with Locke's claim that the natives of America were "poor in all the Comforts of life," and that "A King of a large fruitful Territory there feeds, lodges, and is clad worse than a day Labourer in England." This claim is fundamental to Locke's assertion of a natural right to property and to virtually unlimited acquisition.[39] Franklin's closer observations of pre-agricultural life led him to doubt both the premise and the conclusion.

Obviously Franklin found the inequalities less severe in England, where he had been living, or he would not have shown such shock at the conditions in Scotland and Ireland. But his words on the English society, with its miserable poor and corrupt lords, are harsh as well. What is it, then, that redeems civilization in Franklin's mind? It seems to be two things, in some tension with each other for Franklin, just as they were in classical republicanism: the possibilities that still exist for virtuous freedom, and the advantages of leisure and learning. In the same letter written after the tour of the British Isles, Franklin adds, "I thought often of the Happiness of New England, where every Man is a Freeholder, has a Vote in publick Affairs, lives in a tidy warm House, has plenty of good Food and Fewel, with whole Cloaths from Head to Foot, the Manufactury perhaps of his own Family."[40] But equally striking is another comment he makes about an earlier visit to Scotland, this one addressed to his friend Lord Kames,

On the whole, I must say, I think the Time we spent there, was Six Weeks of the *densest* Happiness I have met with in any Part of my Life. And the agreeable and instructive Society we found there in such Plenty, has left so pleasing an Impression on my Memory, that did not strong Connections draw me elsewhere, I believe Scotland would be the Country I should chuse to spend the Remainder of my Days in.[41]

In the same spirit, Franklin's most revealing words on the progress of civilization are his enthusiastic characterization of his own time as an "age of experiments" and a comment made at the end of his life about science: "The rapid Progress *true* Science now makes, occasions my Regretting sometimes that I was born so soon."[42]

Whereas Franklin showed ambivalence about civilization's proliferation of new comforts and artificial wants, he was wholehearted in his embrace of new learning. It is above all the great pleasure Franklin took in books, in conversation, and in discovery—the highest pleasures of serious leisure—that makes Weber's portrait of him as the quintessential capitalist such a distorting caricature. For Franklin, work is ultimately justified by its contribution to a richer life that includes personal and political liberty and, in the best case, serious leisure as well; yet Franklin understands each of these advantages in a distinctively modern way. In order to see better what is new in his understanding, we will look first at his economic policies and then at his thoughts on leisure.

A Republican Political Economy

Franklin's economic thought is eclectic and not always consistent. At times he voices an almost classical preference for simplicity and an opposition to manufacturing and even to commerce. But in its main currents his thought is decisively modern, showing a pervasive interest in supporting personal independence and economic freedom, a democratic sense of fairness, a confidence in people's ability to improve their lives with diligent effort, and a keen sense of the importance of material rewards in spurring them to make that effort. On the basis of observation and personal experience, he early developed a robust faith in what Adam Smith would later call the "invisible hand" to provide us with all the materials and innate capacities we need and, through free markets, to distribute labor, resources, and products in the way that is most beneficial to all. At a time when economic thinking still mostly followed mercantilist principles, Franklin as an American readily saw both the injustice and the short-sightedness of mercantilism and became one of the first advocates of free trade and of minimizing government interference in the economy. Yet while the dominant current in Franklin's economic thinking is an enthusiastic embrace of economic freedom and growth, and while he generally saw economic and political freedom as mutually reinforcing, Franklin's moral and political concerns occasionally produced far more classical-sounding crosscurrents of reservations about untrammeled economic growth.

In keeping with his penchant for putting first things first and his refusal to scorn the importance of laying low but solid foundations for freedom, Franklin's first serious political writing was his 1729 pamphlet, "A Modest Enquiry into the Nature and Necessity of a Paper-Currency." This essay shows Franklin's concern with the economic basis of a healthy society and his sense of the importance of trade and full employment.[43] In its title the essay also shows a characteristic lack of concern for theoretical precision, for of course there is no currency by nature, currency taking all its worth from the conventional agreements of human beings. But what matters to Franklin is the hope that economic understanding can be reduced to a practical science in a way that will advance both general prosperity and justice. In a 1769 letter to Lord Kames he writes,

> I am glad to find that you are turning your Thoughts to political Subjects, and particularly to those of Money, Taxes, Manufactures, and Commerce. The World is yet much in the dark on these important Points; and many mischievous Mistakes are continually made in the Management of them. Most of our Acts of Parliament for regulating them are, in my Opinion, little better than political Blunders, owing to Ignorance of the Science, or to the Designs of crafty Men, who mislead the Legislature, proposing something under the specious Appearance of Public Good, while the real Aim is, to sacrifice that to their own private Interest.[44]

The early essay on paper currency is an attempt to begin dispelling this ignorance as well as the irrational moral prejudices that Franklin thought had no place in a modern economy. Central among Franklin's assumptions is the modern notion that a growing, dynamic economy is good; central among the prejudices he wished to combat is the prejudice against lending and borrowing at interest, which Aristotle and centuries of Christian thinkers had condemned as usury. In Franklin's eyes moneylending is not a moral evil but a practical necessity, and lending at high rates of interest is not a crime to be deterred with stiff penalties but an inconvenience to be prevented with better monetary policies. "For he that wants Money will find out Ways to give 10 *per Cent.* when he cannot have it for less, altho' the Law forbids to take more than 6 *per Cent.*" By increasing the money supply, the colony can reduce the demand for loans and thus bring down interest rates; by reducing interest rates, it can stimulate economic growth and encourage those with capital to invest it more productively in agriculture and commerce rather than in moneylending.[45]

But national prosperity is not an isolated matter; it is always in some degree a struggle for competitive advantage. Long before the American colonies had any collective sense of themselves as one nation, Franklin was appealing to the interest not only of Pennsylvania but of all America against the narrowly selfish policies of the mother country, which sought to keep all manufactures and trade in British hands. A plentiful money supply would encourage American commerce, ship building, the growth of domestic industries, and immigration, all contributing to colonial strength. A country can never have too much wealth or too many people, Franklin maintains, for labor will naturally find its way to the most productive employment.[46]

In this essay we see the beginning of Franklin's lifelong campaign against mercantilist policies. These policies were based on the belief that a nation's wealth is measured by the amount of gold and silver it can amass. The goal of mercantilist policy was thus to keep a favorable balance of trade, which Britain pursued by encouraging the production of manufactured goods for export. The continual flow of workmen to the cities, low industrial wages, and a neglect of agricultural development were all consequences of this policy. The American colonies were exploited as a source of cheap raw materials and a captive market for British manufactured goods. The colonies' chronically negative balance of trade, which made money scarce and impeded the development of the American economy, was thus part of a deliberate policy that Britain would prove unwilling to change and which set her on a collision course with the colonies.

Franklin was convinced that British restrictions on American economic activity were bad not only for America but also for the long-term interests of Britain herself. He found his thinking converging with that of the French physiocrats, who argued that all political interference with the natural order of economic life is pernicious. In particular, they criticized the mercantilist preoccupation with manufacturing for export that resulted in neglect of a nation's agricultural base.[47] While Franklin knew that agriculture would long be overwhelmingly important for America, he opposed restrictive laws on American trade and manufacturing, regarding them as impediments to the natural flow of economic activity that would be most beneficial for the whole empire.

> [I]n Proportion to the Increase of the Colonies, a vast Demand is growing for British Manufactures, a glorious Market wholly in the Power of Britain, in which Foreigners cannot interfere, which will increase in a short Time even beyond her Power of supplying, tho' her whole Trade should be to her Colonies: Therefore Britain should not too much restrain Manufactures in her Colonies. A wise and good Mother will not do it. To distress, is to weaken, and weakening the Children, weakens the whole Family.[48]

But this comment shows the difficulty of leaving competitive thinking altogether behind. If Americans and British were foolish to regard one another as rivals, they were perhaps not unwise to regard France and other foreigners as such. Even within the empire, the extensive convergences of interest that Franklin found did not overcome all tensions. When the British monopolized colonial shipping, they really did profit at the expense of colonists as well as foreigners, as ancient Athens did when it used revenue from its empire to expand its own navy. To the extent that the colonists followed Franklin's advice to practice frugality, to eschew foreign luxuries, and to support local cottage industries, they really did begin to stand on their own feet economically in a way that would bring less profit to large numbers of British manufacturers and merchants. Free trade policies, if implemented, would be generally but not universally beneficial. Hence, Franklin's policy of reform required a fair and enlightened government that would take the good of the whole empire into account in an impartial way, and to support it a British-American public opinion that would regard the whole as one people.

Franklin would struggle in vain, however, during the decades leading up to the the Revolutionary War, to convince the British to take a broader view. Over time he came to see this injustice to the Americans as only one expression of the decay of an old society in which economic inequality and political corruption went hand in hand. He complained that rich landowners, "who delight no longer to live upon their Estates in the honourable Independence they were born to, among their respecting Tenants, but chuse rather a Life of Luxury, tho' among the Dependants of a Court, have lately raised their Rents most grievously to support the Expence." At that court their arrogance was only increased, while avarice drew them to compete for lucrative offices, further corrupting the political process.[49] Just as a small number of wealthy landowners controlled British agrarian policy, so a cabal of rich merchants dictated imperial trade policies. When Franklin found he could not persuade the crown to look equally to the good of all its subjects on both sides of the Atlantic, he hoped that nonimportation agreements would teach the British the wisdom of free trade. But in the end he concluded that the British political system was simply too corrupt for reform and that independence for America was the only solution.[50]

Looking beyond the empire, Franklin argued with equal vigor for international free trade policies: "Commerce, consisting in a mutual Exchange of the Necessaries and Conveniencies of Life, the more free and unrestricted it is, the more it flourishes, and the happier are all the Nations concerned in it."[51] Even so, Franklin saw that as long as there were nations that considered themselves as separate peoples with separate interests, they would be at odds, even prone to go to war over trade. On the one hand, Franklin thought that warfare was an insane way to pursue wealth, that even peaceful trade restrictions were ineffective ways to secure it, and that the lucrative colonial possessions that European nations fought over would bring more profit to those nations if they simply granted their independence and traded freely with them. To this extent, it seemed to be only short-sightedness that stopped European nations from endorsing total free trade. Yet on the other hand, in the intense rivalries of European politics, keeping one's neighbors relatively poor brought a competitive advantage, even if it meant less absolute profit for one's own country than free trade would bring. And Franklin never disputed the primacy of security concerns. Hence, before the Revolution, he accepted the Navigation Acts' exclusion of foreign ships from colonial ports as good for the British Empire's relative power in Europe.[52]

These judgments left Franklin with a tension in his thinking that he saw could not be resolved within the nationalist assumptions of the eighteenth century. Nations would need to become much more enlightened as to their true interests but also more cosmopolitan in spirit, possibly even convinced of a divine support for free trade policies and the economic rights that they embodied, before they would risk giving up narrow and temporary advantages for the long-term good of everyone. In 1764 he lamented,

> Britain would, if she could, manufacture and trade for all the World; England for all Britain; London for all England; and every Londoner for all London. So selfish is the human Mind! But 'tis well there is One above that rules these Matters with a more equal Hand. He that is pleas'd to feed the Ravens, will undoubtedly take care to prevent a Monopoly of the Carrion.[53]

A few years later he wrote to a leading French physiocrat,

> I am sorry to find, that that Wisdom which sees the Welfare of the Parts in the Prosperity of the Whole, seems not yet to be known in this Country. We are so far from conceiving that what is best for Mankind, or even for Europe, in general, may be best for us, that we are ever studying to establish and extend a separate Interest of Britain, to the Prejudice of even Ireland and our own Colonies! It is from your Philosophy only that the Maxims of a contrary and more happy Conduct are to be drawn, which I therefore sincerely wish may grow and increase till it becomes the governing Philosophy of the human Species, as it must be that of superior Beings in better Worlds.[54]

Franklin was one of the first to begin thinking in terms of a transnational order to make the modern project work for the peaceful prosperity of all, and this theme would reemerge in his conduct of American diplomacy during and after the Revolutionary War.[55]

But even within the colony of Pennsylvania, Franklin implicitly acknowledged that enlightened economic policies would not be for the good of absolutely everyone. He always looked for benefits that were truly common, but when choices had to be made, he preferred the good of many to the good of the few, and the good of the common man to that of anyone else. In the essay on a paper currency, he sought to win poor and middling working men to his cause by arguing that a paper currency would be to their benefit and would find its opposition among the wealthy, moneylenders, and bankruptcy lawyers, together with their poor dependents. The new currency was to be embraced for encouraging decent working men and for increasing the economic activity and interdependence that knit together a healthy society.

In acknowledging such tensions and in taking sides with society's most honest and productive members, however, Franklin found himself pulled in an anticapitalist direction. His moral preference for the decent, simple working man goes with the view that each product has a naturally just value, which is not necessarily the same as the market value. "Trade in general being nothing else but the Exchange of Labour for Labour, the Value of all Things is . . . most justly measured by Labour."[56] Franklin was opposed to economic advantages that accrue to anyone by virtue of privilege or the shrewdness that exploits others' ignorance.

> There seem to be but three Ways for a Nation to acquire Wealth. The first is by *War* as the Romans did in plundering their conquered Neighbours. This is *Robbery.* The second is by *Commerce* which is generally Cheating. The third is by *Agriculture* the only *honest Way;* wherein Man receives a real Increase of the Seed thrown into the Ground, in a kind of continual Miracle wrought by the Hand of God in his Favour, as a Reward for his innocent Life, and virtuous Industry.[57]

The view that each product has an intrinsically just price goes back, of course, to Aristotle, and it contributes to Aristotle's moral objections to usury and commerce as activities that yield profit without creating any new goods. But in his insistence that labor is the true measure of a product's worth, Franklin also anticipates Marx's full development of the labor theory of value, according to which the profits taken by entrepreneurs make wage labor invariably unjust.[58] Franklin, however, shows far more appreciation than either Aristotle or Marx for the economic contribution made by bankers, merchants, and entrepreneurs, and he is far more hopeful about solving the moral problems that economic development tends to bring in its wake. But, like Marx and unlike Aristotle and the American Antifederalists who championed rural simplicity, he sees these problems chiefly as soluble problems of inequity and dependency, and he shows little concern about excessive attachment to material things as such.

In the end, Franklin's enthusiasm for rustic simplicity turns out to be much less than whole-hearted. Just as moderation is more a means to personal and national independence than an end in itself for Franklin, so commerce proves to be only a conditional evil, one whose inequities can be corrected by more freedom, more competition, and more general enlightenment. As Franklin adds, in the same paper in which he calls commerce "generally Cheating," bargains will often be unequal when one party can take advantage of the other's ignorance, but when "the Labour and Expence of producing both Commodities are known to both Parties, Bargains will generally be fair and equal."[59] The most serious problem in the colonial American economy was thus not Britain's restraint of the colonists' manufactures, which cheap land would discourage at any event, or even her domination of colonial trade, but rather the foolishness of American consumers who allowed British merchants to take advantage of them.

> Could our folks but see what numbers of Merchants, and even Shopkeepers here, make great estates by American folly . . . [and] live like Princes on the sweat of our brows . . . I am persuaded that indignation would supply our want of prudence, we should disdain the thralldom we have so long been held in by this mischievous commerce, reject it for ever, and seek our resources where God and Nature have placed them WITHIN OUR SELVES.[60]

But again, the call for national economic independence from Europe is not Franklin's last word: it is a temporary measure aimed at securing more favorable terms. In the bulk of his writings Franklin expresses faith that the unfairness of commerce can be corrected by better knowledge on the part of consumers, by more vigorous competition, which will drive prices to their natural level, and by the self-interest of sellers themselves, if only they will take an enlightened view of it.

> Commerce among nations as well as between Private Persons should be fair and equitable, by *equivalent* Exchanges and mutual Supplies. The taking unfair advantages of a Neighbour's Necessities, tho' attended with a Temporary Success, always breeds ill Blood. To lay Duties on a Commodity exported which our Friends want, is a Knavish Attempt to get something for Nothing. . . . [A]s we produce no Commodity that is peculiar to our Country, and which may not be obtained elsewhere, the Discouraging the Consumption of ours by Duties on Exportation, and thereby encouraging a Rivalship from other Nations in the Ports we trade to, is absolute Folly, which indeed is mixed more or less with all Knavery.[61]

In the doubts Franklin expressed about commerce there was no serious thought of trying to return to a subsistence economy or to the austere self-restraint of ancient republics like Sparta. So important was access to markets for American farmers that control of the Mississippi became a major issue in the peace negotiations after the Revolutionary War, and Franklin was all on the side of pressing for complete control of the river. During preliminary negotiations with Spain, he wrote to John Jay, "I would rather agree with them to buy at a great Price the whole of their Right on the Mississippi than sell a Drop of its Waters.—A Neighbour might as well ask me to sell my Street Door."[62]

Like his contemporary Montesquieu, Franklin sees that the spirit of commerce brings with it a certain toleration for luxuries and a softening or weakening of the stern self-denying morals of the ancient republic, but also that it brings its own virtues of industry, honesty, thrift, and self-control, in a way that does less violence to natural inclination.[63] He even cautiously acknowledges, on occasion, a certain positive role for luxuries: "Is not the Hope of one day being able to purchase and enjoy Luxuries a great Spur to Labour and Industry? May not luxury, therefore, produce more than it consumes, if without such a Spur People would be, as they are naturally enough inclined to be, lazy and indolent?"[64]

Franklin shows a similarly complex but ultimately darker view of manufacturing. When conducted on a small scale by households for domestic consumption or by independent artisans like himself, he regards it as an unmitigated good for society. Manufactures of such a kind can be precisely the counterweight that keeps trade honest, and independent entrepreneurs make good citizens.[65] In one early writing he voices a possible political objection to large-scale industry, with a warning against choosing employments that are "such as make a Man too dependent, too much oblig'd to please others, and too much subjected to their Humours in order to be recommended and get a Livelihood."[66] But whether he would include industrial labor under this description is not clear. In his 1751 "Observations Concerning the Increase of Mankind, Peopling of Countries, &c.," he praises laws to encourage manufacturing as "generative laws."[67] In time, however, he would come to view such laws as unwise on economic and perhaps also on moral grounds. After the war, he applauded the wisdom of American state governments' refusal to subsidize manufacturing:

> [W]hen the Governments have been solicited to support such Schemes by Encouragements, in Money, or by imposing Duties on Importation of such Goods, it has generally been refused, on this Principle, that, if the Country is ripe for the Manufacture, it may be carried on by private Persons to Advantage; and if not, it is a Folly to think of forcing Nature.[68]

Large-scale manufacturing was necessary in old countries that had grown too densely populated, Franklin realized, and it would come to America when it must, but he was glad that America was not and for a long time would not be such a country.

> Manufactures are founded in poverty. It is the multitude of poor without land in a country, and who must work for others at low wages or starve, that enables undertakers to carry on a manufacture."[69]

Franklin puzzled over the question of how industrial workers' lives might be made more decent and comfortable, but he could find no solution. He wrote in a London paper,

> A law might be made to raise their wages; but if our manufactures are too dear, they will not vend abroad, and all that part of employment will fail, unless by fighting and conquering we compel other nations to buy our goods, whether they will or no, which some have been mad enough at times to propose.[70]

Franklin's views on the poor are the dark side of his faith in the hand of nature or free markets to distribute labor and resources most effectively. He is surprisingly harsh in his judgment that charity to feed the poor is a mistake, declaring that without the sharp tooth of want we would all fall into indolence: here is one of his great quarrels with the Christian moral teaching.

> I fear the giving mankind a dependance on any thing for support in age or sickness, besides industry and frugality during youth and health, tends to flatter our natural indolence, to encourage idleness and prodigality, and thereby to promote and increase poverty, the very evil it was intended to cure.

He notes that no country is more generous than England in its provisions for feeding, clothing, educating, and healing the poor, that no one does more to make up the losses occasioned by fire, storms, and floods, and yet that England has only multiplied beggars rather than reducing their numbers.[71] Precisely because the hope for a good return on our efforts can do such wonders to rouse us to activity, removing that hope, he asserts, is a grave error.

But lest we think Franklin cold-hearted, we should also recall that he was one of the first to propose a very different kind of poor relief—the prudent and voluntary pooling of resources to reduce risks proposed in Silence Dogood's life insurance plan. No doubt, all manner of insurance plans and perhaps even Social Security would meet with his hearty approval. Indeed, Franklin even defied his own warnings against charity when he helped to raise money for a hospital for the poor in Philadelphia. Perhaps he found that in early America, where work was so profitable and indigence so rare, the natural tendency to indolence and improvidence was already being replaced by a new ethos that made charity less dangerous.[72]

In sum, Franklin's economic vision is far more nuanced and complex than the wholesale embrace of capitalism that Weber attributes to him. His economic prescriptions were shaped by a deep concern for personal independence and political liberty, and, at least at incisive moments, Franklin made prescient warnings about the dangers of preoccupation with fashionable goods and excessive consumer debt, the pathologies of dependence on public charity, and the social importance of small, independent businesses. He shared with the much more agrarian-minded Thomas Jefferson a keen appreciation for what was best and healthiest in early American society; yet he also shared with Jefferson an enthusiasm for the economic progress, rapid westward expansion, and consequent population growth that could only hasten the day when the continent would grow crowded and industrialization would run rampant.

The Meaning of Leisure

In Franklin's public discussions of economic principles, one important theme that is absent is the classical notion that wealth's highest justification lies in securing a life of leisure, either for study and conversation or for civic participation.[73] Yet, in his own life at least, Franklin retained a great deal of the traditional gentlemanly outlook, according to which happiness consists above all in the thoughtful pursuit of friendship, study, and public service, and such unpaid but serious activities are clearly distinguished from both toil and mere relaxation. The aristocratic gentleman's freedom from toil rested on the unfree labor of others. Franklin combined greater justice with equally high aspirations when he first built his own fortune and then retired from business to live upon its proceeds, but his priorities are strikingly similar to those of the aristocratic gentleman.[74] Are these priorities also in some important way different? If learning and conversation are among civilization's greatest gifts, does Franklin quietly agree with the classical view of leisure, and does his relative silence on it merely reflect his political tact? Does he give learning and leisured conversation and even public service a high status that is nevertheless crucially different from the traditional understanding? Or does he break with that view altogether and regard his own studies as merely an idiosyncratic taste and a fascinating hobby?

In the almanac Franklin gives only the rarest hints of a higher perspective according to which a devotion to moneymaking ought ultimately to be transcended.

> Methinks I hear some of you say, *Must a Man afford himself no Leisure?* I will tell thee, my Friend, what Poor Richard says, *Employ thy Time well, if thou meanest to gain Leisure;* and, *since thou art not sure of a Minute, throw not away an Hour.* Leisure is a time for doing something useful; this Leisure the diligent Man will obtain, but the lazy Man never; so that, as Poor Richard says, *a Life of Leisure, and a Life of Laziness are two Things.*[75]

But he does not explain in the almanac what he means by leisure, or precisely how it differs from labor on the one hand and frivolity on the other. Indeed, the almanac casts some aspersions on the original core meaning of *leisure,* which is "study."[76] Typical sayings are: "He that lives well, is learned enough"; "He that can compose himself, is wiser than he that composes books"; and "The most exquisite Folly is made of Wisdom spun too fine."[77]

We see much more of Franklin's own thoughts about leisure in his private letters. In 1748, soon after his retirement from business, when the press of activity of founding a militia for Pennsylvania had just passed, he congratulated himself on his newfound freedom.

> The Share I had in the late Association, &c. having given me a little present Run of Popularity, there was a pretty general Intention of chusing me a Representative for the City at the next Election of Assemblymen; but I have desired all my Friends who spoke to me about it, to discourage it, declaring that I should not serve if chosen. Thus you see I am in a fair Way of having no other Tasks than such as I shall like to give my self, and of enjoying what I look upon as a great Happiness, Leisure to read, study, make Experiments, and converse at large with such ingenious and worthy Men as are pleas'd to honor me with their Friendship or Acquaintance.[78]

But it was not to be. In 1753 Franklin wrote to John Perkins, apropos of a discussion of waterspouts,

> [H]ow much soever my Inclinations lead me to philosophical Inquiries, I am so engag'd in Business public and private, that those more pleasing pursuits are frequently interrupted, and the Chain

> of Thought necessary to be closely continu'd in such Disquisitions, so broken and disjointed, that it is with Difficulty I satisfy myself in any of them.[79]

In 1755 and again in 1765 he explained his involvement in politics as a response to crises that he hoped would soon pass and leave him leisure for studies and friendship.[80] But in 1782 the litany was still the same:

> As long as the Congress think I can be useful to our Affairs, it is my Duty to obey their Orders: But I should be happy to see them better executed by another, & myself at liberty, enjoying, before I quit the Stage of Life, some small degree of Leisure & Tranquility.[81]

Does Franklin protest too much? Even when Congress finally released him from his duties as ambassador to France, he returned home and immediately accepted employment in the governments of Pennsylvania and the United States, no doubt flattered by his countrymen's desire to keep him in their service. As is common today and was even more common in that more aristocratic age, even those who are most ambitious for public office and honor are prone to deny any such inclination, considering it more honorable to serve with reluctance than to hunger for power. After all, is public service not most noble when it entails a sacrifice of private interest? Franklin doubtless enjoyed the honors and engaging challenges of public service more than he sometimes claimed. But his liberal philosophy, which paid no honor to conquerors like Alexander and which viewed politics as the instrument of the people and the statesman as their servant, must have dimmed those pleasures a little.[82] Franklin's own political successes were mixed with tedious and frustrating efforts that make perfectly credible a countervailing yearning for the freedom to pursue his own studies in the quiet of solitude and private friendship.

And yet, when he speaks of these studies, the same thread of ambivalence is everywhere to be seen. Is the life of the mind valuable as an end in itself or only when and because it is valuable to the world of practical concerns? Is the best life one of independent thought that needs no justification beyond itself and that gives to labor its highest purpose? Or is the best life ultimately one of service, a life that even when devoted to study is fundamentally akin to labor inasmuch as its serious goal is the relief of man's estate? Franklin's thinking is characteristically modern in the stress it puts on scientific advances that bring material benefits to all, but he shares with the gentlemanly ethos of all ages (in contrast to the spirit of philosophy as originally conceived) an essential ambivalence as to how much weight should be given to the enjoyment of beautiful and useless objects—or useless but fascinating studies—and how completely one should devote oneself to public service.

One Franklin biographer, Carl Becker, has argued that science was "the one mistress to whom he gave himself without reserve and served neither from a sense of duty nor for any practical purpose," and Franklin himself certainly echoes this judgment. Writing of his electrical experiments, he relates, "I never before was engaged in any study that so engrossed my attention and my time as this has lately done."[83] But Franklin shows something of a bad conscience about intellectual pursuits that have no possible utility. He rebukes himself for wasting too much time on unhealthy frivolities, including chess. He admits that he is ashamed to confess how much time he has spent making magic squares—though he eagerly writes two detailed letters explaining all the remarkable features of those he has invented—and he defends the mathematicians of England against the charge that they ever waste time on useless studies. Possibly implicit in these reproaches is the distinction—crucial for classical philosophy—between studies that merely amuse the mind and those that teach us about the world we live in and our place in it, whether or not they are of further utility. But tellingly, he refers to his own experiments in physics as "philosophical amusements."[84] When he defends science as something more serious, it is always in terms of its utility, even if he defines utility in the broadest of terms, including what sharpens the mind for other studies or prepares the ground for benefits still unimagined. Once asked what use a hot air balloon could ever have, Franklin queried in turn, "What use is a new born baby?"[85] One senses that his fascination and his pleasure were equally ignited by scientific and mathematical inquires of every kind. But following the modern re-conception of science led by Francis Bacon, which presents the great aim and justification of science as the relief of man's estate, Franklin needed to believe in the eventual utility of his studies in order fully to approve them.[86]

Franklin's most positive comment on leisure as an end in itself comes in a letter to the physician and philanthropist John Fothergill.

> *When do you intend to live?* i.e. to enjoy Life. When will you retire to your Villa, give your self Repose, delight in Viewing the Operations of Nature in the vegetable Creation, assist her in her Works, get your ingenious Friends at times about you, make them happy with your Conversation, and enjoy theirs; or, if alone, amuse yourself with your Books and elegant Collections? To be hurried about perpetually from one sick Chamber to another, is not Living.

The context in which this was written, however, is revealing: Franklin was in a towering dark mood, having just been the impotent witness to a brutal mob's massacre of a group of peaceful, unarmed Indians and to his governor's craven refusal to enforce order. Thus, the letter continues, "Half the Lives you save are not worth saving, as being useless; and almost the other Half ought not to be sav'd, as being mischievous."[87] It was not long before the thundercloud passed and Franklin returned to his characteristically sunny affection for most of humanity. More important context for the Fothergill letter is provided by Franklin's words upon hearing of the death of this friend many years later.

> I think a worthier Man never lived. For besides his constant Readiness to serve his Friends, he was always studying and projecting something for the Good of his Country and of Mankind in general, and putting others, who had it in their Power, on executing what was out of his own reach; but whatever was within it he took care to do himself; and his incredible Industry and unwearied Activity enabled him to do much more than can now be ever known, his Modesty being equal to his other Virtues.[88]

Franklin's most definitive statement on the question of study versus service—one that should be taken all the more seriously inasmuch as it accords with the choices he made throughout his life—comes in a 1750 letter to Cadwallader Colden.

> I wish you all the Satisfaction that Ease and Retirement from Publick Business can possibly give you: but let not your Love of Philosophical Amusements have more than its due Weight with you. Had Newton been Pilot but of a single common Ship, the finest of his Discoveries would scarce have excus'd, or atton'd for his abandoning the Helm one Hour in Time of Danger; how much less if she had carried the Fate of the Commonwealth.[89]

This statement has, with good reason, been contrasted to Jefferson's 1778 letter to David Rittenhouse, which seems a direct answer to it. Jefferson wrote:

> Tho' I have been aware of the authority our cause would acquire with the world from it's being known that yourself and Doctr. Franklin were zealous friends to it, and am myself duly impressed with a sense of the arduousness of government, and the obligation those are under who are able to conduct it, yet I am also satisfied that there is an order of geniuses above the obligation, and therefore exempted from it. No body can conceive that nature ever intended to throw away a Newton upon the occupations of a crown. . . . Are those powers then, which being intended for the erudition of the world, like air and light, the world's common property, to be taken from their proper pursuit to do the commonplace drudgery of governing a single state, a work which may be executed by men of an ordinary stature, such as are always and every where to be found?[90]

Surveying both Franklin's record and his arguments, Edmund S. Morgan has argued compellingly that public service was ultimately what mattered most to Franklin.[91] Certainly it was politics that absorbed the lion's share of his thought, and if his dedication to it involved less spontaneous pleasure and more dutiful effort than his scientific studies did, it was only politics that could engage his passions to such an extent as to rupture friendships and estrange him from his only son. And yet even public service Franklin managed much of the time to turn into high-level play of the broadest and richest kind, such as writing wicked political satires, dining with dignitaries and luminaries, winning over enemies and reconciling rivals with his charming stories, and the whole while carrying on conversations and correspondences with fascinating men and women about human nature, history, the rights of man, and even waterspouts. The human life Franklin offers us as a model is one of diligence and acquisitiveness with a high and broad purpose, aimed at building the powers of application and the comfortable self-sufficiency that can then be turned to use in even more satisfying activities of a political, literary, and scientific nature.

In sum, while the mature Franklin shared much of the traditional gentleman's cherishing of serious leisure and public service, he combined it with the modern capitalist's approval of the moral value of work and he qualified it with a new focus on utility, broadly conceived. This emphasis on utility, which Franklin shared with Jefferson and so many others of their age, was of a piece with the Founders' splendidly philanthropic spirit, but it also served to blur the crucial difference between things we choose as means and things we cherish as ends in themselves. Perhaps it also prevented Franklin from acknowledging, even in his own mind, the high value he placed on understanding the world simply for its own sake.

Be this as it may, if we return to the virtues that Franklin preaches and the story of himself that he self-consciously tells in the *Autobiography*, these higher reaches of his life are much less visible than are his instrumental, more bourgeois pursuits and virtues. Poor Richard does teach a pedestrian ethic of toiling and saving. The *Autobiography*, whether by design or by the accident of its remaining unfinished, emphasizes Franklin's industry and the steady self-improvement that every American can imitate, leaving in the background the political and above all intellectual accomplishments that followed his retirement from business and that are beyond most people's reach. Franklin wants us to focus on attainable goals, and he is convinced that virtually everyone is capable of living a useful and dignified life. But by downplaying the significance of leisure, by putting little in his most popular works about what the positive focus of a life of leisure should be, he leaves his message open to distortion and to the view that wealth is the goal. This danger is increased by the fact that the lower part of his message on gaining wealth is what will naturally resonate most powerfully with most readers. Franklin was keenly aware of our need for exertion to overcome our naturally lazy inclinations; this awareness may have made him less attuned than he should have been to the danger that diligence itself can become an addiction that crowds out serious leisure, as it often does among ambitious Americans today. It is little surprise that among his most ardent disciples we should find men like Thomas Mellon and Andrew Carnegie: Franklin's spirit lends itself perhaps too easily to the capitalist urge that knows no limit to wealth, even if it does eventually turn some of that wealth to philanthropy.[92]

A more impressive disciple than the robber barons is Booker T. Washington, the leading spokesman and proponent of industrial education for freed slaves in the late nineteenth century. Washington grasped the full power of work and of little efforts of self-help to bring dignity and self-respect to a downtrodden people. He followed Franklin's insistence on putting first things first, urging his fellow American freedmen to build a solid foundation of self-discipline and economic strength in farming and manual arts before trying to acquire higher culture. But W. E. B. Du Bois, a student of Max Weber's, launched a thoughtful criticism of Washington that resembles Weber's of Franklin, but with more honesty and penetration. It applauds all that Booker T. Washington had accomplished but expresses concern about the spirit of practicality that can easily be taken too far.

> So thoroughly did he learn the speech and thought of triumphant commercialism, and the ideals of material prosperity, that the picture of a lone black boy poring over a French grammar amid the weeds and dirt of a neglected home soon seemed to him the acme of absurdities. One wonders what Socrates and St. Francis of Assisi would say to this.

Du Bois agreed with Washington that educators of the freed slaves had wasted a great deal of effort by aiming too high too soon, but he still maintained that, compared to the error of Washington, theirs was the wiser mistake to make. These educators, he said, had forgotten the natural "rule of inequality,"

> that of the million of black youth, . . . some had the talent and capacity of university men and some had the talent and capacity of blacksmiths; and that true training meant neither that all should be college men nor all artisans, but that the one should be made a missionary of culture to an untaught people, and the other a free workman among serfs. And to seek to make the blacksmith a

> scholar is almost as silly as the more modern scheme of making the scholar a blacksmith; almost, but not quite.[93]

In the end, Du Bois agreed with Franklin that both practical self-help and thoughtful leisure are essential for a great civilization, but he saw, as Franklin perhaps did not, that it is leisure and not diligence that requires the most careful cultivation.

CHAPTER 2

THE VIRTUOUS CITIZEN

FRANKLIN THOUGHT long and deeply about the virtues needed for self-government and for private happiness. He began by reflecting upon the qualities he himself needed to develop in order to prosper; soon he was working out a systematic program of moral improvement for himself and launching an informal program of moral education for his friends and fellow citizens. As always, he built from the ground up. In placing the foundation of solid morals in personal economic independence, Franklin was joined by many of his contemporaries, especially Thomas Jefferson. But Franklin gave a distinctively modern twist to the old theme of the sturdy yeoman farmer. According to Jefferson,

> Those who labour in the earth are the chosen people of God, if ever he had a chosen people, whose breasts he has made his peculiar deposit for substantial and genuine virtue. . . . Corruption of morals in the mass of cultivators is a phaenomenon of which no age nor nation has furnished an example. It is the mark set on those, who not looking up to heaven, to their own soil and industry, as does the husbandman, for their subsistence, depend for it on the casualties and caprice of customers.[1]

Franklin, however, could never savor the solitude of a Monticello; in this he again reminds us of Socrates, who explains his preference for urban life by the fact that "the country places and the trees are not willing to teach me anything, but the human beings in town are."[2] As Walter Isaacson observes, when the young Franklin set out in good American fashion to make his fortune, he went not to the frontier but to another urban center, where he immediately began to form a community of like-minded people who valued books and conversation.[3] Franklin valued the contribution that independent yeoman farmers made to American liberty, but he saw as others did not the equal and in some ways greater civic possibilities of urban life, and he developed a business ethos of enlightened self-interest that would prove more important in the long run for the developing nation than Jefferson's agrarian spirit, especially in the North. Farmers are good for republics because of their self-reliant and moderate spirit, born of a fidelity to ancestral ways and to ancestral faiths and a sober acceptance of human dependence on heaven or fortune. But Franklin saw different civic possibilities in the more dynamic spirit of free enterprise that was percolating in American cities. In this he displayed the characteristically modern embrace of progress and the hope, planted by Machiavelli, that fortune might be conquered through reason.[4] It is the entrepreneur, not the farmer, who is most open to the thought that his own and his nation's affairs may be improved almost without limit. Franklin also saw the civic possibilities inherent in an urban spirit of salutary interdependence. So influential would Franklin's new ethos of enlightened self-interest be that Alexis de Tocqueville, returning from a tour of the United States in the 1830s, portrayed it as the ethos of America itself.

> In the United States it is almost never said that virtue is beautiful. They maintain that it is useful and they prove it every day. American moralists do not claim that one must sacrifice oneself to those like oneself because it is great to do it; but they say boldly that such sacrifices are as necessary to the one who imposes them on himself as to the one who profits from them. . . .
>
> I think that in this it often happens that they do not do themselves justice; for one sometimes sees citizens in the United States as elsewhere abandoning themselves to the disinterested and unreflective sparks that are natural to man; but the Americans scarcely avow that they yield to movements of this kind; they would rather do honor to their philosophy than to themselves.[5]

Tocqueville captures admirably the spirit of energetic self-help that Franklin inspired. He captures as well a concomitant reluctance, which Fanklin encouraged and may even had shared, to acknowledge one's own deep-seated attachment to older ideas of noble self-overcoming.

The Ethos of the Merchant

We have seen how some of the most obviously profitable virtues, such as industry, thrift, and order, can be good for democracy. Franklin argues further that the wise businessman also understands the value of such moral virtues as civility and honesty, which are even more essential for self-government. Civility, as its name implies, is especially a virtue of cities. The farmer's business will prosper almost equally whether he is polite or surly, but enlightened self-interest demands that prudent merchants and tradesmen learn to curb their pride and anger, giving up small points, even when in the right, to keep peace with their fellows, and showing respect to all their acquaintances and potential customers, wealthy and humble alike. As a young workman in London, Franklin became convinced of "the Folly of being on ill Terms with those one is to live with continually." He wrote rules for the civil conduct of conversation and for the civil behavior of competitors and observers at chess games, similar in spirit to the rules he wrote for the meetings of the Junto and the conduct of public meetings. He excoriated the British Parliament for the madness of using harsh threats to try to induce Americans to submit peacefully to British trade laws, observing that "customers are not naturally brought back to a shop by unkind usage."[6]

In contrast to many of our contemporaries, Franklin had little hope that human beings could be led to respect one another for their differences. Differences, he thought, will always tend more to be a source of disagreement. But, tacitly following Hobbes, Franklin did hope that civility would grow out of an increased recognition of how much humanity has in common. As Hobbes stresses in introducing the new virtue of "complaisance," recognizing our shared vulnerability and mutual need for assistance is essential. But equally important are the fallibility of all human reason and our common vanity, which make it necessary that we offer our opinions in a modest spirit and never make a show of our superiority. Franklin points out that unpleasant and overbearing people try foolishly to win the admiration of others by pushing themselves forward, forgetting that by wounding others' vanity one usually only incurs their resentment. It is by curbing one's vanity that one has the best chance of ultimately gratifying it.[7]

Franklin places even more emphasis on the virtue of honesty. It is one of his oft-repeated sayings that a liar is never safe from detection.

> I believe it is impossible for a man, though he has all the cunning of a devil, to live and die a villain, and yet conceal it so well as to carry the name of an honest fellow to the grave with him, but some one by some accident or other shall discover him.

Again, prudence tells us that our weakness puts us in need of the assistance of others, for which we need to keep their trust.[8] But in enjoining honesty, Franklin does not leave it at that. He speaks of the shame and confusion that attend the discovery of dishonesty, as well as the disadvantage; he appeals to our own disdain for "poor pitiful sneaking Excuses"; he even speaks on occasion (Tocqueville notwithstanding) of the "Beauties of *Truth*," and asks, "[I]f *outward* Reputation could be preserved, what Pleasure can it afford to a Man that must *inwardly* despise himself, whose own Baseness will, in Spite of his Endeavours to forget it, be ever presenting itself to his View." And finally, in case all this does not work, he throws in an occasional appeal to divine justice.[9]

Such a pile of disparate reasonings is just what Kant objects to when he argues that *only* the intrinsic rightness of an act should ever be appealed to as a reason for performing it and that moral education is made weaker the more "heteronomous" reasons are allowed to contaminate it.[10] Franklin of course stands unapologetically at the opposite pole from Kant: the chief point for him is not purity of motive but good results. Prudence should give us reason enough to be honest, but people are not very reasonable; the moral beauty of a good character would also suffice if people understood the convergence between true virtue and true interest, yet moral appeals are even less reliable than prudential ones. Franklin works to steer society towards an ethos that will need as little reliance on nonutilitarian and especially other-worldly sanctions as possible, but in the meantime he does not disdain their support.

If we wished to press Franklin, we might ask whether such a virtue as honesty is really good in itself, apart from all consequences, as Kant thinks, or whether it is good only as a means to further ends, and if the latter, why it would not be rational to abandon honesty in exceptional cases when a very great cost would be incurred by upholding it. It is an important part of Franklin's whole outlook that he never pursues such a line of questioning. Franklin never pressed the exceptional case; he shows no attraction to the view of Thucydides and Machiavelli and Hobbes that the real truth about the human condition is found in extreme situations that put all virtue to the test. Franklin's distance from Kant is clear from the definition he gives to sincerity in his own program of self-improvement: "Use no hurtful Deceit."[11] Franklin would not have hesitated an instant, if confronted by a Nazi at the door, to lie about the Jews in his basement. If asked whether honesty would still be a virtue if it generally proved disadvantageous in the long run to those who practiced it, he might well say not; he might indeed say that our whole understanding of virtue would then need to be rethought. But he would regard the question as academic. The important thing is that there *is* a convergence between what is obviously and immediately good for others and what is in the long run best for ourselves.

Franklin goes a step further, however. Describing his policy of refusing to print personal libel and scurrilous reflections on foreign governments in his newspaper, both of which may be accompanied by the most pernicious consequences, he shows that he thinks the social benefit of a good policy should be reason enough to follow it, so long as doing so does not actually harm us. "These things I mention as a Caution to young Printers, and that they may be encouraged not to pollute their Presses and disgrace their Profession by such infamous Practices, but refuse steadily; as they may see by my Example, that such a Course of Conduct will not on the whole be injurious to their Interests.[12]

In fact, Franklin thinks, true happiness is to be found only in lives that transcend narrow self-interest. He makes this point in a late essay entitled "The Whistle." It tells the story of how as a child he cried with vexation at learning that he had paid for a toy whistle four times what it was worth, and how he then characteristically turned the experience to good use, reminding himself, when tempted to buy some unnecessary thing, "*Do not give too much for the Whistle.*" Franklin continues,

> As I grew up, came into the World, and observed the Actions of Men, I thought I met many *who gave too much for the Whistle.*— When I saw one ambitious of Court Favour, sacrificing his Time in Attendance at Levees, his Repose, his Liberty, his Virtue and perhaps his Friend, to obtain it; I have said to my self, *This Man gives too much for his Whistle.* . . . If I knew a miser, who gave up every kind of comfortable living, all the Pleasure of doing Good to others, all the Esteem of his fellow Citizens, & the Joys of benevolent Friendship, for the sake of Accumulating Wealth, *Poor Man,* says I, *you pay too much for your Whistle.*[13]

Franklin hoped that increasing numbers of merchants and tradesmen like himself, if enlightened about their own happiness, might become pillars of their communities. If he emphasizes the mundane connection of these bourgeois virtues to self-interest rather more than some would wish, it is an essential part of his project to teach us not to deceive ourselves about human selfishness. Trust is good, but he advises us to keep it on a short leash. Friendly partnerships can be of great mutual advantage, but all the terms should be put in writing, so that there can be no room for dispute about what each party's obligations are.[14] Such a practice, Franklin hoped, would save us in the short run from broken friendships and lawsuits and in the long run from the cynicism and misanthropy that unrealistic expectations can spawn.

Franklin's Early Thoughts on Virtue and Vice

This understanding of virtue Franklin seems to have held without wavering for most of his adult life, but he arrived at it only after a period of severe moral skepticism. To better understand his view of virtue and its connection to moral responsibility, it will be useful to examine his early essay, "A Dissertation on Liberty and Necessity, Pleasure and Pain," which argues against the existence of free will and concludes that there is in reality no distinction between virtue and vice.[15] We will then examine the reasons he later gave for repudiating this essay and for making the cultivation of virtue his lifelong study and practice.

Franklin wrote the essay during his first stay in London, at age

19. He tells us that he had already become a thorough doubter of the Presbyterian beliefs of his parents through reading Shaftesbury and his disciple Anthony Collins.[16] Yet even the moral deism of these authors is called into question in this essay. In its dedication Franklin warns that he has written only for discerning readers, who must take care "to distinguish the hypothetical Parts of the Argument from the conclusive." But one hypothetical part of the argument would seem to be its main foundation, for, citing the common belief of "People of almost every Sect and Opinion," Franklin posits that there is a creator and that he is "all-wise, all-good, all powerful." What follows, he says, "being a Chain of Consequences truly drawn from" these propositions, "will stand or fall as they are true or false." It takes Franklin only a few sentences to draw from his pious hypotheses a conclusion that is shocking both to conventional Christian opinion and to deistic moralists—everything that God does and allows to be done must be good, and evil does not exist—for Franklin finds the traditional distinction between what God does and what he permits unpersuasive.

> If God permits an Action to be done, it is because he wants either *Power* or *Inclination* to hinder it; in saying he wants *Power,* we deny Him to be *almighty;* and if we say He wants *Inclination* or *Will,* it must be, either because He is not Good, or the Action is not *evil.* . . .
>
> . . . *If a creature is made by God, it must depend upon God, and receive all its Power from Him; with which Power the Creature can do nothing contrary to the Will of God.*

Franklin takes issue not only with the traditional Christian view of good and evil but also with the account propounded in *The Religion of Nature Delineated* by William Wollaston, who defines as good every action that is done according to truth and as evil all that are done contrary to truth. Franklin replies that everyone acts according to the truth of his nature all the time. If respecting others' property accords with the truth of their ownership, as Wollaston observes, stealing accords equally with the truly covetous nature of the thief. We may note that this argument is not hypothetical, as it depends not on the presumed existence of a perfect God, but on Franklin's own observations of human characters and actions. Yet does not Wollaston's argument, properly refined to take account of Franklin's objection, point to a sensible basis for distinguishing virtue and vice? Virtuous actions would be those that take fully into account the truth of our natures, our needs and desires, our situation in the world and our potential happiness, choosing what is best for us. Vicious actions would be those that accord only with partial truths and thus are short sighted and self-destructive. This is the distinction Socrates draws, and he attributes our varying degrees of success in living well to our varying degrees of clarity about the truth, failures being due to ignorance and passions that cloud the vision. Socrates therefore denies a radically free will (as Franklin evidently wishes to do also), while affirming a real distinction between virtue and vice. But Franklin does not follow this path.[17]

Franklin's explicit denial of free will is made first on religious grounds: A wise God would no more allow free but ignorant beings to mar the order of his creation than a good watchmaker would build such beings into a watch. To claim that God designed the world with perfect wisdom and yet left his best creatures free to become evil is absurd, Franklin avers.[18] He denies not only the moral freedom to choose between good and evil that Christianity asserts but even the far more limited freedom, accepted by all ancient and most modern philosophers, to follow one's own judgment and to choose otherwise when one's judgment changes, for he describes all action as *mechanically* determined. Franklin argues, "*If there is no such Thing as Free-Will in Creatures, there can be neither Merit nor Demerit in Creatures.*" Now, it is true that if human actions are like the movements of clock springs, no one can merit rewards and punishments, although the best might still merit admiration. Franklin concludes, however, that "*therefore every Creature must be equally esteem'd by the Creator.*" This is a strange corollary, for even a master painter does not esteem equally all parts of his great paintings; faces are more important than stones in the background. Franklin argues further that if all creatures are equally esteemed by the Creator, *"so they are, as in Justice they ought to be, equally us'd."* This follows even less. How can clock springs make claims of justice? But perhaps Franklin is continuing to make explicit what is implicit in the Christian notion of a perfect God: Christians can never give up on the idea of God's justice, by which they mean his equal care for the happiness of all human beings who are equally innocent.

Franklin proceeds in the second part of the essay to argue that every life is in fact just as happy as every other. He posits that to be alive is to be subject to pain and uneasiness. He does not say how this applies to plants, but of humans he says,

> We are first mov'd by *Pain* and the whole succeeding Course of our Lives is but one continu'd Series of Action with a View to be freed from it. As fast as we have excluded one Uneasiness another appears, otherwise the Motion would cease. If a continual Weight is not apply'd, the Clock will stop. And as soon as the Avenues of Uneasiness to the Soul are choak'd up or cut off, we are dead, we think and act no more.

Thus Franklin proves again, on very different grounds, that there is no merit or demerit in human beings.

> For since *Freedom from Uneasiness* is the End of all our Actions, how is it possible for us to do any Thing disinterested?—How can any Action be meritorious of Praise or Dispraise, Reward or Punishment, when the natural Principle of *Self-Love* is the only and the irresistible Motive to it?

This hedonistic account of human motivations, resting on grounds independent of the postulation of a perfect God, seems not to be hypothetical: we may take it as Franklin's true view, at this time in his life, of the human soul.[19]

But what follows is a most curious and unsatisfactory argument. As desires are nothing but wishes to be released from pain, so the pleasure that satisfies a desire is always equal in magnitude to the discomfort of that desire. And the conclusion is that in every life there is an exact equality of pleasure and pain, all uneasiness finally ending in the "sweet sleep of death." Franklin makes no mention of unexpected pleasures, fulfillments of desires that turn out to be disappointing, happy anticipations, gnawing anxiety that goes on for years, the pleasures of music, good books, and delicious meals that come just as the appetite is felt and before it becomes uncomfortable, and above all the fear of death, which often ends only in the terror of death itself. He acknowledges that people will think that his argument defies common experience, but he insists that we are not such good judges of others' happiness as we think, that many people are happy in the midst of poverty and many secretly enjoy even their sorrows. True, but as a wiser Franklin would later observe, human beings are still remarkably dissimilar in their capacity for happiness. In a letter written in 1758 he comments on two of his recently deceased friends, William Parsons and Stephen Potts:

> If *Enough* were the Means to make a Man happy, one had always the *Means* of Happiness without ever enjoying the *Thing;* the other had always the *Thing* without ever possessing the *Means.* Parsons, even in his prosperity, always fretting! Potts, in the midst of his Poverty, ever laughing! It seems, then, that Happiness in this Life rather depends on Internals than Externals; and that, besides the natural effects of Wisdom and Virtue, Vice and Folly, there is such a Thing as being of a happy or unhappy Constitution.[20]

The claim that everyone has an equal share of happiness might be simply the work of a clever young mind that has gotten carried away with a penetrating insight into the interdependence of pleasure and pain. But it may also be a deliberate *reductio ad absurdum* of the idea of a perfect and benevolent God. If the existence of such a God precludes evil and if his benevolence extends equally to all, then some such equality of pleasures and pains in every life would be necessary.[21]

Of course the orthodox Christian account of God's providence includes an afterlife, and it is there that the just are made happy and all accounts are set right. But in addition to his proof that no one merits rewards or punishments, Franklin makes strong arguments on naturalistic grounds against the possibility of any state of "uninterrupted Ease and Happiness": "Are not the Pleasures of the Spring made such by the Disagreeableness of the Winter? . . . Were it then always Spring, were the Fields always green and flourishing, and the Weather constantly serene and fair, the Pleasure would pall and die upon our hands." He further adduces the mind's dependence on the bodily senses for its ideas and its tendency to become impaired when the body is impaired as grounds to doubt that disembodied souls could have an active existence. These arguments, too, are independent of the essay's theological premises and seem to be intended with utmost seriousness.

Franklin ends the essay with a recapitulation that introduces one new and important thought. "Since every Action is the Effect of Self-Uneasiness, the Distinction of Virtue and Vice is excluded," and the denial of merit and demerit that was made on the basis of God's perfection "is again demonstrated." As he suggests in his autobiography, this conclusion is the chief point the essay was designed to demonstrate. He seems to prove it twice, first on the religious grounds that in a world made by a perfect God all human actions would be as good as possible, and second on the naturalistic grounds that among human beings motivated solely by the desire to escape pain, there can be no disinterested action and no claims of merit on that basis. This is a correct inference, but it does not follow that there can be no vice and no virtue. There can still be stupidity, cowardice, laziness, and failures of self-control that prevent one from attaining what happiness is available; there can still be cruelty that brings no one any benefit, and steadfastness and kindness that bring good things for oneself and others whose happiness is intertwined with one's own. Virtue and vice are not excluded on the naturalistic premises of the essay's second part unless Franklin seriously intends his implausible claim that all lives are equally happy. And those naturalistic, exclusively hedonistic principles are themselves questionable, as Franklin would soon come to see.

The strained arguments of this essay suggest that the following may have been at work behind it. At a time in his life when he had twice run away from responsibilities and was living a carefree life in London, Franklin set out to prove by every means he could that the Puritan notion of sin and responsibility under which he had grown up was wholly unfounded. But he was uneasy; he could not absolutely refute the possibility that we are free and that heaven and hell await us; he went too far in constructing an argument about happiness that would make the afterlife unnecessary for justice; he went too far in denying the existence of virtue and vice when all that he had shown from his own premises was that no one merits rewards or punishments.[22] Perhaps a part of him thought that he did have duties to others and that he ought to attend to them, and another part was intent on silencing this thought. At the time in his life when he was thinking hardest about freedom and necessity, he had not yet had the insight into the convergence of virtue and happiness that would later give decisive shape to his outlook. Thus, his theoretical critique of moralism or moral indignation was separated in time and thought from his embrace of virtue; he never thought through to the bottom the ramifications for human responsibility of the convergence of virtue and good sense. Be this as it may, the essay provides important evidence of Franklin's early and profound doubts about the Christian view of free will and sin and gives evidence of the centrality of pleasure and pain to his understanding of human motivations.

Franklin's Retreat from His Early Views

Not long after this, most likely in the quiet hours of shipboard musing on the return trip to America in 1726, Franklin decided that virtue and vice are meaningful after all and indeed of utmost importance. Franklin tells us that he came to doubt the cleverness of the essay on liberty and necessity and of the "deism" that inspired it. The impetus for the religious part of this reassessment seems to have been entirely pragmatic. "My arguments" for deism, he says,

> perverted some others, particularly Collins and Ralph: but each of them having afterwards wrong'd me greatly without the least Compunction and recollecting Keith's Conduct towards me, (who was another Freethinker) and my own towards Vernon and Miss Read which at Times gave me great Trouble, I began to suspect that this Doctrine tho' it might be true, was not very Useful. My London Pamphlet, which . . . from the Attributes of God, his infinite Wisdom, Goodness and Power concluded that nothing could possibly be wrong in the World, and that Vice and Virtue were empty Distinctions, no such Things existing: appear'd now not so clever a Performance as I once thought it; and I doubted whether some Error had not insinuated itself unperceiv'd into my Argument, so as to infect all that follow'd, as is common in metaphysical Reasonings. I grew convinced that *Truth, Sincerity and Integrity* in Dealings between Man and Man, were of the utmost

> Importance to the Felicity of Life, and I form'd written Resolutions, (which still remain in my Journal Book) to practice them ever while I lived.[23]

Franklin echoes this criticism of "metaphysical reasonings" in a letter to Benjamin Vaughan written near the end of his life. He tells of another early essay he wrote proving that everything must not be fated by God, because one of the things that God commands is prayer, and if everything were fated, prayer would be absurd. "The great Uncertainty I found in Metaphysical Reasonings, disgusted me, and I quitted that kind of Reading & Study, for others more satisfactory."[24] What are we to make of this turn in his thinking?

The statement that his doctrine was not very useful even if it was true suggests one possible way of understanding Franklin's new outlook. He might have continued to reject all moral standards but decided that one must be more discreet, that one must cultivate the appearance of virtue while concealing one's genuine materialistic and hedonistic views. We would expect such a person quietly to amass wealth and power for himself, while outwardly espousing the reigning moral views of his time. But what Franklin did is quite different. He remained an open doubter of the prevalent Protestant faith of the colonies, incurring the intense disapproval of his family and forgoing the advantages that networking within a dominant church can bring to an ambitious man. On the other hand, he devised for himself a private program of moral self-improvement that he continued to follow for years, examining himself every evening and carrying with him in all his travels the little black book in which he monitored his progress. He formed a club for collective self-improvement, moral as well as intellectual. And at the end of his life he was still seizing every opportunity to teach posterity that virtue is the surest road to happiness. Something much different from a strategic decision to cover his tracks was clearly at work.

Apparently, as the young Franklin gazed back over his life and its errata, he realized more than that his materialistic doctrines had caused others to hurt him and that his denial of a providential God, even if true, was impolitic. He realized that the *moral* conclusion of his essay on liberty and necessity—its denial of any meaningful distinction between virtue and vice—was clearly *not* true. He came to see that even if we are motivated simply by pleasure and pain, there are qualities we can cultivate that make all the difference to our happiness and that of others, of which good sense is one of the most important. It is our own wise or foolish actions, not some inscrutable fate that drives us willy-nilly from without, that do most to determine how happy we are, and human lives do vary enormously in degrees of happiness. But more than that, Franklin began to realize that his thesis that pleasure and pain determine everything we do was not right. Human benevolence exists and cannot be adequately explained on hedonistic grounds. A few years later, he reasoned:

> It is the Opinion of some People, that Man is a Creature altogether selfish, and that all our Actions have at Bottom a View to private Interest; If we do good to others, it is, say they, because there is a certain Pleasure attending virtuous Actions. But how Pleasure comes to attend a virtuous Action, these Philosophers are puzzled to shew, without contradicting their first Principles, and acknowledging that Men are *naturally* benevolent as well as selfish. For whence can arise the Pleasure you feel after having done a good-natured Thing, if not hence, that you had *before* strong humane and kind Inclinations in your Nature, which are by such Actions in some Measure gratified?[25]

And this benevolence is no small matter. Friendship and trust are essential to happiness, and hence a heartfelt concern with the welfare of others is to be encouraged not just in others but in ourselves. Merely feigning virtue would show that one had missed the great lesson that Franklin spent his life trying to teach: that doing real good is essential to happiness and, thus, that virtues like justice and honesty are not ultimately a sacrifice of self-interest but are integral to the richest happiness.

As he found his own way to an appreciation of virtue, Franklin came to have more respect for the teachings of the great religions. It was never plausible to him that virtue is good simply because God commands it, but after his first return from London, in 1726, he became willing to entertain the possibility that God might command it because it is good.[26] As a support for morality, religion can be a force for good in this world; if this is not sufficient reason to believe in any particular revelation, it is reason enough to support religion in general and to take care not to undermine the good opinion anyone has of his own. Since Franklin never retracted the strong logic of the first part of his essay on liberty and necessity, and since he now acknowledged real imperfections in the world, it seems that he must also have rejected the belief in an all-good, all-wise, and all-powerful God who leaves no room for error, if indeed he ever believed in such a being. He remained open to a God who was either omnipotent and unconcerned with individual lives or concerned with individuals but not omnipotent. By now, however, moral truths had come to appear clear and self-evident to Franklin in a way that theological truths never would, and he was confident that one need not know the latter in order to grasp the former.

It seems, then, that the errors that insinuated themselves unperceived into his argument are several. First would be the hypothesis of an all-wise, all-good, and all-powerful God. Second (if indeed he ever believed it) would be the preposterous conclusion that all lives are equally happy. Third would be the hedonistic claims about human motivation, which Franklin did not altogether reject—pleasure and pain remained extremely important in his account of the human heart—but he supplemented them now with an account of the possibility of benevolence. And the fourth and most important error would be the illogical inference from the denial of radical freedom to the denial of any meaningful distinction between virtue and vice.[27]

What remains, then, of the concept of deserving or merit? Franklin raises this question in an essay entitled "Self-Denial Not the Essence of Virtue."[28] In it he challenges the common notion "that without *Self-Denial* there is no Virtue, and that the greater the *Self-Denial* the greater the Virtue." It is possible, he argues in response, to have such a good nature or such good habits that one is never tempted by a given vice. A natural virtue is as much a virtue as one acquired through struggle, and a well-ingrained good habit is more of a virtue than a weak and frequently broken resolution. But does a virtue merit any reward, he allows a hypothetical objector to ask, if it never costs any pains? Franklin's response to this is radical. "We do not pretend to merit any thing of God, for he is above our Services; and the Benefits he confers on us, are the Effects of his Goodness and Bounty." This unorthodox but reverent-sounding note is one that Franklin would strike throughout his life. He is silent on whether anyone merits divine punishment, but the suggestion is that God's kindness is given freely to all. Thus Franklin effectively removes God from his discussion of merit; God does not concern himself with assigning rewards and punishments, nor does justice require that he should.

Instead, merit is nothing but the obligation one human being puts another under by rendering a good service. What matters is not the spirit in which an act is performed but simply how useful we really are to each other. "If a man does me a service from a natural benevolent Inclination, does he deserve less of me than another who does me the like Kindness against his Inclination?" Franklin does not even mind if the motive is mercenary or vain; the obligation to return it (and hence the merit in that act) is the same. The superiority of true virtue lies not in its purity but in its consistency, for the good nature or habits that make virtue easy also make it reliable.

But what is the status of this indebtedness that Franklin speaks of? Is returning a favor anything more than the natural expression of a healthy soul's spontaneous gratitude and the dictate of prudence? Do we have here a duty of justice that the will is free to fulfill or violate? Or is the soul in this as in everything governed by an inner necessity of passions and judgments ultimately as inexorable as the necessities that govern the movements of the stars? Franklin never quite says.[29] In the autobiographical account of his turn to moral seriousness, after discussing his new hypothesis that nothing is bad because it is forbidden but certain actions "might be forbidden *because* they were bad for us," he concludes,

> And this Persuasion, with the kind hand of Providence, or some guardian Angel, or accidental favorable Circumstances and Situations, or all together, preserved me (thro' this dangerous Time of Youth . . .) without any *wilful* gross Immorality or Injustice that might have been expected from my Want of Religion. I say *willful*, because the Instances I have mentioned, had something of *Necessity* in them, from my Youth, Inexperience, and the Knavery of others.[30]

But this implies that these errors had something of freedom, too.

We find the same ambiguity in Franklin's discussion of several lines of Pope earlier in the *Autobiography.* In the suggestive context of an account of the Socratic method of discourse, Franklin argues that a dogmatic style of conversation defeats the purposes of speech, which are mutual information and pleasure. Seconding Pope, he urges us instead "To speak tho' sure, with seeming Diffidence," and adds to it a line from another context, "For Want of Modesty is Want of Sense." This leads him to criticize the original couplet that contained the latter line:

> Immodest Words admit of *no* Defence,
> For Want of Modesty is Want of Sense.

Franklin observes,

> Now is not *Want of Sense* (where a Man is so unfortunate as to want it) some Apology for his *Want of Modesty?* and would not the Lines stand more justly thus?
>
> Immodest Words admit *but this* Defence,
> That Want of Modesty is Want of Sense.[31]

This is almost pure Socratism. But why does Franklin call this unfortunate want of sense only "some Apology," rather than the whole explanation, as Socrates would? Why does he suggest that the defense is still defective? He seems to be hedging, almost willing to grant that souls are governed by inner necessities that do not leave them free to be more sensible than they are, and yet still not prepared to rule out some modicum of freedom that he never explains.

The same ambiguity pervades the *Autobiography.* Franklin shows great gentleness, great understanding of human faults, characterizing his own faults as errata or inadvertent misprints, yet still holding himself to account for them, regarding those of others with the same generous understanding and equanimity, and holding up all human faults for gentle ridicule rather than hatred. After relating the way Governor Keith's duplicity left him stranded and penniless in London, he asks,

> But what shall we think of a Governor's playing such pitiful Tricks, and imposing so grossly on a poor ignorant Boy! It was a Habit he

> had acquired. He wish'd to please every body; and having little to give, he gave Expectations. He was otherwise an ingenious sensible Man, a pretty good Writer, and a good Governor for the People. . . . Several of our best Laws were of his Planning, and pass'd during his Administration.[32]

It is part of Franklin's charm that he shows such understanding; it belongs to the same charming, benevolent spirit to pass over with a light hand the metaphysical question of freedom and necessity and merit.

The Project for Moral Perfection

In the *Autobiography,* Franklin reports, with a perfectly straight face:

> It was about this time [in the early 1730s] that I conceiv'd the bold and arduous Project of arriving at moral Perfection. I wish'd to live without committing any Fault at any time; I would conquer all that either Natural Inclination, Custom, or Company might lead me into. As I knew, or thought I knew, what was right and wrong, I did not see why I might not *always* do the one and avoid the other. But I soon found I had undertaken a Task of more Difficulty than I had imagined. While my *Attention was taken up* in guarding against one Fault, I was often surpriz'd by another. Habit took the Advantage of Inattention. Inclination was sometimes too strong for Reason. I concluded at length, that the mere speculative Conviction that it was our Interest to be compleatly virtuous, was not sufficient to prevent our Slipping, and that the contrary Habits must be broken and good ones acquired and established, before we can have any Dependance on a steady uniform Rectitude of Conduct. For this purpose I therefore contriv'd the following Method.[33]

Franklin's method is carefully to define the virtues he wants to cultivate and then to work on them systematically, one at a time. His spirit could not be more American: the difficult we do immediately; the impossible takes a little longer. But with method all things are possible.[34] Franklin evidently had no difficulty determining what virtue demands. His qualification, "I knew, or thought I knew," is not followed up by any critique of virtue here or elsewhere; we find no evident doubts as to whether what passes for virtue might be naïve simple-mindedness, as Thrasymachus charges in Plato's *Republic,* no explicit revaluation of traditional virtue after the fashion of Jesus or Machiavelli or Nietzsche. Franklin does not even acknowledge that such revaluations of the canon of virtues have taken place; he writes as if all the disagreements in human conceptions of virtue come down to different ways of slicing up the same pie. Nor does Franklin spend any time on the question that Socrates wrestled with for so long, the question of whether the many virtues people honor or should honor are all ultimately one and the same. Behind this question is the question of whether virtue is reducible to prudence or whether it ever requires a sacrifice of prudent self-interest. Instead, he suggests that the differences in moralists' catalogues of virtues all arose "as different Writers included more or fewer Ideas under the same Name." He says he decided, for his own part, "to use rather more names with fewer Ideas annex'd to each, than fewer Names with more Ideas; and I included under Thirteen Names of Virtues all that at that time occurr'd to me as necessary or desirable."[35]

But Franklin was more subtle than this breezy introduction to his catalogue of virtues would suggest. In publishing late in his life the scheme that he devised for his own use as a young man, he wished to make his conception of virtue seem as uncontroversial and universally applicable as possible. In fact, his list includes many deliberate and fascinating modifications of traditional virtues, and equally important omissions.[36] His thirteen virtues, with their definitions, are these:

1. Temperance. Eat not to Dulness. Drink not to Elevation.
2. Silence. Speak not but what may benefit others or yourself. Avoid trifling Conversation.
3. Order. Let all your Things have their Places. Let each Part of your Business have its Time.
4. Resolution. Resolve to perform what you ought. Perform without fail what you resolve.
5. Frugality. Make no Expence but to do good to others or yourself: i.e. Waste nothing.
6. Industry. Lose no Time. Be always employ'd in something useful. Cut off all unnecessary Actions.

7. Sincerity. Use no hurtful Deceit. Think innocently and justly; and, if you speak, speak accordingly.
8. Justice. Wrong none, by doing Injuries or omitting the Benefits that are your Duty.
9. Moderation. Avoid Extreams. Forbear resenting Injuries so much as you think they deserve.
10. Cleanliness. Tolerate no Uncleanness in Body, Cloaths or Habitation.
11. Tranquility. Be not disturbed at Trifles, or at Accidents common or unavoidable.
12. Chastity. Rarely use Venery but for Health or Offspring; never to Dulness, Weakness, or the injury of your own or another's Peace or Reputation.
13. Humility. Imitate Jesus and Socrates.

This is a thorough and thoroughly bourgeois recasting of the canon of virtues that Franklin had inherited from aristocratic Europe and Puritan New England, shorn of everything pious and heroic but not of good sense or humanity. Here we find our old friends frugality and industry, prefaced now by the order and resolution needed to put them fully into practice. But here also is a constant resolve to be useful to others: silence, frugality, sincerity, justice, and moderation are all defined in a way that bespeaks benevolence. If the list is morally suspect, it is not because it is narrowly selfish but because it is so comfortably accommodating of worldly pleasures. Temperance and chastity make the new direction clear: moderation demands that at all costs we avoid the folly of asceticism. Franklin drives home the point in a song entitled "The Antediluvians Were All Very Sober."

> 'Twas honest old Noah first planted the Vine,
> And mended his Morals by drinking its Wine;
> He justly the drinking of Water decry'd;
> For he knew that all Mankind, by drinking it, dy'd
> Derry down . . .

And he defends it in a letter in which he demonstrates scientifically, with appropriate diagrams, that mankind was meant to drink wine, for while the animals were all given straight legs and hooves or paws that leave them no choice but to drink water from the ground, man was provided with an elbow, at just the right point in his arm, clearly signaling the divine intention that we should all lift wine glasses to our mouths.[37]

True chastity Franklin regarded as even more unreasonable than teetotaling. The limits he in fact put upon his own desires are sometimes difficult to discern, but for all his attempts to bed charming females, young and old, perhaps we may say that he enjoyed the half-serious attempt and the serious flirtation as much as or more than the thing itself, and surely that he was an untiring advocate of marriage as the best remedy for "that-hard-to-be-govern'd Passion of Youth."[38] As he put it in one piece so scandalous that it was suppressed by all editors of Franklin's works during the nineteenth century, "A single Man has not nearly the Value he would have in that State of Union. He is an incomplete Animal. He resembles the odd Half of a Pair of Scissars." Failing this remedy, Franklin goes on to recommend to his nameless bachelor friend an old mistress over a young one, on account of her greater discretion and on other grounds both scientific and moral:

> 5. Because in every Animal that walks upright the Deficiency of the Fluids that fill the Muscles appears first in the highest Part: The Face first grows lank and wrinkled; then the Neck; then the Breast and Arms; the lower Parts continuing to the last as plump as ever: So that covering all above with a Basket, and regarding only what is below the Girdle, it is impossible of two Women to know an old from a young one. And as in the dark all Cats are grey. . . .
>
> 7. Because the Compunction is less. The having made a young Girl *miserable* may give you frequent bitter Reflections; none of which can attend the making an old Woman *happy*.[39]

For himself, however, he seems to have chosen only women who were charming in every light. To one of these, the faithful widow Helvétius, he sent a story in which he visited the Elysian Fields, where he met her former husband and discovered that the husband had consoled himself for the loss of his delightful wife by marrying another, as much like her as he could find—who turns out to be Franklin's own deceased wife. Franklin closes with the appeal, "Let us revenge ourselves." To the still married Madame Brillon, whom he loved equally well and at practically the same time, he wrote,

> People commonly speak of *Ten* Commandments.—I have been taught that there are *twelve*. The *first* was, Increase and multiply & replenish the Earth. The *twelfth* is, A new Commandment I give unto you, *that ye love one another.* It seems to me that they are a little misplaced, and that the last should have been the first. However, I never made any Difficulty about that, but was always willing to obey them both whenever I had an Opportunity.[40]

Franklin's laxness in sexual morals goes hand in hand with his great gift of charm, his unequaled ability to understand and to find common ground with all people, old and young, male and female, learned and simple, proud and humble. He had an instinctive knowledge of how to reach people, disarm them, draw them out, and win them over, and it is perhaps inevitable that a man with such talents would be incorrigibly flirtatious. In this Franklin only carried to an extreme an ability and a corresponding weakness common to many great political men.

But we return to our list of virtues. It should be reasonably clear by now that excellence, for Franklin, does not dictate that one crucify the self or even that one put others first, but it does demand an enlightened attention to the ways in which the good of others dovetails with one's own. Franklin's comments on silence and sincerity show that he was still struggling to make his conversation constructive and to get his prattling, punning, and satirizing under control. His belated addition of humility to the list, made at the insistence of a Quaker friend who kindly informed him that he was generally thought proud and overbearing in conversation, raises another side of the same problem. Long after he first encountered the Socratic style of discourse as an apprentice and resolved to adopt it, and well after forming his young tradesman friends into a club for mutual improvement and persuading them to conduct their debates "in the sincere Spirit of Enquiry after Truth, without Fondness for Dispute, or Desire of Victory," forbidding themselves all expressions of "Positiveness in Opinion, or of direct Contradiction," Franklin was still fighting his own tendency to pursue victory at the expense of instructing both himself and others.[41]

His definitions of moderation and tranquility are also revealing, especially his injunction to "Forbear resenting Injuries so much as you think they deserve." When Franklin wrote the *Auto-*

biography, with the advantage of time and distance, he was able to relate such stories as Governor Keith's betrayal with splendid equanimity, giving the impression of a soul naturally philosophic in spirit. But we see in this injunction the effort it took to bring his temper under control. And indeed, although the massive impression the *Autobiography* leaves us with is that of its twinkling-eyed narrator, he gives many hints of the lively resentment the younger Franklin felt at injustices. These include his responses to the violence of his brother James, but also to the colonial government that imprisoned James for his opposition; to the insults of his employer Keimer; to his rival Bradford, who as postmaster refused to let his newspaper be carried in the mail; to the family of a girl he courted, whose machinations provoked him to break off relations abruptly and irrevocably, despite a reportedly strong attachment; and to the Pennsylvania proprietors for their refusal to allow their massive dominions to be taxed.[42]

In his efforts to moderate his anger Franklin had impressive success. We see him using his reason and sympathy to turn his resentment into constructive channels, as in his response to Bradford's injustice: "I thought so meanly of him for it, that when I afterwards came into his Situation, I took care never to imitate it."[43] We see his anger tempered by a habit of affectionate bemusement at human foibles and by sheer, insatiable curiosity about human nature. So well did he keep his perspective that he could dine amicably with great political rivals and offer generous support to them in causes on which they could agree. So habitually did he adopt an unruffled spirit that a French friend would report, in awe, "His eyes reflect a perfect equanimity, and his lips a smile of unalterable serenity."[44] Despite the bitterness of his country's rupture with Great Britain, he preserved most of his personal friendships across the ocean. But he did not preserve all, and significantly not his friendship with his loyalist son William. Nor did Franklin demand of himself that he overcome all anger, but only that he give it less scope than he thought was deserved. He was certain that anger clouds the vision and drives people to irrational acts, but whether anger itself is irrational in every case he never said, and perhaps never made up his mind.

Franklin's account of justice, too, is less fully worked out than we might wish. He does not develop in a systematic way the relation of justice to natural rights and positive law; he never defines whether the duty of benevolence goes beyond simple reciprocity to include an obligation to contribute to the common good or to assist those less fortunate. Above all, he never treats systematically those cases in which justice seems to demand a serious sacrifice. But the suggestion is that it never really does. Typical are Franklin's assertions that it is "our Interest to be compleatly virtuous" and that, as his father taught him, "nothing was useful which was not honest."[45] How, we might ask, could this be categorically true? Honesty should not be defined too broadly, for even sincerity demands only that we use "no hurtful deceit," and it surely does not apply to national enemies. The thought seems to be that, at least in personal affairs between fellow citizens, the apparent utility of any dishonest short-term gain pales beside the solid good of having a community based on lawfulness and trust; the true material needs of life are slight, but the satisfactions of being a pillar of a thriving community are immense. Franklin's views about justice on a broader scale are revealed most fully only in his judgments of political events and especially in his actions, and a full unfolding of these views must await our examination of his thoughts on government and diplomacy.

Franklin's catalogue of virtues is as interesting for what it omits as for what it includes. Missing are the Christian virtues of faith, hope, and charity. In place of faith and hope Franklin seems to put a reasonable, cheerful prudence that came so naturally for him that he never had to work at it. He was altogether wary of charity for its tendency to breed dependency, and perhaps also for its tendency to make us think of virtue as something costly to ourselves. Of the rare proverbs about generosity in the almanac, these two are characteristic: "Be not niggardly of what costs thee nothing, as courtesy, counsel, & countenance"; and "*Liberality* is not giving much but giving wisely."[46] He subtly criticizes the Bible for failing to understand the pitfalls of charity. Describing the book he has long intended to write on moral virtue, he explains,

> I should have called my Book the ART *of Virtue*, because it would have shown the *Means* and *Manner* of obtaining Virtue, which would have distinguished it from the mere Exhortation to be good, that does not instruct and indicate the Means; but is like the

> Apostle's Man of verbal Charity, who only, without showing to the Naked and the Hungry *how* or where they might get Cloaths or Victuals, exhorted them to be fed and clothed. *James* II, 15, 16.

But the biblical passage cited in fact rebukes the mere well-wisher for failing to *provide* food or clothing; it is Franklin who corrects this to say that true service consists in teaching the needy how to provide for themselves.[47]

Of course, there are cases where simple handouts are called for. As ambassador to France during the Revolutionary War, Franklin sent what assistance he could to relieve the sufferings of Americans in British prisoner-of-war camps, with such remarks as the following:

> Sometime or other you may have an Opportunity of assisting with an equal Sum a Stranger who has equal need of it. Do so. By that means you will discharge any Obligation you may suppose yourself under to me. Enjoin him to do the same on Occasion. By pursuing such a Practice, much Good may be done with little money.—Let kind offices go round. Mankind are all of a Family.[48]

Franklin was likewise unstinting with his expertise. When his brother in Boston suffered a urinary blockage, he designed a flexible catheter, went to a silversmith to see it properly made, and sent it the same day, with instructions. When his sister requested reading glasses and Franklin did not know her prescription, he made her thirteen pairs, sending them with instructions for choosing the right one, advising her to keep those that were stronger for future use and to "oblige your Friends with the others." Thanked by a friend for another medical device, he responded with the same appeal "to let good Offices go round," observing that "For my own Part, when I am employed in serving others, I do not look upon myself as conferring Favours, but as paying Debts." It is not charity but thoughtless charity to which he objects.[49]

Franklin omits not only the Christian virtues of faith, hope, and charity but the aristocratic virtues of wisdom, courage, magnificent generosity, loyalty or friendship, and magnanimity or justified pride, which figure so prominently in Aristotle's classic compendium of virtues in the *Nicomachean Ethics* and were long honored in the aristocratic tradition. Wisdom is not for

Franklin the core of virtue in the Socratic sense, since *knowing* what is right seems easy to Franklin and applying it seems the difficult part; yet wisdom does have an important place, as we shall see. Courage is a most revealing omission. Franklin is of course compiling the virtues he thinks he needs as a young tradesman making his way in a peaceful society, but he is also setting a model for others, a model he presents with the injunction that it is always in one's interest to be virtuous. Courage is the virtue that presents the greatest challenge to this claim; it is altogether characteristic that Franklin, the peaceful salesman and networker and negotiator, should minimize its importance. But his implicit denigration of courage is much more than an evasion. What past societies celebrated as heroic courage was in Franklin's eyes just proud, bloody inhumanity. Of Louis XV *Poor Richard* reports, "he bids fair to be as great a mischief-maker as his grandfather; or in the language of poets and orators, a Hero."[50] Loyalty and friendship fade in importance in a world in which tight-knit, ancient alliances between aristocratic families have given way to a fluid democratic society. Magnificent generosity is not within the working man's reach and is inferior anyway to collective projects for self-help and public improvement. But pride or magnanimity is the most interesting omission, for it is here that Franklin transforms both classical and Christian conceptions of virtue and vice in a new, democratic direction.

Humility, Pride, and Vanity

We have noted Franklin's belated addition of the Christian-looking quality of humility to his catalogue of virtues. He says that he has given "an extensive meaning to the word," yet this does not seem to entail any serious demand that he lower his own opinion of himself, only that he curb outward expressions of pride. His inner pride is evident even in the way he frames the goal: "Imitate Jesus and Socrates." Jesus seems humble only if we believe him divine; his characteristic mode of discourse is to cite ancient scripture and then to give his own alternative declaration of what God demands of mankind. Socrates is famous for an ironic condescension that covers with the thinnest of veils his contempt for the thoughtlessness of great men all around him. But Franklin still finds the audacious task of imitating these two models more achievable than trying to acquire true Christian humility. Mastering the appearance of humility he finds useful and good, but eradicating pride itself is against nature.

> In reality there is perhaps no one of our natural Passions so hard to subdue as *Pride*. Disguise it, struggle with it, beat it down, stifle it, mortify it as much as one pleases, it is still alive, and will every now and then peep out and show itself. You will see it perhaps often in this History. For even if I could conceive that I had compleatly overcome it, I should probably be proud of my Humility.[51]

Nor is there much point, in Franklin's mind, in trying to eradicate pride. He tells the story of an elderly Catholic recluse who inhabited the garret of his landlady's house in London, living on water-gruel and imitating the life of a nun as best she could in that Protestant country. She had given away her fortune, reserving to herself a tiny pittance, and out of that still gave a great deal to charity. "A Priest visited her, to confess her every Day. I have ask'd her, says my Landlady, how she, as she liv'd, could possibly find so much Employment for a Confessor? O, says she, it is impossible to avoid *vain Thoughts*." Others in the house were in awe of the maiden lady's pious self-abnegation, but the moral which Franklin draws from the story is different. "She look'd pale, but was never sick, and I give it as another Instance on how small an Income Life and Health may be supported."[52] Natural needs are small, as young Franklin found when he kept a plain table to save money for books, but nature also intends us a full and active life, and the effort to empty ourselves of ambition and pride is pointless.

Jonathan Edwards, the contemporary who in so many ways stands at the opposite pole from Franklin, claims of course that the tenacity of human pride is but proof of our fallen nature. Franklin's cheerful and perhaps too comfortable acceptance of human limitations indicates that he is closed to the profound possibility that Edwards represents, the possibility that human nature is corrupted by radical evil, for which the only remedy is the grace of God. But it is striking that although Edwards, in his

Personal Narrative, shows the same lifelong concern with self-improvement and self-examination that we find in Franklin, only the easy-going Franklin is able to report substantial progress in virtue. Edwards finds himself growing in faith but stubbornly unable to overcome his vices; were he to judge himself successful in doing so, this would only display his lapse into deplorable pride.[53] Franklin, as we have seen, embraces a healthy self-respect as the foundation for all virtue, and a patient realism as the proper spirit in which to build it. His success in gently and methodically taking himself in hand is some evidence for his belief that ordinary men and women are not evil but only mired in bad habits from which they do not know how to extricate themselves.[54]

But if a reasonable degree of pride is good, Franklin insists equally that stubborn pride is foolish. His whole program of self-improvement and public enlightenment depends on the willingness to admit shortcomings, try new approaches, and change one's mind. In vain he inveighs against Parliament's stubborn pride in refusing to correct its mistaken policies towards the colonies: "It is the persisting in an Error, not the Correcting it, that lessens the Honour of any Man or Body of Men." At the end of his life, in his closing speech in the Constitutional Convention of 1787, he summed up his thinking on stubbornness of opinion.

> I confess that there are several parts of this constitution which I do not at present approve, but I am not sure I shall never approve them: For having lived long, I have experienced many Instances of being obliged by better information or fuller consideration, to change opinions even on important Subjects. . . . It is therefore that the older I grow, the more apt I am to doubt my own judgment, and to pay more respect to the judgment of others. Most men indeed as well as most sects in Religion, think themselves in possession of all truth, and that wherever others differ from them it is so far Error. . . . But . . . few express it so naturally as a certain French lady, who in a dispute with her sister, said, "I don't know how it happens, Sister, but I meet with no body but myself, that's always in the right."[55]

Franklin always advocated reserving the right to decide one is wrong and refraining from celebrating one's victories before they are won, and he welcomed objections to his theories. To one scientific correspondent he wrote,

> Nothing certainly can be more improving to a Searcher into Nature, than Objections judiciously made to his Opinions, taken up perhaps too hastily: For such Objections oblige him to restudy the point, consider every Circumstance carefully, compare Facts, make Experiments, weigh Arguments, and be slow in drawing Conclusions. And hence a sure Advantage results; for he either confirms a Truth, before too slightly supported; or discovers an Error and receives Instruction from the Objector.
>
> In this view I consider the Objections and Remarks you sent me, and thank you for them sincerely.[56]

In keeping with this philosophy, Franklin decided not to respond publicly when his book on electricity was attacked by the Abbé Nollet, but instead to "let my Papers shift for themselves," believing that if his experiments could not be confirmed, they did not deserve to be defended. This did not stop him from chuckling with open enjoyment when his own book prevailed and "[t]he Doctrine it contain'd was by degrees universally adopted by the Philosophers of Europe in preference to that of the Abbé, so that he liv'd to see himself the last of his Sect."[57]

Unwarranted pride is clearly a vice in Franklin's pragmatic eyes, but even fully justified pride is problematic for such a dynamo of energy and talent as Franklin who wishes to make his way in a democratic society; hence the need for humor and irony. Consider the pages that surround the presentation of his audacious plan to achieve moral perfection and that culminate in what would normally be an insufferable description of how his good plan has brought him health, fortune, repute among the learned, the honor and trust of his countrymen, and personal popularity. Introducing the plan, he emphasizes his own surprise at how incorrigible his vices proved to be. Summing up his method, he reiterates his surprise at the number of black spots he had to record in his book and dwells at length on the one virtue that he has had the most trouble with, order. Then, in a masterful passage, he makes fun of both his own perfectionism and the temptation to abandon it.

> I was almost ready to give up the Attempt, and content my self with a faulty Character in that respect. Like the Man who in buying an Ax of a Smith my neighbor, desired to have the whole of its Surface as bright as the Edge; the Smith consented to grind it

> bright for him if he would turn the Wheel. He turn'd while the Smith press'd the broad Face of the Ax hard and heavily on the Stone, which made the Turning of it very fatiguing. The Man came every now and then from the Wheel to see how the Work went on; and at length would take his Ax as it was without farther Grinding. No, says the Smith, Turn on, turn on; we shall have it bright by and by; as yet 'tis only speckled. Yes, says the Man; but—*I think I like a speckled Ax best.* And I believe this may have been the Case with many who having for want of some such Means as I employ'd found the Difficulty of obtaining good, and breaking bad Habits, in other Points of Vice and Virtue, have given up the Struggle, and concluded that *a speckled Ax was best.* For something that pretended to be Reason was every now and then suggesting to me, that such extream Nicety as I exacted of my self might be a kind of Foppery in Morals, which if it were known would make me ridiculous; that a perfect Character might be attended with the Inconvenience of being envied and hated; and that a benevolent Man should allow a few Faults in himself, to keep his friends in Countenance.

Is this thought something that merely pretends to be reason, or is it true reason? Franklin seems to have resisted the thought and continued to strive, but he also conceded it some ground and cut himself a certain amount of slack.

At any rate, he knows how to keep us in countenance. He continues,

> In Truth I found myself incorrigible with respect to *Order;* and now I am grown old, and my Memory bad, I feel very sensibly the want of it. But on the whole, tho' I never arrived at the Perfection I had been so ambitious of obtaining, but fell far short of it, yet I was by the Endeavour a better and a happier Man than I otherwise should have been.[58]

Nothing could distinguish Franklin more sharply from the Puritans than this cheerful acceptance of imperfection. Cotton Mather, who advocates a project of self-examination and self-improvement much like the one Franklin adopts, condemns all pride as a vice, but Franklin judges justified pride problematic only if it provokes ill-will. Mather warns that even undertaking a project of moral self-improvement will provoke the envy and ridicule of less upright neighbors, but Franklin learned to deflect the envy and preempt the ridicule by adroitly poking fun at himself.[59] He found that by disguising his pride as the more democratically acceptable vice of vanity, he could give it satisfying scope.[60] After all, vanity on the part of another, adroitly managed, can flatter our vanity while pride merely wounds it, for vanity values our opinion. Franklin courts his readers' admiration with such charming openness and with such deft attention to our own vanity that we are disarmed. Nothing could be more audacious than his insertion of two laudatory letters at the beginning of the second part of the *Autobiography,* urging him to complete the work so that his life may provide a fitting model for all future ages. Yet he gets away with it by openly appealing to us to indulge the vanity of an old man who loves to reminisce, who knows he may bore some, whom he invites to set the book aside, who comes before us in his slippers as if to a family supper. Franklin has exquisite timing: he knows that he will receive credit for his accomplishments in due time, even if he does not claim it immediately; he knows that, as an old man with no further ambitions in the world, he can now indulge his vanity a bit and receive a fair hearing.

Nor does Franklin lose an opportunity to point out vanity's good effects. His own generosity to fellow travelers at a time when he is almost penniless and afraid of being thought so is one example; his pleasure in secretly launching philanthropic schemes and later winning credit for them is another.[61] In a comic essay for the *Pennsylvania Gazette,* Franklin even praises that unpleasant child of vanity, the habit of backbiting.

> There is scarce any one Thing so generally spoke against, and at the same time so universally practic'd, as *Censure* or *Backbiting.* All Divines have condemn'd it, all Religions have forbid it, all Writers of Morality have endeavour'd to discountenance it, and all Men hate it at all Times, except only when they have Occasion to make use of it.[62]

But Franklin sets out boldly to prove that in fact backbiting is a virtue, by the same means "as we commonly use to demonstrate any other Action or Habit to be a Virtue, that is, by shewing its Usefulness." With a little vanity of his own, he adds, "What can be said to the contrary, has already been said by every body; and indeed it is so little to the purpose, that any body may easily say it: But the Path I mean to tread, has hitherto been trod by no body," and so he asks the reader's indulgence if the path is a little rough.

The first great advantage of backbiting he proposes is that "it is frequently the Means of preventing powerful, politick, ill-designing Men, from growing too popular for the Safety of a State." These men always attempt to shine "with false or borrowed Merit," but "all-examining CENSURE, with her hundred Eyes and her thousand Tongues, soon discovers and as speedily divulges in all Quarters, every the least Crime or Foible that is a part of their true Character."

Second,

> the common Practice of *Censure* is a mighty Restraint upon the Actions of every private Man; it greatly assists our otherwise weak Resolutions of living virtuously. *What will the World say of me, if I act thus?* is often a Reflection strong enough to enable us to resist the most powerful Temptation to Vice or Folly. This preserves the Integrity of the Wavering, the Honesty of the Covetous, the Sanctity of some of the Religious, and the Chastity of all Virgins.

Third, censure promotes self-knowledge. Friends are too kind to tell us our faults,

> [b]ut Thanks be to Providence (that has given every man a natural Inclination to backbite his Neighbour) we now hear of many Things said *of* us, that we shall never hear said *to* us; (for out of Goodwill to us, or Illwill to those that have spoken ill of us, every one is willing enough to tell us how we are censur'd by others,) and we have the Advantage of mending our Manners accordingly.

Fourth, backbiting "helps exceedingly to a thorough *Knowledge of Mankind*," and last but not least, gossip and backbiting are the reins and spurs that maintain general good mores, censuring vices too petty for the law to take cognizance of or impossible to punish without oppressive intrusion into private life.

In this light-hearted essay Franklin continues his serious indictment of Christianity for failing to understand human nature and hence failing to give morality the support that it should. Christianity demands that we be pure, selfless and humble; nature makes us impure, selfish, and vain. Christianity scorns good deeds done for the wrong reason, but for Franklin, virtue is virtue, and we should welcome it and welcome supports to it wherever we find them. Christianity demands that we crucify our pride and welcome the grains of truth in others' malicious gossip as a spur to improvement, while forgiving the rest; Franklin demands no such forbearance but is happy if vices are mended in any spirit and for any reason at all.[63] This essay was written in the same month as the essay "Men are Naturally Benevolent as Well as Selfish" and is very much of a piece with it. Franklin exposes people's mixed motives with such gusto not only because he finds it amusing but because he finds it useful. Demanding and expecting unreasonable purity makes us blind to skillful imposters, but it also makes us see mere hypocrites where the truth is rather more complex and less sinister. Unreasonable expectations breed extremes of gullibility and cynicism that are equally bad for republican self-government.

Franklin's catalogue of modest, sober, bourgeois virtues does not describe the whole of the excellence he possessed or wished to teach, but it was an early effort that Franklin in old age still judged an excellent guide for anyone looking to take himself in hand. While explicit mention of the rich philanthropy and public-spiritedness that we see in the mature Franklin are missing from the list, the simple industry, frugality, and order the list commends give them their best foundation. If the deep human wisdom that Franklin later possessed is nowhere to be found among the catalogue of virtues, learning to hold one's tongue, to listen, to curb one's pride, and to engage in close self-observation will give one a substantial start on that virtue as well. Precisely what wisdom is, according to Franklin, and what part it plays and does not play in his method for attaining virtue need now to be considered.

The Art of Virtue

If virtue is as important for happiness in this life as Franklin says it is, why do human beings practice it as little as they do? Central to Franklin's thesis about virtue is the thought that mere intellectual persuasion that it is good to be virtuous is not enough to make one become so. Virtue, he says,

> is as properly an Art, as Painting, Navigation, or Architecture. If a Man would become a Painter, navigator, or Architect, it is not enough that he is *advised* to be one, that he is *convinc'd* by the Arguments of his Adviser that it would be for his Advantage to be one, and that he *resolves* to be one, but he must also be taught the Principles of the Art, be shewn the Methods of Working, and how to acquire the *Habits* of using properly all the Instruments; and thus regularly and gradually he arrives by Practice at some Perfection in the Art.[64]

At the root of human failing is not sin or even ignorance about what is good, but habit, passions too strong for reason, and lack of method, no different at bottom from the lack that has prevented shipbuilders and sea captains from discovering the optimal way to build, load, and rig a ship. Franklin, that famous champion of experimentation and enlightenment, was in fact a most careful observer of the weaknesses of human reason. His observations on it, which provide endless grist for his humor, are also fundamental to his method of moral education. The key is to be forewarned and forearmed against reason's characteristic failings.

In his "Dialogue Between the Gout and Mr. Franklin," dated "midnight, October 22, 1780," Franklin endures a tongue-lashing from his gout for his indulgences at table, his insufficient use of exercise, and above all for the flimsy excuses with which this purportedly reasonable man keeps defeating his own good resolutions.[65] Brought face to face with his own sophisms, Franklin replies, "Your reasonings grow very tiresome." Lady Gout asks him how often he has broken his resolutions to take morning walks, "alleging, at one time, it was too cold, at another too warm, too windy, too moist, or what else you pleased; when in truth it was too nothing but your own insuperable love of ease." He replies, "That I confess may have happened occasionally, probably ten times in a year." She answers, "Your confession is very far short of the truth; the gross amount is one hundred and ninety-nine times." He feebly evades a few more questions and then contritely intones, "I am convinced now of the justness of Poor Richard's remark, that 'Our debts and our sins are always greater than we think for.'" The gout replies, "So it is. You philosophers are sages in your maxims, and fools in your conduct."

The source of the folly is clear: the immediate attractions of pleasure and the distance and abstractness of the long-term good that temperate living and exercise might (or might not) bring to this portly and convivial seventy-four-year-old. Thus, when Franklin promises a complete reform if only the gout will leave him, she says, "I know you too well." She agrees to leave for now, but "with an assurance of visiting you again at a proper time and place; for my object is your good, and you are sensible now that I am your *real friend.*"

Franklin is forever remarking on the bad consequences of thoughtless habit on human life, from unhealthy diets to bad construction practices to poorly designed streetlamps that fill with soot in a few hours and that no one has thought to build differently. Because reason is so weak in the face of passion and habit, most moral exhortation alone is all but useless. "There is, perhaps, no other valuable Thing in the World, of which so great a Quantity is *given,* and so little *taken.*"[66] Human beings love comfortable habits and hate being exposed to challenges that wound the vanity and instill painful doubts. There can be little hope of reform without a method that finds a way around our impulses, our inertia, our inattention, our need for respect and self-respect, and our outright self-deceptions.

To outwit self-deception, Franklin advises appointing a friend to monitor our actions: even another person's rebukes are not so bad when that person is our own deputy. But Franklin's preferred method is close self-examination. He uses it to keep his head clear and his impulses in check while making difficult practical decisions. In a 1772 letter to Joseph Priestley he explains his invention of "*Moral* or *Prudential Algebra,*" which turns out to be nothing but the now-classic expedient of dividing a sheet of paper into columns of pros and cons and recording all the considerations that occur to one on either side, striking out those that balance one another until every consideration has been duly weighed and the preponderance of arguments becomes clear.[67]

Above all, Franklin uses self-examination to attack his bad habits, training a floodlight of attention on one vice at a time, so that no occurrence of it is allowed to creep by unnoticed. With this method Franklin turns the stubborn power of habit to his own advantage. Habit matters so much because life is a cumulative thing. The use of small moments, the indulgence in small extravagances, the seizing of small opportunities to take control of one's fate, all add up to dissipated resources or to a life well lived. The right habits become a bulwark against irrational propensities and ensure that in the grip of passion we will still do what calm reason previously judged sound. Franklin explains the principle in advising a friend on learning to swim. He offers one of his lucid scientific accounts of why a human body with full lungs is lighter than water and what the posture is that can keep it indefinitely afloat, but he does not count on this knowledge to be of any help in a sudden accident. The habit of trusting the water to support one is essential, "For though we value ourselves on being reasonable knowing creatures, reason and knowledge seem on such occasions to be of little use to us; and the brutes to whom we allow scarce a glimmering of either, appear to have the advantage of us." But with a little practice the art of swimming is soon learned even by human beings and is never forgotten.[68] Learning good moral habits is harder than learning to swim, because bad habits must be unlearned, but the fruits of the effort are even greater.

Like Aristotle, then, Franklin places habit at the center of moral education. He agrees with Aristotle that anyone decently brought up knows what virtue is; the hard thing is to follow it. But Franklin does not accept Aristotle's gentlemanly contention that the good man must choose what is right for its own sake, or the consequent suggestion that only those who have been schooled from childhood to love virtue have any hope of attaining moral excellence. And thus, for Franklin even more than for Aristotle, enlightenment has an important role to play in strengthening the motive to be good, in helping us see past duty's stern frown to grasp the convergence of virtue and self-interest.[69] While Franklin never thought to turn to God for guidance about what he should do, he did prefix to his table of daily examination a prayer to God to "Increase in me that Wisdom which discovers my truest Interests," and to "Strengthen my Resolutions to perform what that Wisdom dictates."[70]

In a dialogue entitled "A Man of Sense," Franklin explores

further the connection between enlightenment and virtue, pressing the question of whether a man who is not honest can be called a man of sense.[71] The character "Socrates" quickly gets his interlocutor, "Crito," to agree that the knowledge that characterizes a man of sense is "the Knowledge of our *true Interest;* that is, of what is best to be done in all the Circumstances of Humane Life, in order to arrive at our main End in View, HAPPINESS." Crito claims that one may know one's true interest and not do it, but Socrates replies that knowledge of virtue is like knowledge of shoemaking, and that one who speaks well about it but does not make good shoes really does not have the requisite knowledge. A man is virtuous only when he has "a thorough sense" that the argument for virtue is true, and "knows how" to put it into practice. Those who "talk well of it" but do not put it into practice "speak only by rote." Most strikingly of all, Franklin has Socrates say that this lack of good sense is itself rooted in ignorance and not perverse willfulness, for the person who lacks an efficacious knowledge of virtue "is ignorant that the SCIENCE OF VIRTUE is of more worth, and of more consequence to his Happiness than all the rest put together."

This reasoning is all very Socratic. But while Franklin agreed with Socrates about both the power of knowledge when it is complete and the power of passion against it when it is not, he was less curious as to *why* our understanding so often is so woefully incomplete; he gave little attention to the inner ambivalence that makes us both embrace and deplore the insight that vice is rooted in ignorance. Lacking this curiosity, Franklin never tracked down and confronted the small part of himself that was still inclined to view vice as just willful perversity. Thus, much later in his life, he would develop such a resentment of his son's stubborn allegiance to England that nothing could heal the breach between them. Franklin tried. In a wrenching letter of 1784 to William he wrote,

> I received your letter of the 22nd past, and am glad to find that you desire to revive the affectionate Intercourse, that formerly existed between us. It will be very agreeable to me. Indeed nothing has ever hurt me so much and affected me with such keen Sensations, as to find myself deserted in my old Age by my only Son; and not only deserted, but to find him taking up Arms against me, in

> a Cause wherein my good Fame, Fortune, and Life were all at Stake. You conceived, you say, that your Duty to your King and Regard for your Country requir'd this. I ought not to blame you for differing in Sentiment with me in Public Affairs. We are Men, all subject to Errors. Our Opinions are not in our own Power; they are form'd and govern'd much by Circumstances, that are often as inexplicable as they are irresistible. Your Situation was such that few would have censured your remaining Neuter, *tho' there are Natural Duties which precede political ones, and cannot be extinguish'd by them*. This is a disagreeable Subject. I drop it.

But the bitterness he could never really drop; the attempted reconciliation failed.[72]

Franklin still saw both the importance and the fallibility of human understanding, but he did not now pursue the insights of "A Man of Sense." He did not ask himself whether, perceived interest and mistaken principle having allied to recommend the loyalist side, William could really be blamed for taking it, or whether, if William's knowledge of his duty to his father was merely abstract, a truth known only "by rote," he could really be expected to follow it, or whether the failure to pursue a well-understood good would not evince a lack of understanding of *how* to be good, like the theoretical shoemaker of Franklin's dialogue who does not know how to make shoes. Or again, if William was careless in thinking the whole matter through, did that not betray an ignorance "that the SCIENCE OF VIRTUE is of more worth, and of more consequence to his Happiness than all the rest put together"?[73] Neither at this nor any time did Franklin seize upon such evident conflicts of duties as that between following one's own judgment and bowing to one's father as a challenge requiring us to rethink the question of whether common-sense notions of justice are wholly coherent. Lacking Socrates' doggedness in pursuing these questions, Franklin never attained the perfect equanimity of a philosopher in the face of bitter disappointment.

However, it would not be fair to dwell upon the rare failures of Franklin's wise, gentle humanity. Even in "A Man of Sense" he insists that men must be judged not by the exceptions but by the general tenor of their lives. In his own life the gentle good sense is in abundant supply and the lapses are impressively few.

Above all, it would be wrong to lose sight of the way Franklin habitually turns even his failings to his friends' and readers' advantage, using his impressive but reassuringly flawed self to inspire and encourage us, making the virtuous life look like surprising fun, but still winking and showing that he understands the pleasure of a little indulgence and a little outrageous irreverence as well. The more we reflect on his humor, the more we see that it goes to the heart of what Franklin wants to teach.

Franklin's humor is intriguing partly in the way that it continually threatens to undercut his moral message but never quite does. In the almanac, Franklin makes all his best advice about honesty, thrift, and diligence flow from the pen of the fictitious Richard Saunders, a paragon of good-humored shiftlessness and specious frankness.

> I might in this place attempt to gain thy Favour, by declaring that I write Almanacks with no other View than that of the publick Good; but in this I should not be sincere; and Men now a-days are too wise to be deceiv'd by Pretences however specious soever. The plain Truth of the Matter is, I am excessive poor, and my Wife, good Woman, is, I tell her, excessive proud; she cannot bear, she says, to sit spinning in her Shift of Tow, while I do nothing but gaze at the Stars; and has threatened more than once to burn all my Books and Rattling-Traps (as she calls my Instruments) if I do not make some profitable Use of them for the good of my Family.[74]

Of course this "plain Truth" is a complete fabrication, but Richard Saunders plays with this irony too: he takes umbrage at envious "Ill-willers" who charge him with being a mere cover for his printer, Ben Franklin. "They say . . . that there is no such a Man as I am; and have spread this Notion so thoroughly in the Country, that I have been frequently told it to my Face by those that don't know me. This is not civil Treatment, to endeavour to deprive me of my very Being." So freely does Franklin pile lies upon lies, unmasking Saunders' pretensions only to replace them with fresh frauds, that we grow dizzy trying to keep track. First Saunders predicts the death of his rival almanac writer, Titan Leeds. The next year he claims to prove Leeds' death by the fact that in the current Leeds almanac Saunders is called "*a false Predicter, an Ignorant, a conceited Scribler, a Fool, and a Lyar,*" although "Mr. Leeds was too well bred to use any Man so indecently and so scurrilously, and moreover his Esteem and Affection for me was extraordinary." The next year Saunders complains again at the bad manners of Leeds' ghost, whose continued abuse he takes "patiently," but "very unkindly." None of this slackens his own abuse of Leeds, whose latest almanac he says contains doggerel that "no Astrologer but a *dead one* would have inserted," adding that "no Man living would or could write such Stuff as the rest." Meanwhile, Saunders thanks his gentle readers for purchasing his work, giving a grateful report of the pot, the provisions, the shoes, and the new warm petticoat his profits have allowed him to buy his wife, and of the consequent improvement in her temper, their domestic tranquility, and his sleep.[75] These jests are an excellent way to sell almanacs, and Franklin, like the nonexistent Saunders, openly enjoyed the profits. But at the same time this is all part of the serious point: generous motives are seldom pure, nor need they be, for virtue is not the overcoming of self-regard.

Franklin threatens again to undercut his own moral instruction in his final almanac in 1758, where he assembles the most famous of Poor Richard's proverbs into a sermon by Father Abraham. Reprinted separately under the title "The Way to Wealth," this sermon became a runaway best-seller in reprint editions and foreign translations. After a large dose of impeccably good advice about prudence and thrift, Franklin concludes with the ironic observation that when "the old Gentleman ended his Harangue, The People heard it, and approved the Doctrine, and immediately practiced the contrary, just as if it had been a common Sermon." Yet the story has one last twist. The almanacs' "author," Richard Saunders, is himself in the audience, and he comments:

> The frequent mention he made of me must have tired anyone else, but my Vanity was wonderfully delighted with it, though I was conscious that not a tenth Part of the Wisdom was my own which he ascribed to me, but rather the *Gleanings* I had made of the Sense of all Ages and Nations. However, I resolved to be the better for the Echo of it; and though I had at first determined to buy Stuff for a new Coat, I went away resolved to wear my old One a little longer. *Reader,* if thou wilt do the same, thy Profit will be as great as mine.

As Richard Saunders shows, the advice we take to heart is the advice we have given ourselves. It matters little that it be original, but it matters a great deal who administers it. Rebukes from our own wiser self are far less galling than those from anyone else.[76]

Franklin wins our trust by showing that he knows our resistance to his preachings and likes us all the same. If one who is so wise to us still does not give up on improving us, what does he know that we do not? We are intrigued; we read on; we begin to fall under his spell. Little by little we come to see the world through his eyes. We laugh at moral pretensions, but without bitterness; we notice the constant disproportions between aspiration and reality, yet we come to appreciate small kindnesses and look with Franklin for ways to make small improvements in a life that is still very much worth living. In mingling laughter with our ragged efforts to be good, we remember that goodness is, after all, meant to be pleasant and not sour.

The combination of ironic detachment and hopeful, realistic engagement that is Franklin's unique wisdom is nowhere expressed more characteristically than in an early unsigned piece in the *Pennsylvania Gazette,* identified by the editors of the Franklin papers as his because it could be no one else's. This little epistle brings onto the stage yet another of Franklin's colorful panoply of hapless characters, this time an old man who has just "caught two terrible falls" on the icy sidewalks of Philadelphia.

> I am a stiff old fellow, and my Joints none of the most pliant. At the Door before which I fell last, stood a Gentleman-like Looby, with a couple of Damsels, who all made themselves wonderful merry with my Misfortune: And had not a good Woman, whose Door I had just passed, come and helped me up, I might for ought I know, have given them an Hour's Diversion before I found my Legs again. This good Woman, Heaven bless her, had sprinkled Ashes before her Door. I wish her long Life and better Neighbors. . . . Strange Perverseness of Disposition! to delight in the Mishaps which befall People who have no way disoblig'd us. . . . I am resolved, I will not so much as civilly salute one of them, I will not give one of them the Wall, I will not make Room for any of them at a Fire [a deliciously apt punishment for offenders so full of schadenfreude], nor hand them any Thing at a Table. . . . In short, I will be as cross-grain'd towards them as 'tis possible for a good natur'd old Man to be.[77]

Here we have the epitome of Franklin's moral instruction: he acknowledges the presence of human malice but hopes that gentle, mocking rebukes will make more headway against it than angry condemnation; he seizes every small opportunity for education and improvement; he never forgets to leave us smiling and eager to read more.

CHAPTER 3

PHILANTHROPY AND CIVIL ASSOCIATIONS

FRANKLIN'S ADVOCACY of virtue begins with qualities needed for individual happiness, but it always aims at a broader social good. Franklin shares with his early modern predecessors an insistence on the convergence of private and public interests in a well-ordered polity, but he places less emphasis than they on the need for coercive laws and more on the satisfactions of public-spirited activity. How does he understand human sociability, and how does he ground his hopes for a harmonious civic life? What is at work in the fact that, where Hobbes portrays human sociability as fundamentally chaotic and violent and dominated by the dangerous love of vainglory, Franklin presents humans as more benign and tractable, and vanity as a mere foible that is easily harnessed to good purposes?

MAN AS A POLITICAL ANIMAL

Franklin certainly does recognize a danger in human pride, but like Locke and Montesquieu, he hopes that in the modern political economy the attractions of commercial gain and political liberty may deflect warlike and tyrannical ambitions into more constructive channels. In place of the glory of bloody triumph, he extolls the solid satisfactions of self-respecting independence and collective self-rule, a solution to the problem of vainglory that Hobbes does not pursue. But what of the restlessly ambitious who will never be content with an equal share of power? Did Franklin truly understand the ambitions that drove George

III, like greater emperors before him, to seek the glories of dominion even at great economic cost? In dismissing these leaders as blindly irrational, did Franklin take the full measure of their souls?

There is some evidence that Franklin never did completely understand extreme human ambition. Consider the third of the essays he wrote in 1729 under the pseudonym "Busy-Body." Here he claims that "*Virtue alone is sufficient to make a Man Great, Glorious, and Happy,*" and that everyone in his heart of hearts would "rather chuse, if it were in his Choice," to merit the character of a decent, honest, trusted citizen, "than be the richest, the most learned, or the most powerful Man in the Province without it."[1] But if Franklin was naïve on this point, he was less so than first appears. In his *Autobiography* Franklin comes on the stage as a man eminently practical, reasonable, and modest in ambition, though eager for admiration, a man who could never understand why anyone would butcher anyone out lust for power. But his own ambition was greater than this persona suggests. He yearned to make his mark, if only as a writer; he suffered often from envy of others, fought hard and not always successfully to conceal his pride, and thought deeply about how he could gratify his ambition constructively within the constraints of his modest upbringing and the increasingly egalitarian society in which he lived. In the end, he found a way to satisfy this ambition and to win honor—even the honor of being the most famous man of his age—that was uniquely suited to a democratic society.

At the bottom of Franklin's thinking about ambition are his conviction that being a mover and shaker for good is the thing that best satisfies the restless desire for preeminence and his hope that education can persuade others of the truth of this. Ambitious people want power and riches, to be sure, but they want even more the adulation mingled with gratitude that comes of being a force for good in the world. Even the worst tyrants want to be honored as the fathers of their countries. "Almost every Man has a strong natural Desire of being valu'd and esteem'd by the rest of his Species; but . . . few fall into the Right and only infallible Method of becoming so."[2] Franklin is at his best in showing how everyone, great and small, can have some share in these solid political satisfactions. If he underestimates the extent to which many would welcome power even without gratitude and uncoerced honor, surely he is right that it is best to have all of these together, and that this cannot be done without attention to the true good of others.

Franklin's judgment as to the natural satisfactions of benevolent activity grows out of his belief that "Man is a Sociable Being." He ridicules those who pompously quote Cicero on the charms of solitude.

> [I]t is for aught I know one of the worst of punishments to be excluded from society. I have read abundance of fine things on the subject of solitude, and I know 'tis a common boast in the mouths of those that affect to be thought wise, *that they are never less alone than when alone.* I acknowledge solitude an agreeable refreshment to a busy mind; but were these thinking people obliged to be always alone, I am apt to think they would quickly find their very being insupportable to them.[3]

To be a social being is not only to crave company and honor but to feel a natural sympathy with others. As little as he was willing to rely on this sympathy in the absence of stronger passions, Franklin saw in self-interest allied with natural sociability a powerful force for good that had hitherto been undervalued and underutilized.

From his first scribblings for his brother's newspaper until his last public efforts on behalf of abolition, Franklin was a tireless supporter of voluntary associations and philanthropic projects. The projecting spirit was in the air, and Franklin reports that he was influenced especially by two of its chief sources, Daniel Defoe's *Essays on Projects* and Cotton Mather's *Bonifacius,* or *An Essay upon the Good.*[4] Defoe sketched many ideas for public works, insurance, and charitable projects, but he implemented none of them; Mather's pious work provided inspiration for Franklin's program of moral self-improvement; but the adaptation of both sources into a concrete series of secular projects aimed at social, moral, and educational ends was Franklin's own. A comparison of Mather's advice with Franklin's accomplishments is most instructive. Mather strikes many notes that Franklin, a generation later, would make familiar: the insistence on overcoming idleness, using small moments, and building good habits; the stress on the good that diligent men of ordinary status and abilities may achieve; the advocacy of associations for mutual support in self-improvement and philanthropy. But, the Puritan tone of Mather is alien to Franklin, and Mather's chapter on associations must have come as a particular disappointment to the young Franklin, for the whole thrust of all the associations Mather proposes is to encourage piety and suppress vice.[5] It is Franklin who took the idea of the voluntary association and gave it a humanistic and thoroughly constructive direction.

In the end, a life spent organizing voluntary associations was not enough for Franklin: his ambitions stretched higher, and he found himself concerned with causes that could only be advanced by entering public life. Yet between his first small club of apprentices for self-education in Philadelphia and his celebrated ambassadorship to France lies a seamless progression of public-spirited efforts, the habits and skills learned in the earlier projects proving invaluable for the prosecution of those that followed. Most important of these was Franklin's mastery of the art of setting others' opinions and efforts in motion without seeming to lead, which allowed him to avoid their envy and soothe their vanity even as he directed everyone to a goal of his choosing. If, in the event, his own vanity was abundantly gratified, so much the better. Franklin assumed, and American history seems so far to confirm, that vanity remains only vanity, and does not become dangerous vainglory, so long as a polity gives lawful scope for those with the highest ambitions to win honors through service. But Franklin urged even such men as himself to begin their political education at the bottom, with projects that almost anyone could undertake, as it is these efforts that bring the greatest benefits for everyone, including their sponsors.

Franklin and Tocqueville on Associations

So successful was the voluntarism Franklin spearheaded that in the next century Alexis de Tocqueville would observe, "America is, among the countries of the world, the one where they have taken most advantage of association and where they have applied that powerful mode of action to a greater diversity of objects."[6] Tocqueville found in the device of secular, voluntary associations a quintessentially American solution to the social problems that beset every society. Tocqueville noted with evident bemusement that while in England one invariably found a great lord behind any philanthropic project and in France the government, in America every perceived problem, however trivial, seemed to produce a new benevolent association. With their jealousy of government and dearth of great lords, it was natural that Americans should find another way; Franklin would add that it was a better way, in preventing dependency and giving citizens practice in conducting public business.[7] But Tocqueville went much further: he found in the political associations of local self-government and especially in voluntary associations a cure for the worst congenital disorder of democracy, a syndrome to which he would give the name individualism.[8]

Tocqueville distinguishes the new phenomenon of individualism from the age-old vice of selfishness. Whereas selfishness is "a passionate and exaggerated love of self," individualism is "a reflective and peaceable sentiment that disposes each citizen to isolate himself from the mass of those like him and to withdraw to one side with his family and his friends, so that after having thus created a little society for his own use, he willingly abandons society at large to itself." Tocqueville here develops one of his most penetrating contrasts between democracy and aristocracy.

> In aristocratic peoples, families remain in the same state for centuries, and often in the same place. That renders all generations so to speak contemporaries. A man almost always knows his ancestors and respects them; he believes he already perceives his great-grandsons and he loves them. He willingly does his duty by both, and he frequently comes to sacrifice his personal enjoyments for beings who no longer exist or who do not yet exist.
>
> In addition, aristocratic institutions have the effect of binding each man tightly to several of his fellow citizens.
>
> Classes being very distinct and immobile within an aristocratic people, each of them becomes for whoever makes up a part of it a sort of little native country, more visible and dearer than the big one.
>
> As in aristocratic societies all citizens are placed at a fixed post,

> some above the others, it results also that each of them always perceives higher than himself a man whose protection is necessary to him, and below he finds another whom he can call upon for cooperation.
>
> Men who live in aristocratic centuries are therefore almost always bound in a tight manner to something that is placed outside of them, and they are often disposed to forget themselves. It is true that in these same centuries the general notion of *those like oneself* is obscure and that one scarcely thinks of devoting oneself to the cause of humanity; but one often sacrifices oneself for certain men.
>
> In democratic centuries, on the contrary, when the duties of each individual toward the species are much clearer, devotion toward one man becomes rarer: the bond of human affections is extended and loosened.[9]

In America, the constant churning of geographic and social mobility weakens the sense of connection with ancestors and descendants; only the bonds of the immediate family remain as strong as before.

> Aristocracy had made of all citizens a long chain that went from the peasant up to the king; democracy breaks the chain and sets each link apart.
>
> As conditions are equalized, one finds a great number of individuals who, not being wealthy enough or powerful enough to exert a great influence over the fates of those like them, have nevertheless acquired or preserved enough enlightenment and good to be able to be self-sufficient. These owe nothing to anyone, they expect so to speak nothing from anyone; they are in the habit of always considering themselves in isolation, and they willingly fancy that their whole destiny is in their hands.
>
> Thus not only does democracy make each man forget his ancestors, but it hides his descendants from him and separates him from his contemporaries; it constantly leads him back toward himself alone and threatens finally to confine him wholly in the solitude of his own heart.[10]

Tocqueville goes on to show how political freedom counteracts this malady.

> From the moment when common affairs are treated in common, each man perceives that he is not as independent of those

like him as he at first fancied, and that to obtain their support he must often lend them his cooperation. . . .

The legislators of America did not believe that, to cure a malady so natural to the social body in democratic times and so fatal, it was enough to accord to the nation as a whole a representation of itself; they thought that, in addition, it was fitting to give political life to each portion of the territory in order to multiply infinitely the occasions for citizens to act together and to make them feel every day that they depend on one another.

This was wisely done.[11]

But even local government is, in a sense, too far away from the individual for it to do the work required. Yet another, more fundamental intermediary is needed, and this is the voluntary association.

Sentiments and ideas renew themselves, the heart is enlarged, and the human mind is developed only by the reciprocal action of men upon one another. . . . This is what associations alone can do. . . .

In democratic countries the science of association is the mother science; the progress of all the others depends on the progress of that one.[12]

Franklin provided no such far-reaching and theoretical diagnosis of the problem as Tocqueville's, but almost instinctively he grasped and addressed it. Even while he led Americans in promoting the new ethos of personal independence that broke apart old social chains, he gave equal energy to the task of forging new social cohesions. In the first installments of his *Autobiography,* addressed to his son, he tries to strengthen William's sense of connection to his family by restoring the narrative chain that his own removal from Boston and his ancestors' removal from England left in fragments. In good aristocratic fashion he shows William how his family members have set a standard to live up to, but in good democratic fashion he also shows that there is much room for younger generations of Franklins to improve on what their forebears have done. As the *Autobiography* evolves into a book for all young Americans, the appeal to family pride drops away and the inspiring image of the self-made man rises correspondingly in importance. But in sketching this picture Franklin is at pains to show that no man is so utterly self-made as to outgrow his need for his fellows: as the trust and respect of others are essential for success, so their companionship is essential for happiness. The message of all his stories is that joining and especially leading others in cooperative projects is really great fun.

Franklin's Benevolent Projects

The Junto and the Library Company

Franklin's first experiment in democratic self-rule was his Junto, a little club he formed in 1727 in order to give himself better access to conversation and books. Franklin conceived the project, chose the members, drew up the rules, and selected the topics for weekly discussion, which reflect his omnivorous hunger for learning and especially his interest in morals and politics. Franklin relates with pride that many of the Junto's members rose to prominence in the colonies, and the most enduring of the friendships formed there lasted "upwards of forty years." He adds,

> And the club continu'd almost as long and was the best School of Philosophy, Morals and Politics that then existed in the Province; for our Queries which were read the Week preceding their Discussion, put us on Reading with Attention upon the several Subjects, that we might speak more to the Purpose: and here too we acquired better Habits of Conversation, every thing being studied in our Rules which might prevent our disgusting each other.[13]

The Junto was a way of harnessing the human sociability that Franklin had faith in and the incessant energy that Tocqueville observed in the American character and directing them to a multitude of good purposes. The club did not neglect the most mundane benefits that a circle of friends can provide its members, but its focus was on useful conversation. Discussions were structured in such a way that everyone's desire to appear to advantage before his friends would spur him to apply himself, especially when his turn came to take the lead. Topics were chosen with a view to both personal and social utility.

Franklin's list of "Proposals and Queries to be Asked the Junto" bears a striking resemblance to and contains equally striking departures from the queries Cotton Mather proposes for young men's gatherings in New England.[14] The central question that both propose for weekly discussion is "What good is to be done?" But where Mather calls for examinations of the injustices that should be righted, the duties that have been neglected, the comfort that may be brought the afflicted, and above all the opportunities to promote piety, Franklin's more capacious, humanistic, and proactive inclinations appear in his own catalogue of queries for discussion. He begins with the question "Have you met with any thing in the author you last read, remarkable, or suitable to be communicated to the Junto? particularly in history, morality, poetry, physic, travels, mechanic arts, or other parts of knowledge." He goes on to ask members to consider what they have learned about how people thrive and fail in business, who has done a worthy action, deserving of praise and imitation, what noteworthy cures members have experienced or heard of for illnesses, what novices deserve encouragement, and in general, how "the Junto may be serviceable to mankind . . . to their country, to their friends, or to themselves." Where Mather warns young men to steer their discussions clear of backbiting, vanity, and "matters that do not concern them," including politics, Franklin boldly asks them to report any defects they observe in the laws and "any encroachments on the just liberties of the people."[15] Franklin was an indefatigable source of new queries for consideration, including puzzling facts in nature, problems of justice and economics, the reasons for the zealotry of new converts to a religion, and the degree to which human nature may be perfected.

The Junto was in many ways Franklin's own academy, providing the intellectual stimulation and training and camaraderie that he no doubt felt he had lost by never attending college. Clearly he hoped the Junto would do the same for others; what he perhaps did not foresee was the training it would give him in public service. To improve the efficacy of this little school, he persuaded his friends to pool their meager collections of books into a common library. After experiencing the benefits but also the inconveniences of this first informal library, he was inspired to seek a charter and formal membership for what would become the Library Company of Philadelphia, the first of many subscription libraries in the colonies. Franklin reports with satisfaction, "These Libraries have improved the general Conversation of the Americans, made the common Tradesmen and Farmers as intelligent as most Gentlemen from other Countries, and perhaps have contributed in some degree to the Stand so generally made throughout the Colonies in Defence of their Privileges."[16] Papers Franklin wrote for the Junto later found their way into his newspaper and began to influence public opinion. Proposals for public improvements that he first made in Junto meetings laid the groundwork for projects that he would later lead and that other members would support. The more he undertook, the more he saw that needed doing.

Both temperament and calculation led Franklin to insist from the beginning that the Junto be kept secret. "The Intention was, to avoid Applications of improper Persons for Admittance, some of whom perhaps we might find it difficult to refuse." But as the club proved useful and satisfying to its twelve original members, they pressed for permission to include their friends. Franklin persuaded them instead to take advantage of their secrecy and found twelve subordinate clubs, all unknown to one another. Several were successfully launched, and he used them in masterful fashion to shape public opinion further, contriving to introduce ideas into each of them that would seem to have arisen spontaneously from their own members, so as to prepare the soil for projects he had afoot.[17]

Franklin long dreamed of founding a great, international secret society based on the Junto. This society would bring together lovers of virtue everywhere who would support one another in their private businesses and in advancing the common good of their countries and of mankind. Franklin hoped that the partisan character of politics might be overcome by one party that would have only the common good at heart. He called his envisioned society the "society of the free and easy," reflecting his belief that virtue, once habitual, would cease to be a struggle.[18] It was one of only a few of Franklin's schemes that never went anywhere, and perhaps it is well that it did not. A voluntary club of do-gooders and self-improvers will always attract a few hypocrites, which is part of the reason the Junto was kept secret, but a party that aspires to real power, and that therefore must come into the open, will be as much a magnet for ambitious men as any other, and quickly infected with the same partisan spirit.

With this hope for a cosmopolitan party to transcend all partisanship, we see an unusual but revealing lapse of Franklin's ordinarily sober realism. Franklin hated partisanship with a vehemence that did not well accord with his recognition of people's natural self-interestedness. He called it madness when it seized Pennsylvania politics, he called it wicked and corrupt when he encountered it in British politics, and he was deeply dismayed to find that it infected even the Royal Society of London.[19] He seems to have sensed that partisan narrowness, if it could not be transcended, would prove fatal to the whole modern liberal project in which he was thoroughly invested. For this project demands a degree of self-denial, fair-mindedness, and statesmanship that even enlightened self-interest does not invariably support. Hence, while Franklin could regard most human flaws with detached bemusement, against partisanship his moral fervor blazed forth in full force.

The Newspaper

Soon after forming the Junto, Franklin began publishing the *Pennsylvania Gazette.* Like his club, the newspaper had its immediate origin in Franklin's self-interest, for a newspaper was an important source of revenue and visibility for a printer. But it was also a natural outgrowth of efforts begun in the Junto to inform and shape public opinion. Franklin comments upon the power of the press to do this, comparing it favorably to the more fleeting power of oratory in the ancient republics.

> The ancient Roman and Greek Orators could only speak to the Number of Citizens capable of being assembled within the Reach of their Voice. Their Writings had little Effect because the Bulk of the People could not read. Now by the Press we can speak to Nations; and good Books & well written Pamphlets have great and general Influence. The Facility with which the same Truths may be repeatedly enforc'd by placing them daily in different lights in Newspapers which are everywhere read, gives a great Chance of establishing them. And we now find that it is not only right to strike while the Iron is hot, but that it is very practicable to heat it by continually striking.[20]

Franklin in fact perfected the art of preparing the public mind for new ideas with timely columns and pamphlets, often supported by public discussion begun in the Junto and its subordinate clubs. In Tocqueville's judgment, the value of this device can scarcely be exaggerated.

> When men are no longer bound among themselves in a solid and permanent manner, one cannot get many to act in common except by persuading each of them whose cooperation is necessary that his particular interest obliges him voluntarily to unite his efforts with the efforts of all the others.
>
> This can be done habitually and conveniently only with the aid of a newspaper; only a newspaper can come to deposit the same thought in a thousand minds at the same moment.
>
> A newspaper is a counselor that one does not need to go seek, but that presents itself of its own accord and that speaks to you briefly each day and of common affairs without disturbing your particular affairs.
>
> Newspapers therefore become more necessary as men are more equal and individualism more to be feared. It would diminish their importance to believe that they serve only to guarantee freedom; they maintain civilization.[21]

In good Enlightenment fashion, Franklin extols the vigorous exchange of ideas through a free press, just as he does the free exchange of goods.

> Printers are educated in the belief, that when Men differ in Opinion, both Sides ought equally to have the Advantage of being heard by the Publick; and that when Truth and Error have fair Play, the former is always an overmatch for the latter: Hence they cheerfully serve all contending Writers that pay them well, without regarding on which side they are of the Question in Dispute.
>
> It is likewise unreasonable what some assert, *That Printers ought not to print any Thing but what they approve;* since if all of that Business should make such a Resolution, and abide by it, an End would thereby be put to Free Writing, and the World would afterwards have nothing to read but what happen'd to be the Opinions of Printers.

Franklin does claim, although not with perfect consistency, that there are limits to what he will print even for private use, and that he has always refused to print anything that "might countenance Vice" or that "might do real Injury to any Person."[22] Newspapers, however, he holds to a higher standard: their publishers have a positive duty to educate the public.

> I consider'd my Newspaper also as another Means of Communicating Instruction, and in that View frequently reprinted in it Extracts from the Spectator and other moral Writers, and sometimes publish'd little pieces of my own which had been first compos'd for Reading in our Junto. . . . In the conduct of my Newspaper I carefully excluded all Libelling and Personal Abuse, which is of late Years become so disgraceful to our Country.

Franklin takes issue with the claim that a newspaper is like a stagecoach, in which all who pay have a right to a place, arguing that he has a duty to his subscribers to furnish them only with what is either useful or harmlessly entertaining. Likewise, he asserts that printers have a duty to their country not to print "scurrilous reflections on the Government of neighboring States, and even on the Conduct of our best national Allies, which may be attended with the most pernicious Consequences."[23] There is no suggestion here of any appropriate role for government in censoring such pieces; the utility of the press depends upon its freedom, and therefore upon the good judgment and self-restraint of publishers.

In one of his Busy-Body papers Franklin explores another positive role that a free press can play: it can serve as a *censor morum*.

> There are little Follies in the Behaviour of most Men, which their best Friends are too tender to acquaint them with: There are little Vices and small Crimes which the Law has no Regard to, or Remedy for: There are likewise great Pieces of Villany sometimes so craftily accomplish'd, and so circumspectly guarded, that the Law can take no Hold of the Actors. All these Things, and all Things of this Nature, come within my Province as CENSOR.[24]

Unfortunately, most American newspaper publishers of the late eighteenth century did not hold their censoriousness to Franklin's standards of self-restraint. Rather than gently correcting public morals and exposing the rare villainies of great charlatans, most of them made their papers into party rags full of slander. In 1789 Franklin would compare the American press with the Spanish Court of Inquisition, so freely did it condemn men to infamy without due process and without any right to confront and question the witnesses against them.

> If by the *liberty of the press* were understood merely the liberty of discussing the propriety of public measures and political opinions, let us have as much of it as you please: But if it means the liberty of affronting, calumniating and defaming one another, I for my part, own myself willing to part with my share of it, whenever our legislators shall please so to alter the law; and shall chearfully consent to exchange my liberty of abusing others for the privilege of not being abused myself.[25]

In advancing his moral and political views in his own paper, Franklin maintained a light touch and a warm welcome for dissenting views. In fact, there is every reason to suspect that in the absence of such dissent he often provided it himself, especially for some of his more playful discussions of morals and manners, such as the complaint of "Cecelia Single" that Franklin's newspaper had been unfair to women, and other letters to the editor that sound in style suspiciously like the editor himself. We also have among his papers multiple and competing answers he wrote for the *Gazette* for queries of his own posing. He assails himself with cheerful vigor in these pieces, knowing that controversy will sell papers.[26]

Franklin also made a serious effort, however, to encourage independent judgment in his readership. When his attempts to keep readers informed about important developments in the far-flung empire were frustrated by the evident bias of the sources available to him, he used the occasion to provide lessons in critical reading. In 1729 he reprinted four different London newspapers' reports of Britain's peace negotiations with Spain, noting the general leaning of each paper, so that readers might consider all of them and draw their own conclusions. On other occasions he provided detailed maps of military campaigns and multiple accounts of the same battle, "so that the Reader may be the better enabled to form a true Judgment."[27] If a free press is essential to keep the public informed, a critical public is in the end the only sure guardian of that press's integrity. Franklin's newspaper was one of the important vehicles by which he endeavored to build a spirit that we might call vigilant good will, combining realism with a willingness to trust and enter into the good purposes of other friends of liberty. This spirit is an essential antidote both to fanatical hopes and to the equally unreasonable susceptibility to conspiracy theories that makes democratic self-government impossible.

The City Watch and the Fire Company

Success in organizing people in a small way strengthened Franklin's confidence in his ability to influence events and his interest in politics. His first foray into "public Affairs" was a proposal to reorganize the ineffectual city watch of Philadelphia. Here again Franklin showed his unerring sense for starting at the foundations, this time by attending to the most basic issues of security before contemplating more far-reaching reforms. The details of his proposal also reflect his characteristic concern for equity and for the underdog, in this case the "poor widow" who had to pay as much towards the watch to protect her meager property as did a rich householder. Again Franklin started by presenting his ideas to the Junto and its offshoots, to set public opinion in motion. But as his aim was to reform an existing public institution rather than to found a private one, success would take more time. "And tho' the Plan was not immediately carried into Execution, yet by preparing the Minds of People for the Change, it paved the Way for the Law obtain'd a few Years after, when the Members of our Clubs were grown into more Influence."[28] But a similar proposal for a fire company made at the same time and in the same way bore immediate fruit, one company of volunteers setting the example for the formation of others until "they became so numerous as to include most of the Inhabitants who were Men of Property."[29]

The Academy

Observing that Philadelphia lacked a good academy of the sort that was common in New England, Franklin set about, when he had time, to remedy this deficiency with his characteristically encyclopedic attention to detail. His "Proposals relating to the Education of Youth in Philadelphia" and "Idea of the English

School" reveal careful thought about the kind of citizens a free society needs and the key role that schools must play in forming them.[30] Franklin himself arguably benefited on balance from being informally educated and largely self-taught: this experience doubtless increased his confidence and his willingness to consider bold and unconventional ideas. His plans reflect a desire to encourage in others the same spirit of self-sufficiency, independent thought, and civic participation that he valued in his own life. But Franklin did not wish to leave his countrymen to the uncertainty of self-education; he regretted his lack of systematic training in mathematics, and he knew that his own knack for self-education was unusual, as was his success in self-improvement as a grown man. Even the finest formal education carries no guarantees, of course, but Franklin judged the odds of success to be better with it than without.

> I think with you, that nothing is of more importance for the public weal, than to form and train up youth in wisdom and virtue. Wise and good men are, in my opinion, the *strength* of a state. . . . And though the culture bestowed on *many* should be successful only with a *few*, yet the influence of those few and the service in their power, may be very great. Even a single woman that was wise, by her wisdom saved a city.
>
> I think also, that general virtue is more probably to be expected and obtained from the *education* of youth, than from the *exhortation* of adult persons; bad habits and vices of the mind, being, like diseases of the body, more easily prevented than cured.[31]

Yet schooling in Franklin's thinking remained in that realm of voluntary collective action that lies between the public and the strictly private. The new academy took many of John Locke's ideas on private education for gentlemen and applied them to a school setting, but the academy was unusual for its time in being governed not by the state or by an established church but by an independent board of trustees. Franklin considered it an advantage that the school be its own small community, supported by leading citizens "of Leisure and publick Spirit," who would make it their business to supervise and encourage the students while they were enrolled and to help promote their careers when they graduated.[32] The academy itself prospered and grew into the University of Pennsylvania, but Franklin was disappointed in his hopes of ongoing personal involvement from the prominent citizens appointed to the board; as he later admitted with chagrin, he was as derelict as the rest.[33] This failure of oversight illustrates an important limitation of purely voluntary associations: energy and enthusiasm for them are fickle and hard to sustain, as they fall too easily into the void where everyone's responsibility becomes no one's responsibility. They become professionalized in order to survive, and their energetic founders move on to other projects and into public life, where they can hope to have a more enduring impact. Yet this middle ground of voluntarism, however unstable, remains critical as a training ground and a link between the public and private realms.

In most of his public writings Franklin spoke boldly on his own authority, if often not in his own name; but his educational proposals he filled with learned footnotes citing the authority of past writers on education, including Milton, Locke, David Fordyce, Obadiah Walker, Charles Rollin, and George Turnbull. By this means the unschooled Franklin no doubt hoped to still the criticism of conservative, learned divines. But this flood of erudition also covered a radical departure from tradition, as Franklin attempted to turn the educational focus away from both Christian piety and Greek and Latin classics. While his proposals bowed to authority, the school was to train students in the persuasive expression of their own thoughts. Franklin enjoined teachers to cultivate not a stern sense of duty but a pleasure in learning and in practicing benevolence. In all of this, he followed the new educational path forged by Locke, which was gaining increasing but uneven acceptance in the eighteenth century, while appearing only to apply the consensus of the ages.

Perhaps the most striking of Franklin's innovations in this project is his extensive substitution of secular for religious texts. He engaged in some fancy footwork to persuade clergymen, whose support he sought, that the school would be quite traditional in this respect, claiming to one would-be rector of the school, "The Sacred Classics are read in the English School, tho' I forgot to mention them."[34] But equally important is his advocacy of the study of English. Latin and Greek, for centuries the mainstay of gentlemanly education, were still to be available for those who needed and wanted them, but they were no longer to form the core of education. The study of one's own native language was to come first and the English School was to be given equal dignity with the school of classical studies. In this Franklin was taking up a change suggested by Locke and motivated by a desire to focus education on what is most truly useful. To this consideration Franklin added two political ones, especially relevant in an American context that was more democratic than Locke's England: the wish to bring dignity to studies that would be within the reach of many more citizens, and the desire to give a training in clear, persuasive speaking and writing that would prepare students for the conduct of public as well as private affairs. In place of a traditionalist, antiquarian education that revered the ancients and denigrated the present, Franklin sought to reignite the kind of education actually practiced in the republics of Greece and Rome: an education for active men of affairs who would take their own country with utmost seriousness and cultivate their own language with skill and pride.[35]

In the "Idea of the English School" Franklin sums up his goal for the first six grades of education:

> Thus instructed, Youth will come out of this School fitted for learning any Business, Calling or Profession, except such wherein Languages are required; and though unacquainted with any antient or foreign Tongue, they will be Masters of their own, which is of more immediate and general Use; and withal will have attain'd many other valuable Accomplishments; the Time usually spent in acquiring those Languages, often without Success, being here employ'd in laying such a Foundation of Knowledge and Ability, as, properly improv'd, may qualify them to pass thro' and execute the several Offices of civil Life, with Advantage and Reputation to themselves and Country.

Among the professions for which the school would offer preparation, Franklin wished to erase all invidious distinctions between those deemed suitable and those deemed unsuitable for gentlemen. The study of technical drawing and the mechanical arts was to be encouraged for everyone. Citing Locke, Franklin urged that all students also learn accounting, arguing that "if it is not necessary to help a Gentleman to *get* an estate, yet there is nothing of more Use and Efficacy to make him *preserve* the estate he has."[36] Although Franklin did not yet break with tradition to the extent of proposing that the academy be opened to girls, he did recommend similar studies for them in their private education, including accounting. He tells the story of the widow of one of his South Carolina partners, who, through her knowledge of accounting, "manag'd the Business with such Success that she not only brought up reputably a Family of Children, but at the Expiration of the Term was able to purchase of me the Printing House and establish her Son in it."[37] Such solid skills are far more valuable, Franklin avers, than the social polish of music and dancing, taught with the tacit assumption that once a girl has found a husband she is secure for life.

While Franklin looked relatively little to the classics and even less to the Christian scriptures to provide moral and political wisdom for the scholars, he did advocate the extensive study of history.

> [I]f HISTORY be made a constant Part of their Reading, such as the Translations of the Greek and Roman Historians, and the modern Histories of antient Greece and Rome, &c. may not almost all Kinds of useful Knowledge be that Way introduc'd to Advantage, and with Pleasure to the Student? As . . .
>
> MORALITY, by descanting and making continual Observations on the Causes of the Rise or Fall of any Man's Character, Fortune, Power, &c. mention'd in History; the Advantages of Temperance, Order, Frugality, Industry, Perseverance, *&c.* Indeed the general natural Tendency of Reading good History, must be, to fix in the Minds of Youth deep Impressions of the Beauty and Usefulness of Virtue of all Kinds, Publick Spirit, Fortitude, &c.
>
> *History* will show the wonderful Effects of ORATORY, in governing, turning, and leading great Bodies of Mankind, Armies, Cities, Nations. When the Minds of Youth are struck with Admiration at this, then is the Time to give them the Principles of that art. . . .
>
> *History* will also give Occasion to expatiate on the Advantage of Civil Orders and Constitutions, how Men and their Properties are protected by joining in Societies and establishing Government; their Industry encouraged and rewarded, Arts invented, and Life made more comfortable: The Advantages of *Liberty,* Mischiefs of *Licentiousness,* Benefits arising from good Laws and a due Execution of Justice, &c. Thus may the first Principles of sound *Politicks* be fix'd in the Minds of Youth.[38]

To further the study of politics Franklin recommends reading ancient jurists and such widely accepted theorists as Grotius and Pufendorf; readings in more modern and controversial political writings, such as the *Spectator*, are folded into the program for improving English style, which includes readings in "the best *English* Authors," including "*Tillotson, Milton, Locke, Addison, Pope, Swift,*" and "the higher Papers in the *Spectator* and *Guardian*."[39]

Indeed, throughout his proposals Franklin links the study of history and politics to the cultivation of a vigorous, persuasive English style, both being essential tools of citizenship.

> On *Historical* Occasions, Questions of Right and Wrong, Justice and Injustice, will naturally arise, and may be put to Youth, which they may debate in Conversation and in Writing. When they ardently desire Victory, for the Sake of the Praise attending it, they will begin to feel the Want, and be sensible of the Use of *Logic*, or the Art of Reasoning to *discover* Truth, and of Arguing to *defend* it, and *convince* Adversaries.

Whetting the appetite for learning through public contests is an important part of Franklin's educational method: ambition is not to be opposed but encouraged and directed.[40]

The program of study, as Franklin presents it, culminates in science, agriculture, and the history of commerce and manufactures. These subjects give students the capacity to be useful; they also are perhaps even more important in showing students the convergence between individual and collective interests in an enlightened political economy. Thus, the study of science, technology, and commerce plays a key role in encouraging students actively to seek out ways to benefit their fellow citizens and mankind, confident that such benefits will redound, by and large, to their own good as well.

> With the whole should be constantly inculcated and cultivated, that *Benignity of Mind,* which shows itself in *searching for* and *seizing* every Opportunity *to serve* and *to oblige;* and is the Foundation of what is called GOOD BREEDING; highly useful to the Possessor, and most agreeable to all.
>
> The Idea of what is *true Merit,* should also be often presented to Youth, explain'd and impress'd on their Minds, as consisting in an *Inclination* join'd with an *Ability* to serve Mankind, one's

> Country, Friends, and Family; which *Ability* is (with the Blessing of God) to be acquir'd or greatly increas'd by *true Learning;* and should indeed be the great *Aim* and *End* of all Learning.

Or as Franklin slyly adds in a footnote, "To have in View the *Glory* and *Service of God,* as some express themselves, is only the same Thing in other Words.[41] Piety is useful for support in this educational project, but the aim and focus of education are to be fixed firmly on this world.

The Philosophical Society

In keeping with his views on the primacy of labor and the choiceworthiness of leisure, Franklin in 1743 proposed an American philosophic society to encourage and share discoveries in science. Franklin's keenness for scientific discourse is reflected in the unusual fact that he signs this proposal in his own name, argues that the centrality of Philadelphia makes it the ideal meeting place, and even volunteers to serve as the society's first secretary. But in typical Enlightenment fashion he stresses the utility of science for humanity.

> The first Drudgery of Settling new Colonies, which confines the Attention of People to mere Necessaries, is now pretty well over; and there are many in every Province in Circumstances that set them at Ease, and afford Leisure to cultivate the finer Arts, and improve the common Stock of Knowledge. To such of these who are Men of Speculation, many Hints must from time to time arise, many Observations occur, which if well-examined, pursued and improved, might produce Discoveries to the Advantage of some or all of the British Plantations, or to the Benefit of Mankind in general.

Studies to be encouraged include agriculture, medicine, geology, mathematics, chemistry, technology, manufactures, geography, "and all philosophical Experiments that let Light into the Nature of Things, tend to increase the Power of Man over Matter, and multiply the Conveniencies or Pleasures of Life."[42]

Franklin's own studies in electricity are one example of what he is trying to encourage; his improved wood stove is another. At a deeper level, the habit of open-minded willingness to question all received opinion and subject it to experimentation for the sake of bettering man's estate is his central goal. The "benignity of mind" mentioned at the end of his proposal for an academy is nowhere better illustrated than in his eagerness to spread the benefits of the Franklin stove without profiting himself (though of course not without increasing his fame).

> Govr. Thomas was so pleas'd with the Construction of this Stove . . . that he offer'd to give me a Patent for the sole Vending of them for a Term of Years; but I declin'd it from a Principle which has ever weigh'd with me on such Occasions, viz. *That as we enjoy great Advantages from the Inventions of others, we should be glad of an Opportunity to serve others by any Invention of ours, and this we should do freely and generously.*[43]

Few gifts are so widely useful, at so little cost to oneself, as the inventive mind, he thought. There could be no better way to promote Franklin's ethos of enlightened self-interest than by encouraging a spirit of scientific inquiry.

The Pennsylvania Militia

The militia was the last major voluntary project undertaken by Franklin in the years prior to his entry into political life. In this daring undertaking Franklin pushed the concept of voluntary association as far as it could be taken, testing the limits of what private citizens could accomplish and stopping little short of an open assault on the authority of government itself. The occasion was a crisis in colonial defense, brought on because the pacifist, Quaker-dominated Pennsylvania assembly refused to take any action against the growing threat of French and Spanish privateers during the War of the Austrian Succession. Franklin's language was reassuring and his manner scrupulously respectful; he presented the militia as nothing but a stop-gap expedient until the government should provide something better. But already in 1748 he was demonstrating his willingness to act on the same revolutionary principle that would bring America to war with Britain a quarter-century later: the conviction that when a government fails in its duty to secure the lives and the liberties of its subjects, it is the people's right to take whatever means they judge necessary to provide that security for themselves.

Franklin took the lead at every turn, organizing the militia, proposing an association for the purpose, drawing up and publicizing the membership agreement, explaining where to get arms, selling muskets in his shop, organizing a lottery to pay for a battery, printing the tickets and an explanation of the lottery, designing the standards for the companies, and talking a neighboring governor into lending cannon. Through the *Gazette,* he kept the population continually apprised of the association's progress and of small ways in which they could help. Franklin's arguments—and as always he provided an abundance of patient, thorough arguments long before he issued a call to action—were directed mainly against the pacifist Quakers, urging those in the assembly to pass defensive legislation or step aside so that others might do so. But his calls for arms and especially his leadership in the militia association brought him ultimately into more serious conflict with the Pennsylvania proprietors, who neglected the colonists' appeals for ships and cannon but were only too ready to recognize any threat to their own prerogatives. After the death of the colony's enlightened Founder, William Penn, his heirs had fallen into selfish policies that would come to embody for Franklin the injustices of hereditary privilege and irresponsible government. Franklin's experiences with the problems of founding the militia spearheaded a process of thought that ultimately led him to advocate full democracy and independence.

Franklin began his agitation for colonial defense in 1733 by publishing in the *Gazette* a short series of "queries" as to the wisdom of Pennsylvania's failure to arm itself. Beginning with an appeal to reason, he asks whether "they who are against fortifying their Country against an Enemy, ought not, by the same Principle to be against shutting and locking their doors a Nights," And whether "it be not as just to shoot an Enemy who comes to destroy my Country, and deprive the People of their Substance, Lives and Liberties, as to sit (being either Judge or Juryman) and condemn a Man to Death for breaking open a House, or taking a Purse?" But he does not confine himself to arguments from reason; he willingly grants the Quakers' fundamental presupposition as to the authority of scripture and argues on those grounds also. Most significant is the way he combines the two types of arguments, working always from the implicit assumption that God must be reasonable and must demand of us only reasonable things. Thus, he asks "whether the ancient Story of the Man, who sat down and prayed his Gods to lift his Cart out of the Mire, hath not a very good Moral?"[44]

Pressing the same thought in "Plain Truth," the 1747 pamphlet that finally galvanized the colony into action, Franklin cites the story in the Book of Judges of the people of Laish, rich and careless and thoughtlessly trusting in their gods rather than in human prudence. Franklin does not quite say that it is folly to trust in the true God, but he does question the fairness as well as the wisdom of relying on special favors from outside powers. Should we tell the Quakers, he asks rhetorically,

> That tho' *they* themselves may be resigned and easy under this naked, defenceless State of the Country, it is far otherwise with a very great Part of the People; with *us*, who can have no Confidence that God will protect those that neglect the Use of rational Means for their Security; nor have any Reason to hope, that our Losses, if we should suffer any, may be made up by Collections in our Favour at Home?[45]

Franklin makes many arguments for the economic importance of protecting the colony's shipping, for the deterrent effects of military preparedness, and even for the stimulating effect of military expenditures on the local economy. But he also interweaves his arguments from interest with appeals of another sort. It is base as well as foolish, he argues, to imagine that only those on the river are in danger from privateers, or only those on the frontier from Indians. "[A]re these the Sentiments of true Pennsylvanians, of Fellow-Countrymen, or even of Men that have common Sense or Goodness? . . . When the Feet are wounded, shall the Head say, *It is not me; I will not trouble myself to contrive Relief?*"[46] He never raises the question of whether a sensible person, after sensibly voting for a vigorous defense, would also be sensible to stand his ground in a desperate battle. It is easy enough to point out that without an organized militia there is slender hope that one's neighbors will offer resistance, and hence little sense in doing so oneself. Franklin implies that with an organized force in the field, fighting bravely is prudent. But whatever he counted upon to keep citizens in the field if deterrence did not work, it was presumably something more than mere calculation.

Since remonstrances failed to produce government action on public defense, Franklin began to defend the legitimacy of voluntary action. In "Plain Truth" he urged the assemblymen to consider "if not as Friends, at least as Legislators, that *Protection* is as truly due from the Government to the People, as *Obedience* from the People to the Government." Once he resolved to form a militia with or without government involvement, he went further, justifying the unauthorized association by, among other things, the fact "that thro' the Multiplicity of other Affairs of greater Importance (as we presume) no particular Care hath hitherto been taken by the Government at Home of our Protection, an humble Petition to the Crown for that purpose, sign'd by a great Number of Hands, having yet had no visible Effect." He explains, "Where a Government takes proper Measures to protect the People under its Care, such a Proceeding might have been thought both unnecessary and unjustifiable: But here it is quite the Reverse."[47]

So moderate and respectful was Franklin's mode of proceeding that he won the full support of the Philadelphia city council, who granted regular commissions to all the officers the militia association chose. But Thomas Penn considered Franklin's actions "little short of treason," commenting, "I am sure the people of America are too often ready to act in defiance of the Government they live in, without associating for that purpose." Penn added, misjudging the present but with prescient forebodings,

> This Association is founded on contempt to Government, and cannot end in anything but Anarchy and Confusion. The People in general are so fond of what they call Liberty as to fall into Licenciousness, and when they know they may Act . . . by Orders of their own Substitutes, in a Body, and a Military manner, and independent of this Government, why should they not Act against it.[48]

In another letter, Penn writes of Franklin, "He is a dangerous man and I should be very Glad he inhabited any other Country, as I believe him of a very uneasy Spirit. However as he is a Sort of Tribune of the People, he must be treated with regard."[49]

Especially troubling to Penn, with good reason, was a clause in the association's rules that bound the members to obey as laws the regulations of a military council established by the association. This provision might equally well have been criticized from the opposite side, for Franklin was strongly inclined to believe that the regulations needed to govern an army could be upheld without force, and the rules had no teeth. Franklin was the quintessential civilian, as he readily admitted. He stressed repeatedly that he had no expertise in military matters, declining to serve when his organizational skill won him election as colonel in the militia. Although he willingly did his part as a common soldier, he had no taste for a good fight, no love of danger, no attraction to the glories of heroic self-overcoming. So much did he hate tyranny and love liberty, reason, and gentle persuasion that he could not see the need for military discipline. As a young man on his first trip to England, after touring the fortress and dungeon of Portsmouth, where one governor of the town used to confine his disobedient soldiers, Franklin mused in his journal,

> 'tis a common maxim, that without severe discipline it is impossible to govern the licentious rabble of soldiery. I own indeed that if a commander finds he has not those qualities in him that will make him beloved by his people, he ought by all means to make use of such methods as will make them fear him, since one or the other (or both) is absolutely necessary; but Alexander and Caesar, those renowned generals, received more faithful service, and performed greater actions by means of the love their soldiers bore them, than they could possibly have done, if instead of being beloved and respected they had been hated and feared by those they commanded.[50]

The same hopeful, egalitarian spirit pervaded his later thinking about military discipline. In organizing the militia he provided that men be assigned to companies by neighborhood so as to prevent any segregation by class, that the officers all be chosen by election, and that their terms be kept very short. Recognizing that this policy of election departed from standard military practice and that military discipline may be thought to suffer when officers are made dependent on their men, he defends his policy with an appeal to the custom of electing officers in the Roman Republic. Yet Franklin ignores the crucial difference that Rome was an aristocratic society in which the plebian soldiers could be depended upon to elect patrician officers and to defer to them. Franklin goes furthest in slighting the need for military discipline in his provisions for the General Military Council, to be elected by all the regiments. He provides on the one hand that "whatever Orders and Regulations shall be so made by the said Council, or the Majority of them, shall have the Force of Laws with us." But he immediately undercuts this provision by forbidding the military council to impose any fines or corporal penalties "on any account whatever; We being determined, in this whole Affair, to act only on Principles of Reason, Duty and Honour." In the same spirit, his draft of a 1755 act for a state militia rejects the use of conscription on the grounds that cowards in arms do more harm than good.[51]

The discipline of Franklin's militia was fortunately never put to a serious test, and the danger against which it was formed was soon to pass. But Washington would later experience in full measure the limitations of a volunteer, democratic army and the difficulties of maintaining discipline among men who had grown up believing that they should choose their own leaders and be governed only by reason and their own sense of duty and honor. Washington was most critical of the democratic naïveté that failed to understand the need for force and fear. It was only by dint of Washington's enormous dignity and military reputation that he managed to prevail against these obstacles. By the same token, only a military hero and savior of his country's cause could show such unbending pride and reserve and still be beloved by his country. The equally talented but more sinuous and diplomatic Franklin found an altogether different route to his country's affection and trust.

Democratic Leadership

In the course of launching and leading his voluntary associations, Franklin developed a unique style of leadership, partly out of the peculiar nature and limits of his talents and circumstances, but partly out of his deep insight into human nature and the democratic spirit. This style depended not on public oratory, with all its potential for demagoguery and for the development of personality cults, but rather on rational appeals, the power of example, the use of indirect approaches, and moral and political education gently administered.

Franklin was fascinated by the power of both written rhetoric and spoken oratory. As a youth he was consumed with the ambition to become a great prose stylist; as a man he was intrigued by the way George Whitefield could keep an audience enthralled to his every word. But this was a talent he did not have. Instead, he perfected the art of friendly, informal persuasion.

> The modest way in which I propos'd my Opinions, procur'd them a readier Reception and less Contradiction; I had less Mortification when I was found to be in the wrong, and I more easily prevail'd with others to give up their Mistakes and join with me when I happen'd to be in the right. And this Mode, which I at first put on, with some violence to natural Inclination, became at length so easy and so habitual to me, that perhaps for these Fifty Years past no one has ever heard a dogmatical Expression escape me. And to this Habit (after my Character of Integrity) I think it principally owing, that I had early so much Weight with my Fellow Citizens, when I proposed new Institutions, or Alterations in the old; and so much Influence in public Councils when I became a Member. For I was but a bad Speaker, never eloquent, subject to much Hesitation in my choice of Words, hardly correct in Language, and yet I generally carried my Points.[52]

It is at first surprising that such a master of English style should have lacked eloquence, but oratorical fire usually depends upon the speaker's fiery passions and his willingness to ignite them in others; Franklin's instinct was always to douse such passions with reason, wry wit, and skepticism.

Franklin's claim about leadership is that it really requires no extraordinary talent, but only extraordinary diligence.

> I have always thought that one Man of tolerable Abilities may work great Changes, and accomplish great Affairs among Mankind, if he first forms a good Plan, and, cutting off all Amusements or other Employments that would divert his Attention, makes the Execution of that same Plan his sole Study and Business.

This claim is no doubt partly true, but it is also a deliberately adopted part of Franklin's public persona. Franklin carefully cultivated an image of pedestrian diligence, pushing his own wheelbarrow through the streets, wearing his American fur cap even in Europe, and always, despite his many honors, signing his name "Benjamin Franklin, Printer." Here was the tradesman's son who was taught that a man who is diligent in his calling will stand before kings, and who proved the saying literally true, much to his own surprise.[53]

The young Franklin was encouraged in this line of thinking not only by his father but by Cotton Mather, who wrote that "Plain men dwelling in tents, persons of a very ordinary character, may in a way of bright piety, prove persons of extraordinary usefulness."[54] But Franklin may also have been prompted by Mather to reflect upon the problem that when ordinary men set out to do extraordinary things, they invariably provoke the envy of their neighbors. "A man of *good merit,* by engrossing a great many applauses, which would serve to gratify a great many others, . . . cannot but be envied." Mather offers no solution to the problem except to treat it with cold scorn: "I must press you to do good, and be so far from affrighted at, that you shall rather be generously delighted in, the most envious deplumations," as a confirmation of one's own excellence.[55]

Tocqueville, looking more broadly at the envy that attaches to wealth, power, and fame, observes that the problem of envy only grows worse as society grows more democratic.

> One must not conceal from oneself that democratic institutions develop the sentiment of envy in the human heart to a very high degree. It is not so much because they offer to each the means of becoming equal to others, but because these means constantly fail those who employ them. . . .
>
> While the natural instincts of democracy bring the people to keep distinguished men away from power, an instinct no less strong brings the latter to distance themselves from a political career, in which it is so difficult for them to remain completely themselves, and to advance without debasing themselves.[56]

But Franklin, who ran full tilt into the problem of envy from a young age, pondered it, refused to condemn the natural vanity that spawned it, and patiently found an admirable way through. As a spirited and precocious boy apprenticed to his envious brother James, he suffered unjust beatings, though on reflection he later admits he was perhaps "too saucy and provoking." His own keen sense of emulation was stirred up by James's friends, who sometimes contributed to the *New England Courant.*

> Hearing their Conversations, and their Accounts of the Approbation their Papers were receiv'd with, I was excited to try my Hand among them. But being still a Boy, and suspecting that my Brother would object to printing any Thing of mine in his Paper if he knew it to be mine, I contriv'd to disguise my Hand, and writing an anonymous Paper I put it in at Night under the Door of the Printing House.[57]

Thus were launched the Silence Dogood letters, and a lifetime habit of anonymous satires and colorful pseudonyms. The next day Franklin had the unexpected pleasure of hearing his work frankly praised to his face by the unsuspecting company and hearing their flattering surmises as to who the author might be. When he eventually disclosed his authorship, he attracted more respect but also more fraternal envy. The lessons learned here would be relearned and refined in later ventures, as Franklin's "saucy" impudence was gradually replaced by the mature charm of his puckish but disarmingly self-deprecating humor.

In his first philanthropic venture, forming a subscription library, Franklin encountered again the problem of envy and devised what would become his customary way around it.

> The Objections, and Reluctances I met with in Soliciting the Subscriptions, made me soon feel the Impropriety of presenting one's self as the Proposer of any useful Project that might be suppos'd to raise one's Reputation in the smallest degree above that of one's Neighbours, when one has need of their Assistance to accomplish the Project. I therefore put myself as much as I could out of sight, and stated it as a Scheme of a *Number of Friends,* who had requested me to go about and propose it to such as they thought Lovers of Reading. In this way my Affair went on more smoothly, and I ever after practic'd it on such Occasions; and from my frequent Successes, can heartily recommend it. The present little Sacrifice of your Vanity will afterwards be amply repaid. If it remains a while uncertain to whom the Merit belongs, some one more vain than yourself will be encourag'd to claim it, and then even Envy will be dispos'd to do you Justice, by plucking those assum'd Feathers, and restoring them to their right Owner.[58]

When one learns, like Franklin, to give vanity fair quarter wherever one meets with it, the cold satisfactions of Mather's "deplumations" may thus be replaced by pleasures of an altogether more delicious kind.

Franklin's sensitive handling of vanity won him the affection of his colleagues. In the meeting of the Continental Congress to revise Jefferson's draft of the Declaration of Independence, watching Jefferson's growing dismay at the number of deletions that were being made, Franklin smoothed his ruffled feathers with a story about a young hatmaker composing a sign for his shop.

> He composed it in these words, "John Thompson, hatter, makes and sells hats for ready money," with a figure of a hat subjoined. But he thought he would submit it to his friends for their amendments. The first he showed it to thought the word "Hatter" tautologous, because followed by the words "makes hats," which showed he was a hatter. It was struck out. The next observed that the word "makes" might as well be omitted, because his customers would not care who made the hats . . . He struck it out. A third said he thought the words "for ready money" were useless, as it was not the custom of the place to sell on credit. Everyone who purchased expected to pay. They were parted with; and the inscription now stood, "John Thompson sells hats." "Sells hats!" says his next friend; "why, nobody will expect you to give them away. What then is the use of that word?" It was stricken out, and "hats" followed, the rather as there was one painted on the board. So his inscription was reduced ultimately to "John Thompson," with the figure of a hat subjoined.[59]

Franklin also won people's loyalty by praising their contributions while keeping out of sight his own crucial role in setting them in motion. Richard Peters, the secretary of the Philadelphia city council, reports an early meeting on the proposed militia that Franklin in his autobiographical account says nothing about. After the agreement to form the militia was drafted and before the general assembly of citizens met to sign it, Franklin held a rally for his closest supporters.

> On Saturday there was a Meeting of 150 Persons, mostly Tradesmen, in Chancellor's Sail Loft, and Franklyn after having address'd them as the first Movers in every useful undertaking that had been projected for the good of the City—Library Company, Fire Com-

> panys &c., he pull'd a Draught of an intended Association out of his Pocket and read it, all approv'd and offer'd to sign. No says he let us not sign yet, let us offer it at least to the Gentlemen and if they come into it, well and good, we shall be the better able to carry it into Execution."[60]

Here, clearly, were the secret Junto and its secret offshoots, marshaled by Franklin without their full understanding of the springs setting them all in motion. Franklin stoked their pride by giving them credit for his favorite projects, whetted their eagerness to lead in this one, but held them back, so as to appeal more effectively to the pride of the city's gentlemen, on whom he wanted to confer the honor of thinking themselves the first to volunteer.

In all his voluntary projects, Franklin preferred the well-laid plan and the rational appeal to interest over obtrusive moral exhortation; and even when his appeal was to charity, he found a way of weaving prudent calculation into the mix. A fine example is his invention of the device of the matching grant. The occasion was the establishment of a hospital for the poor in Philadelphia, a project that was foundering until Franklin came to its aid, for people had become so accustomed to seeing him behind every philanthropic project that they suspected there must be something wrong with one he did not support. The expense of building a hospital drove him to seek help from the legislature; the stinginess of the legislature put him in mind of a way to appeal to its members' vanity—their desire to seem generous—while hiding from them the likelihood of their actually having to pay the conditionally granted funds. Persuading them to promise £2000 if the friends of the hospital should raise the same amount privately, he then drew upon his deep wells of support to bring in the requisite donations in short order—helped, as he explains, by his ability to urge the legislative grant as an additional motive to give, "since every Man's Donation would be Doubled." "I do not remember any of my political Maneuvers, the success of which gave me at the time more Pleasure. Or that in after-thinking of it, I more easily excus'd my-self for having made some use of Cunning."[61] Today we think nothing of such cunning, but then Franklin has long since taught us to be content with any gift in a good cause, even when vanity and calculation are inextricably entangled with its purer motives.

Nor was Franklin averse to using outright lies, if he really must, to cajole people into acting wisely and well. A little-remembered aspect of Braddock's campaign into the American wilds is Franklin's pivotal intervention to provide him with wagons. Braddock was on the point of returning to England in disgust when the wagons he had ordered failed to appear. Franklin, with characteristic generosity, spent his time and credit arranging for transport to be hired in Pennsylvania, printing and distributing advertisements for the wagons and drivers and advancing the requisite funds to pay the farmers. But he did not stop there; he also backed up the generous offer he had persuaded Braddock to make for the wagons with a threat that Braddock would take them by force if they were not voluntarily offered on his generous terms. This was a sheer fabrication. Clearly Franklin did not trust the farmers, who knew of Braddock's "violent prejudices" against the Americans, to overlook this fact and act calmly in their own best interest.[62]

In other ways, too, Franklin skillfully wove his way around people's passions and prejudices, always giving respectful berth to their vanity and pride, always making use of these passions when he could. He observed that the pleasure of being the source of benefit to others strengthens our good will towards them, whereas being in others' debt is painful. Thus, when he wanted to win over a powerful rival in the Pennsylvania assembly, he did so not by servility, nor by argument, nor by ostentatious shows of goodwill, but by "this other Method": he asked the favor of borrowing a book from the man's library, and returning it promptly and with thanks, he made the man his benefactor.

> And he ever afterwards manifested a Readiness to serve me on all Occasions, so that we became great Friends, and our Friendship continu'd to his Death. This is another Instance of the Truth of an old Maxim I had learnt, which says, *He that has once done you a Kindness will be more ready to do you another, than he whom you yourself have obliged.* And it shows how much more profitable it is prudently to remove, than to resent, return and continue inimical Proceedings.[63]

But of course all of this requires not only a sensitivity to the pride of others but a capacity to keep one's own in check. It requires, that is to say, a certain cool distance on oneself and a cool and even ironic distance on others. In Franklin's elaborate appeals to the pride and self-interest of his fellow citizens we are reminded of Locke's advice on the education of children, which Franklin studied so closely. As Locke observes, children love to be treated as rational creatures—and so of course do adults. We can get great mileage out of that fact, especially if we keep clearly in mind that much of the time people are not as reasonable as they would like to be thought. Thus, it is often not just reason that we must appeal to but an unreasonable pride in being treated as reasonable. In the same spirit, Franklin appeals not only to people's generosity but to the pride they take in a generosity they do not entirely possess. If we are troubled by his manipulations, we must remember at least that his ethic was consistent in raising no objections to them. The freedom he loved and wanted to advance was not the Kantian freedom of a radically undetermined human will, regarded with solemn respect by other free wills who leave each other the greatest possible autonomy. Rather, it was the difficult freedom of living according to what is naturally reasonable and good, following a rationality that often eludes us and does not come naturally at all but requires careful education that begins with habituation in childhood.

By Franklin's own account, these insights into human irrationality, vanity, and pride were the reason for his first reported use of subterfuge, his secret authorship of the Silence Dogood papers. The same insights were clearly a major source of his lifelong love of masks, impersonations, and behind-the-scenes manipulations. One must use indirection in leading people to live rationally and act fairly because human beings are so stubborn and prickly and proud that a direct assault will never do. Franklin's love of self-concealment has led some to suspect that he was ironic all the way down.[64] Perhaps he was never frank about his views on religion, but in his understanding of human nature and the moral and political principles he drew from it, Franklin expressed himself with convincing force and remarkable consistency over a lifetime of writing, both public and private. More tellingly, in his energetic pursuit of public-spirited projects, in his conduct of diplomacy, and even in his flaws, he behaved just as a man would who joined such a forgiving view of human imperfection with a profound belief in liberty, democracy, and virtue as enlightened self-interest. Franklin's subterfuge was fundamentally tactical; goal of a more decent and enlightened world he paints for us in glowing colors.[65]

And thus, while Franklin was willing to use manipulation to cajole people into reasonable actions and good habits, he never stopped there. His first and last recourse was always to persuade, to enlighten, to nudge people by small but continual steps towards more sober and critical judgment about themselves and their situations. His newspaper was the most important tool of all his philanthropic projects, and an enlightened readership was the newspaper's constant goal. After all, his first use of duplicity in a public project was to hide his own importance in the scheme for founding a subscription library to promote literacy and knowledge. When he signed his name "Benjamin Franklin, Printer," he did so in a show of solidarity with the simple working man, but also as an act of pride.

Yet while Franklin's style of leadership was well crafted to avoid the envy characteristic of democracy, and in its ultimate purpose was not undemocratic at all, we may still be concerned that his spirit of benevolent detachment is difficult to reproduce. Indeed, his peculiar combination of shrewdness, humor, integrity, and public spiritedness is matchless. Franklin could not engender other Franklins, but he did what he could to persuade others who might enter public life to keep some perspective on its charms and disappointments and not be overcome by the yearnings for power and fame that tempt people to use their cleverness in unscrupulous ways. One should temper one's ambition, he suggests, with a quiet pride in one's own ability to smile at the storms of applause that come one's way and to shrug off the equally unpredictable thunderclaps of public disfavor. Here is his response to a wave of bad publicity in 1776:

> I have often met with such Treatment from People that I was all the while endeavouring to serve. At other times I have been extoll'd extravagantly when I have had little or no Merit. These are the Operations of Nature. It sometimes is cloudy, it rains, it hails; again 'tis clear and pleasant, and the Sun shines on us. Take one thing with another, and the World is a pretty good sort of a World; and 'tis our Duty to make the best of it and be thankful. One's true

> Happiness depends more upon one's own Judgment of one's self, on a Consciousness of Rectitude in Action and Intention, and in the Approbation of those few who judge impartially, than upon the Applause of the unthinking undiscerning Multitude, who are apt to cry Hosanna today, and tomorrow, Crucify him.[66]

Likewise he writes to Joseph Galloway, responding to a calumnious essay that has charged them both with responsibility for the Stamp Act,

> Your Consolation, my Friend, and mine, under these Abuses, must be *that we do not deserve them*. . . . Let us, as we ever have done, uniformly endeavour the Service of our Country, according to the best of our Judgment and Abilities, and Time will do us Justice. Dirt thrown on a Mud-Wall may stick and incorporate; but it will not long adhere to polish'd Marble.[67]

No less striking than the equanimity in these two comments is the vaunting pride; perhaps it is not possible to have the one without the other. Surely it was the same pride that helped Franklin to rise above petty resentments so as to remain on good terms with political enemies and to give them his support in every good cause. It also gave him the fortitude to maintain a complete, dignified silence in his greatest political humiliation, when Alexander Weddenburn publicly excoriated him in the "cockpit" of the House of Lords in London—although for that offence Franklin was glad to get his quiet revenge. Such freedom from public opinion, or at least a patient faith that opinion will always in the long run settle in favor of the true friends to the public good, is most difficult for the bourgeois spirit to attain, as Rousseau so trenchantly observed. Franklin even in some degree undercut it: his advocacy of this spirit of independence is in tension with his constant advice to cultivate good relations with everyone and never to underestimate the value of their esteem. Nor did Franklin give significant thought to the problem of how to resist the tyranny of the majority and its opinions that Tocqueville makes such prescient warnings against. But even if he could not reliably bequeath his independent spirit to others, Franklin provided a fine example of it for American statesmen to contemplate; and even if they cannot quite attain his inner equanimity, they have much to learn from his superb, unfailing tact.

CHAPTER 4

THOUGHTS ON GOVERNMENT

WE HAVE now examined Franklin's reflections on the economic and moral foundations of liberty and the most fundamental civic expressions of that liberty in free associations, which in turn teach the skills necessary for self-government. In doing so, we have largely followed the progression of Franklin's own interests and activities, beginning with his early efforts to establish himself in business and moving through his projects for moral perfection and civic improvement in Philadelphia, up to the moment of his entry into public life in 1751. In this chapter we will continue from that point, tracing the development of Franklin's thoughts on government and diplomacy as they emerged from his practical confrontations with the great issues of his day, in this last, longest, and most illustrious chapter of his career. But here we find a change in tone. Franklin relates with gusto his civic projects in Philadelphia: he has had fun with all of them, and he invites everyone else to do the same in their own communities. But serving in office, especially high office at a level removed from the people, does not seem to have held the same natural satisfactions for Franklin.[1] For all the fame it brought him, he found working at diplomacy and lawmaking a dark and frustrating business in which his faith in human nature was tried and most of his best hopes bore little fruit.

Franklin gave so much time to politics because he recognized its importance, and he was of course pleased that his country thought well of his talents. Yet the importance of politics, in his thinking as in that of many of his contemporaries, was largely negative. As he saw it, happiness requires liberty and prosperity and a thriving civil society, which governments can protect or thwart; in the worst case, tyranny enslaves a people so thoroughly that virtue is corrupted as well.[2] The true tasks of government are few and simple. It should do for society only those things that individuals and voluntary associations cannot, such as defending against criminals and enemies and constructing large public works.

While most of Franklin's efforts before his entry into politics involved launching new projects, the lion's share of his efforts afterwards had the goal of curtailing excessive and pernicious assumptions of governmental power. Franklin should not, however, be classed with the revolutionary radicals who saw government as only a necessary evil that a society should minimize as much as possible. His early experiences with colonial governments that were too weak and divided to provide for their own defense inoculated him against the naïve wish for minimal government. It would be more accurate to say that Franklin favored simple government: government with strictly curtailed ends, powers fully adequate to meet those ends, and lines of responsibility of maximum directness and clarity.

Simplicity is a virtue that recurs in Franklin's thoughts on a myriad of subjects, including colonial dress and republican manners, English spelling, relations between business partners, and governmental structure.[3] Simplicity of form and function in government is good because it prevents the duplication, contradictory policies, and overlapping jurisdictions that make it hard to assign responsibility for problems and resolve them. Franklin's advice that the king appoint a single postmaster for America, his preference for direct royal governance over proprietary rule in Pennsylvania, his request to Congress to put the mission to France under one ambassador, and his endorsement of unicameral legislatures are all expressions of this love of simplicity.

Yet in one respect Franklin's politics departed markedly from the general inclination of Americans who loved simplicity and prized local self-government. Many who shared these views found themselves among the Antifederalists, who wished to maximize local autonomy, in imitation of the ancient small republics of Greece and Rome. Franklin, however, was an inveterate foe of narrow localism, finding it prone to prejudice, suspicion of outsiders, and fiercely circumscribed loyalties. Throughout his life he worked to combat such narrowness, with his press and his post office, his numerous schemes for national and international associations of learned men, and his bold advocacy of continental union, a well-integrated British Empire, and later a vigorous national government for the United States. Franklin believed that many tasks of government are best fulfilled by unified policies under firm central control and that the wisest perspective is the least parochial and the most cosmopolitan. It is no accident that his greatest practical contribution to the new American nation was as an ambassador of international understanding to the court of Versailles and as negotiator of the Peace of Paris. The uneasy balance he sought might be characterized as vigorous local involvement with a cosmopolitan perspective.

The realm of politics, like the military realm, was to prove an important test of Franklin's faith in enlightened self-interest. As armies call upon men to risk their lives, so in the political arena justice often seems to demand that they voluntarily forego profits and powers that they might easily seize. How consistently was Franklin able to hold to his thesis about the convergence of virtue and happiness, and how far would he be forced to maintain that human beings also have duties to society that do not accord with their self-interest?

The Albany Plan of Union

Even before he first accepted public office, and far ahead of most Americans, Franklin became convinced that a political union of the colonies was essential. The French and their Indian allies were launching well-coordinated attacks on frontier settlements, while the colonial governments remained weak, indecisive, niggardly, and short-sighted in their divisions and failures to assist one another. In 1751 Franklin observed, "It would be a very strange Thing, if six Nations of ignorant Savages should be capable of forming a Scheme for such an Union" and that it "should be impracticable for ten or a Dozen English Colonies, to whom it is more necessary . . . and who cannot be supposed to want an equal Understanding of their Interests."[4] When a colonial commission was convened at Albany in 1754 by the British Lords of Trade to discuss means to provide a common defense, many delegates came with thoughts of a political union, but Franklin arrived with a detailed plan of union already drafted. His plan served as the basis of discussion and of the proposal that was in the end unanimously adopted by the convention.[5]

The plan was moderate in scope, granting to the central government a carefully delineated sphere of authority, which was to include relations with the Indian tribes, coordinating the common defense, purchasing lands, and regulating their settlement. It did, however, give the new government a power that the Americans were most jealous of, the power to tax. It provided for a president general to be appointed by the king and a grand council of delegates drawn from the colonies, the representation of each colony being proportional to the contributions it made to the treasury of the whole. Franklin explained that this arrangement was meant to maintain the same balance between royal prerogative and popular representation as was found in each of the colonial governments.[6] He advertised the proposed union with his famous cartoon of a snake cut into thirteen segments and the motto, "Join, or Die."[7]

Yet the plan was quickly rejected on all sides. In his *Autobiography,* Franklin attributes the opposition of the colonial assemblies to their opinion that there was "too much *Prerogative* in it," and the disapproval of Parliament to the belief that there was "too much of the *Democratic.*" From such diverse objections he concludes that the plan in fact struck the right balance and would have been to the benefit of all.

> The Colonies so united would have been sufficiently strong to have defended themselves; there would then have been no need of Troops from England; of course the subsequent Pretence for Taxing America, and the bloody Contest it occasioned, would have been avoided. But such Mistakes are not new; History is full of the Errors of States and Princes.
>
> "Look round the habitable World, how few
> Know their own Good, or knowing it pursue."[8]

Franklin's willingness to embrace such a scheme in 1754 shows his penchant for bold thinking. He was far more attuned to the realities of the global power struggle than were other colonial leaders, and he saw more clearly the importance of a unified, expanding British-American empire to counter the threat of the French. Accompanying this plan of union was a plan for settling two new western colonies in the Ohio country, which was long a favorite project of Franklin's.[9] He was fully prepared to embrace the means necessary to achieve his goals: he shared neither the growing American wariness of royal power nor the fear of centralized government that would later make so many of his fellow leaders reluctant to arm the Continental Congress with the force necessary to fulfill its tasks. Already he saw that a union dependent only on requisitions and without its own powers of taxation could never be effective. Equally striking at this period, however, is his deference to parliamentary authority, for the plan provides that the American union be brought about by an act of Parliament, not by American governors or a royal decree. Was Franklin's trust in every case well placed?

The balance Franklin sought to establish between popular and royal power was essentially a pragmatic accommodation to the reality of the latter. "As the choice . . . of the grand council by the representatives of the people, neither gives the people any new powers, nor diminishes the power of the crown, it was thought and hoped the crown would not disapprove of it."[10] If the king's power would be extended in America, so would the people's ability to act on their own behalf. The royal power, delegated to the president general, was in Franklin's mind not an unlimited authority to legislate for the colonies but only a circumscribed authority to direct military actions and to veto legislation passed by the people. Franklin was as appalled as any of his countrymen would have been when in 1757 Lord Granville claimed to him in a private interview that the king's instructions to his governors were laws for the colonies.[11]

Nevertheless, there is some evidence that, in addition to accepting royal prerogative as a reality to be dealt with, Franklin welcomed it as a counterweight to impulsive legislatures.

> It was thought that it would be best the President General should be supported as well as appointed by the crown; that so all disputes between him and the Grand Council concerning his salary might be prevented; as such disputes have been frequently of mischievous consequence in particular colonies, especially in time of public danger.[12]

Democratic assemblies as well as "States and Princes" act all too often with narrow, foolish selfishness: Franklin's whole account of the need for union is a litany of charges against the elected colonial assemblies for holding the common defense hostage to their jealous quarrels with one another and with their governors.[13] His thought at this time seems to have been that a firm, independent executive gives more energy to government and that a single executive in charge of colonial defense would take a broad view and look to the long-term needs of British America in a way that elected assemblies often did not. For as long as Franklin acquiesced in the power of the king—that is, up until the early 1770s—he did so with a similar thought about the advantages of a leader who would take a keen interest in the future of his realm and a "Family-interest" in the prosperity of all parts of it. As Gerald Stourzh points out, although Franklin's love of liberty otherwise put him in the camp of the English Whigs, who were champions of parliamentary power against the king, his experience as an American made him cognizant of the ways in which even elected legislatures can fall prey to class and regional biases from which a monarch may be more free.[14]

But Franklin never systematically worked through his thoughts on executive power in the British Empire to arrive at a satisfactory way of attaining the advantages of a mixed government without the disadvantages of governors who were not responsible to their constituents. In a 1754 letter he explains the need for an elected grand council by expanding on the defects of many of these governors, who

> often come to the colonies merely to make Fortunes, with which they intend to return to Britain, are not always Men of the best Abilities and Integrity, have no Estates here, nor any natural Connections with us, that should make them heartily concern'd for our Welfare; and might possibly be sometimes fond of raising and keeping up more Forces than necessary, from the Profits accruing to themselves, and to make Provision for their Friends and Dependents.[15]

For these reasons, he would later protest when governors' salaries were taken *out* of the hands of colonial assemblies, arguing that this removed the one check assemblies had upon governors' self-interested behavior.[16] He saw the problem, but he did not see the solution that Madison would find—to establish separate branches of government that would all rest their power ultimately upon the consent of the people.

A similar question may be asked about the wisdom of Franklin's willingness to allow the American union to be established by an act of Parliament, in light of the bitter contest he would later wage to deny Parliament any power to legislate for America. This, even more than his concessions to royal authority, was just a matter of pragmatism. The new union, speaking with one voice for the North American part of the empire, could be expected to stand on its own and hence to reduce future occasions for Parliament to meddle in American affairs, but initially Parliament's role seemed indispensable. Franklin saw that he and the other commissioners at Albany were in a distinct minority in recognizing the need for a continental union; the colonial governments were in large measure the problem, so they could never be expected to take the lead in applying the remedy. The pivotal colony of Virginia had not even sent a delegation to Albany, and in the event none of the colonial governments supported the plan. In his 1789 commentary on the plan Franklin gives another, equally prescient reason for looking to a higher authority than the colonial governments to establish the union: if that union were simply created by the acts of the separate colonies, they might well withdraw from it again when it came to seem burdensome to them. Franklin saw at once the problem of a confederation, although again he had no satisfactory solution.[17]

On the whole, however, Franklin's plan of union was a bold, forward-looking project that anticipated the federalist structure and the limited grant of powers to the central government that the Constitutional Convention of 1787 would finally adopt as cornerstones of its work.[18] Had it been ratified in 1754, the Albany Plan would have been a distinct improvement over the status quo. It was perhaps the best effort ever made to secure English liberties for the American colonists and to set them on an equal footing with their brethren in the old country within an intact empire.

Of Proprietors and Kings

Franklin's next effort to reform British imperial government to make it more equitable to American subjects began soon afterwards, back home in Pennsylvania, although it would carry him to London and eventually into the center of the storm between the colonies and the British government. At issue was a long-running battle between the Pennsylvania Assembly and the governor over taxes.

> These public Quarrels were all at bottom owing to the Proprietaries, our hereditary Governors; who when any Expence was to be incurr'd for the Defence of their Province, with incredible Meanness instructed their Deputies to pass no Act for levying the necessary Taxes, unless their vast Estates were in the same Act expressly excused; and they had even taken bonds of these Deputies to observe such Instructions.[19]

Franklin's unusually heated expression of the problem betrays an animus that would draw him into a protracted struggle to replace Pennsylvania's proprietary government with direct royal government; this same animus would drive him into a rare misjudgment of public opinion at home and even of his fellow Pennsylvanians' interests.[20] Why this unusual and costly eruption of anger?

All of Franklin's sentiments as a democrat, a proud defender of English liberties, and a self-made man were offended by the fabulously wealthy proprietors who claimed special hereditary rights to rule over their fellow subjects. In Franklin's mind, no one had any need or reasonable claim to that much property; hence, their attempt to exempt it from all taxes was doubly unreasonable.[21] Implicit in Franklin's actions with regard to the proprietors is the judgment that no one had a hereditary right to so much power, either, although this thought is inimical to monarchy and would long remain unspoken by Franklin, perhaps even unformulated in his mind. But after the Revolution Franklin would oppose not only hereditary monarchic and aristocratic powers but even the hereditary honors that Washington and other Revolutionary War leaders wished to establish in the Society of the Cincinnatus.

> For Honour worthily obtain'd, as for Example that of our Officers, is in its Nature a personal Thing, and incommunicable to any but those who had some Share in obtaining it. Thus among the Chinese, the most ancient, and from long Experience the wisest of Nations, Honour does not *descend*, but *ascends*. If a Man from his Learning, his Wisdom, or his Valour, is promoted by the Emperor to the Rank of Mandarin, his Parents are immediately intitled to the same Ceremonies of Respect from the People, that are establish'd as due to the Mandarin himself, on this Supposition, that it must have been owing to the Education, Instruction, and good Example afforded him by his Parents that he was rendered capable of serving the Publick. This *ascending* Honour is therefore useful to the State as it encourages Parents to give their Children a good and virtuous Education. But the *descending Honour*, to Posterity who could have no Share in obtaining it, is not only groundless and absurd, but often hurtful to that Posterity, since it is apt to make them proud, disdaining to be employ'd in useful Arts, and thence falling into Poverty and all the Meannnesses, Servility and Wretchedness attending it; which is the present case with much of what is called the *Noblesse* in Europe.[22]

Despite his instinctive antipathy to all powers and honors that did not come from the earned trust of one's fellow citizens, Franklin long made an exception for the king, who in his mind was essential to holding together an empire comprising freely self-governing parts. When his protests against the exemption of proprietary lands from taxation failed to win a permanent change of policy, he began to agitate for a new charter for Pennsylvania, to replace proprietary government with direct royal rule, as the Carolinas and New Jersey had done. What he failed to take sufficiently into account was the strong support the proprietors enjoyed among London insiders; their retention was even favored by many in Pennsylvania, where they formed a rallying point for Anglican, Presbyterian, and western resistance to the entrenched coastal Quaker domination of the Assembly. Nor did Franklin give sufficient weight to the ways in which royal authority had, by the 1760s, become intertwined with the claimed authority of Parliament, which was moving to increase its control over America and American revenues. These developments made the project of replacing the proprietors both impracticable and dangerous to American liberties; it was a rare lapse of Franklin's usually excellent political judgment.

Statesmanship and Public Relations

While Franklin remained in London as representative of the Pennsylvania Assembly—an extra-constitutional office that the British government never recognized as legitimate—he quickly was given other equally awkward but equally critical duties as the representative of the assemblies of Georgia, New Jersey, and Massachusetts. With these charges he found a task worthy of his enormous energies and talents, one for which no one was better suited and for which the stakes could not have been higher. Franklin regarded himself as an ambassador of friendship, sent to negotiate crucial reforms but even more importantly to explain two branches of the British family to one each other and to remove the misunderstandings and suspicions that were beginning to tear the empire apart. His dream was the harmonious Anglo-American empire that he had sketched in his 1751 "Observations Concerning the Increase of Mankind," an entity that would grow rapidly in prosperity and power as its center of gravity shifted peacefully across the Atlantic.[23] We might say in retrospect that British pride would never have allowed this to happen, but Franklin's pragmatism was flexible; if Americans could continue enjoying the core of English liberties, it mattered little if they were not legally on quite the same footing as the English; if Franklin could only make himself heard, was there not hope that British pride would eventually attach itself to the vision of one great, extended people, as Franklin's own had done? He thought it was only narrow parochialism that prevented this. Franklin himself tended to speak of "we Englishmen" and "we Americans" interchangeably, and in 1762 he seriously considered making England his permanent home and running for Parliament. Only slowly and late did he begin to speak of Britain and America as two countries.[24]

To encourage the British to take a broader view, he reminded them of the increase in trade and wealth that would come if the colonies were well peopled and well defended. He urged English authors to take pride in the spread of their language and writings "beyond the narrow bounds of these islands" to a great continent filled with literate Englishmen, and he urged British patriots to rejoice "in observing that the *children* of Britain retain their native intrepidity to the third and fourth generation in the regions of America; together with that ardent love of liberty and zeal in its defence, which in every age has distinguish'd their progenitors among the rest of mankind."[25] Franklin tirelessly rebutted the slanderous accounts of American cowardice, boorishness, ignorance, and disloyalty that filled British newspapers, warning of the dangers of stoking such petty animosities "with insolence, contempt, and abuse."[26] He explained the harm that excessive taxation of the colonies would cause to Englishmen themselves, the harm that contemptuous treatment of American officers by the British would cause to deep-seated American loyalty and affection for the mother country, and the madness of trying by violence to force Americans to buy British goods.[27] He warned repeatedly against the danger of *creating* rebellion by blaming a whole people for the lawlessness of a few and attributing mutinous motives to loyal subjects engaged in peaceful protests. As time went on he would have more and more such follies to remonstrate against, which he continued to do with untiring logic and patience.

But most of all, Franklin simply tried to explain the Americans to their British brethren, sometimes as a gentle advocate, sometimes in a spirit of complete detachment, but always as a messenger providing information that it would be reckless to disregard. In a typical 1765 letter to a London newspaper, he wrote,

> The Americans, I am sure, for I know them, have not the least desire of independence; . . . they desire only a continuance of what they think a *right,* the privilege of manifesting their loyalty by granting their own money, when the occasions of their prince shall call for it. This right they say they have always enjoyed and exercised, and never misused; and they think it wrong that any body of men whatever, should claim a power of giving what is not their own . . . by granting away the property of others who have no representatives in that body, and therefore make no part of the *common consent in parliament,* by which alone, according to *magna charta* and the *petition of right,* taxes can legally be laid upon the

> subject. These are their notions. They may be errors; 'tis a part of our common constitution perhaps not hitherto sufficiently considered. 'Tis fit for the discussion of wise and learned men, who will, I doubt not, settle it wisely and benevolently.[28]

In similar spirit Franklin told of the dismay and alarm with which the colonists were receiving news of the Quartering Act and of the king's suspension of the New York Assembly for refusing provisions to British troops. He explained that the laws passed by Parliament ordering that quarters and provisions be given the British troops in America appeared to the colonists to be nothing more than "a law made here, directing that the assembly in America should make another law," in contravention of their character as deliberative bodies charged with exercising their own judgments in pursuit of the public good.[29]

In addition to providing an insightful window on American opinions and concerns, Franklin warned the British that their usual sources of information about the colonies were systematically skewed. The royal governors, so often at loggerheads with the colonial assemblies, had every motive to exaggerate their loyalty and their exertions on behalf of the crown in their reports to London and to lay all problems at the door of colonists they described as recalcitrant and disloyal, even when it was only the governors' own greed or incompetence that was to blame.[30] Franklin likewise warned the British against listening to the intemperate language of their own "coffee house orators," who were eager to inflame British opinion against Americans but lacked the stomach for the bloody war in which such vitriol might well embroil them. He urged the British instead to give some thought to American opinion of them, to consider the effects that their "ravings" against the Americans were likely to have, and to realize that

> It is only from a redress of grievances and an equitable regulations of commerce, with mild and reasonable measures of government, permitting and securing to those people the full enjoyment of their privileges, that we may hope to recover the affection and respect of that great and valuable part of our fellow-subjects, and restore and confirm the solid union between the two countries.[31]

As he put it in a 1764 letter, "Dominion is founded in Opinion, and . . . if you would preserve your Authority among us, you must preserve the Opinion we us'd to have of your Justice."[32] In order to maintain this opinion, he pointed out, it is important for governments to attend kindly to the people's petitions, even when they are misguided. "It has been thought a dangerous thing in any state to stop up the vent of grief. Wise governments have therefore generally received petitions with some indulgence, even when but slightly founded."[33]

But Franklin knew that talking the proud British out of their high-handed ways would be no small task.

> Give me leave, Master John Bull, to remind you, that you are *related to all mankind;* and therefore it less becomes you than any body, to affront and abuse other nations. But you have mixed with your many virtues, a pride, a haughtiness, and an insolent contempt for all but yourself, that, I am afraid, will, if not abated, procure you one day or other a handsome drubbing.[34]

Franklin rebuked the British people for trying to climb into the throne with their king and treating his subjects in America as subjects of their own. He regarded the stronger expressions of British pride towards the colonies as nothing less than insanity.[35]

All of these efforts at public relations were, of course, a spectacular failure. Even if Franklin had succeeded in turning British public opinion, it might have done little good, for public opinion counted for much less in Britain than it did in America. Indeed, British opinion was harder to influence in part because it did count for less. Franklin was right to insist on the insight of Lockean liberalism that the legitimacy and hence to some real degree the security of all government rests on opinion, but this truth was already much more palpable in America than in Britain. Americans knew that a government that had ceased to care about its constituents' concerns was a government that had entered treacherous waters; but members of the British ruling class, which felt little need to answer to a broad public at home, cared even less about colonial public opinion.

Gradually, as failure accumulated, Franklin's patience wore out and his gentle remonstrances gave way to biting sarcasm, culminating in such writings as "Rules by which a Great Empire May be Reduced to a Small One," exposing the imprudence of all British colonial policy since the Stamp Act a decade before.

His old puckish humor occasionally reappeared, as in "An Edict by the King of Prussia," a delicious forgery in which King Frederick of Prussia imperiously imposes on the British Isles, former colonies of his dominion which have long failed to pay their proper respect and obedience, just such disciplinary measures as the British were using against America. But in the last decade before the declaration of independence, the usual equanimity and playfulness of Franklin's writings was largely eclipsed by smoldering anger.[36] It would be almost inhuman for Franklin not to have felt such anger, especially since the invective against America so often carried personal barbs aimed at him. And yet his indignation betrays an important difference between him and his old hero Socrates. While the enlightened Franklin did not demand that anyone in power give up his true interest for the sake of justice, and hence did not demand retribution when they failed to do so, still he was exasperated with their blindness; he had hoped for something more and was bitter at not finding it. He had, at least at moments, an un-Socratic faith in human reason and even a covert belief that people are responsible for seeing clearly, a faith that could ill endure the trials of mean-spirited and short-sighted imperial policy.

Natural Right and Human Opinion

Ultimately Franklin would decide that reasoned persuasion alone was insufficient to correct the inequities of imperial policy and that stronger measures were needed. When repeated petitions to the king and protest to his ministers fell on deaf ears, he supported an embargo to get the attention of British merchants and their friends in Parliament. When he saw the futility of the embargo and other efforts at peaceful persuasion, he was among the first Americans to call for independence and to accept the inevitability of war. What turned his patient endurance into resolute resistance? How did he distinguish among merely imprudent policies, true injuries that should nevertheless be patiently tolerated, injuries that should be firmly resisted by the king's loyal subjects, and outright tyranny that dissolved all bonds of loyalty to an ancient throne and a great people?

How Franklin made these distinctions is difficult to discern. In contrast with men of a revolutionary temperament, such as Thomas Paine and Thomas Jefferson, he was always inclined to cautious language and pragmatic accommodation. He tended to speak more of privileges and of opinions about rights than of rights themselves, more of the historical rights of Englishmen than of the natural rights of man, and more of simple human decency and the common good of peoples than of rights at all. In insisting that "[d]ominion is founded in opinion," he seems to have endorsed the Lockean notion that government derives its rightful authority from the consent of the governed, as well as the seemingly more radical claim of David Hume that the power of *all* governments rests on opinion.[37] In fact, Franklin long failed to make quite clear whether he accepted the argument of Locke, and therefore whether, in calling upon the British government to rule and tax only with the consent of American legislatures, he was stating a requirement of justice or only a counsel of prudence.[38] Although he never argued that moral matters are historically contingent or that reason can give no universally applicable guidance, he was enormously reluctant to use the language of rights, evidently because he sensed that claims of rights are polarizing and render pragmatic accommodation difficult. Even if the theory of natural rights is a theory about liberties that all may share, conflicts about rights are often open battles for power, which Franklin wanted to prevent. To assert a right is to claim a good for oneself and to demand self-restraint from others; to speak in terms of wise policy and the common good is to emphasize the convergence of justice with the interests of all concerned. Yet in avoiding the language of natural rights, Franklin also avoided having to make precisely clear in his own mind what the ultimate truth about them was.

Franklin's habit was to speak as if rights were nothing more than human beliefs of which a wise government does well to take cognizance. In discussing the Albany Plan of Union, he wrote of the colonists, "Where heavy burdens are to be laid on them, it has been found useful to make it, as much as possible, their own act," for "it is suppos'd an undoubted Right of Englishmen not to be taxed but by their own Consent given thro' their Representatives."[39] In the struggle over the power of Parliament to tax the colonists, he voiced the same thought more strongly.

> It has been thought wisdom in a Government, exercising sovereignty over different kinds of people, to have some regard to prevailing and established opinions among the people to be governed, wherever such opinions might in their effects promote or obstruct public measures. . . . If public service can be carried on without thwarting these opinions . . . they are not unnecessarily to be thwarted, how absurd soever such popular opinions may be in their natures.[40]

He goes on to praise former British ministries for respecting the colonists' "opinion" that "no money could be levied from English subjects, but by their own consent, given by themselves or their chosen Representatives." On the same grounds, he censures the Grenville ministry for pushing through the Stamp Act of 1765 and its successors, thus "thwarting unnecessarily the fixed prejudices of so great a number of the King's subjects."[41]

At times Franklin seems to have worried as much about American beliefs—that they were being oppressed—as about oppression itself. Contemplating the damage that was likely to result from the dispatch of British troops to quell American resistance, he wrote,

> When I consider the warm resentment of a people *who think themselves injured and oppressed,* and the common insolence of the soldiery, who are taught to consider that people as in rebellion, I cannot but fear the consequences of bringing them together. It seems like setting up a smith's forge in a magazine of gunpowder.[42]

This attention to moral opinion was a significant and sophisticated part of Franklin's pragmatism: he knew that to advance the common good, prudent statesmen must take into account not only the power of weapons and finance but the power of moral opinion. He contrasted this wise pragmatism with the shallow and hence unrealistic "realism" of British ministers who thought only in terms of power and failed to see that people are willing to put up with great burdens if they believe those burdens to be fairly imposed, but are unwilling to endure even the most trifling ones if they believe them to be unjust. In the dispute over the duties on tea he remarked that the British ministers "have no Idea that any People can act from any Principle but that of Interest; and they believe that 3*d.* in a Pound of Tea, of which one does not drink perhaps 10 lb in a Year, is sufficient to overcome all the Patriotism of an American!"[43]

By focusing on claims and opinions about rights rather than rights themselves, Franklin was trying to give the proud British government a way to address American protests without conceding itself to be in the wrong. But this was more than a rhetorical device. As early as 1732 we see Franklin himself identifying rights with opinions of rights. In one of the queries for the Junto he asks, "If the Sovereign Power attempts to deprive a Subject of his Right, (or what is the same Thing, of what he thinks his Right) is it justifiable in him to resist if he is able?"[44] Now, this way of considering rights is, up to a point, quite sensible. Franklin recognizes that to be fully effective, a people's rights must be believed in and claimed, and likewise that wise governments will pay careful attention to all such claims its people make. The obvious problem is that this approach fails to distinguish true rights from foolish prejudices. It also lends itself to a certain spirit of condescension that can make it difficult to take seriously the very opinion Franklin was insisting should be taken seriously.

Edmund Morgan illuminates the first of these problems when he writes,

> In thinking of colonial rights as opinions or beliefs, Franklin deprived them of any absolute character and made them merely instrumental and thus, by implication, negotiable. His task in England would be to prevent Parliament from making the mistake of taxing the colonies. If Parliament persisted in that mistake, his task would be to reduce the damage.

But for the colonists, unlike for Franklin, "rights were sacred," and Franklin's excssively good-natured resolution to make the best of the Stamp Act provoked a firestorm of protest that caught him unawares.[45] Ironically, it was precisely Franklin's attention to opinion and his reluctance to think in terms of absolute rights that kept him from being fully in touch with the American feelings and opinion that he thought he took so seriously. So much was he disinclined to speak in terms of universal claims that he had difficulty attributing to such claims the importance that they were coming to have for Americans.

Franklin's tendency to view rights claims in pragmatic terms lay at the root of his chief political miscalculations of this period. The first was failing to oppose the Stamp Act of 1765 with sufficient vigor. The second concerned the distinction between external taxes, or tariffs, and internal taxes. Franklin himself saw little sense in the distinction that conceded to Parliament the right to impose external but not internal taxes on the colonies. But in testimony before the House of Commons in 1766, he made much of that distinction, believing that the Americans generally did subscribe to it and would therefore accept tariffs in place of the stamp tax. In fact, the colonists cared too much about the truth of their claims to rest content for long with that flimsy distinction, a fact that Franklin might have realized had he taken the discourse of rights more seriously himself. The disastrous Townshend Act of 1767, imposing duties on a wide range of American imports, were in part a direct result of Franklin's testimony. The third miscalculation was his too-ready acquiescence in the Declaratory Act, which accompanied the repeal of the Stamp Act and asserted Parliament's right to legislate for the colonies "in all cases whatsoever." While Franklin was little troubled by a bare assertion of authority that had no more practical consequences than the British's king's claim to the throne of France, both Parliament and the Americans took it with utmost seriousness, and it set them on a collision course.

In Franklin's own mind, then, were rights nothing but politically potent fictions? Before about 1768 he seems to have regarded all claims about natural rights—claims of absolute entitlements entailing corresponding duties on the part of others—as mere opinions, but ones that reflected important truths. Like religious beliefs, the beliefs in absolute rights of nature were powerful and sometimes dangerous; but also like religious beliefs they contained real insights into the moral relations of human beings and the requisites for human happiness. Certain claims of rights had come to be habitually asserted by the English because they had been found in practice to conduce to good government, which is to say, to policies that really were good because they were of true benefit to the people. Thus, there existed for Franklin a rough correlation between opinions of absolute rights and truths about good policy, such as the wisdom of allowing the people's representatives to determine the amount and kind of taxes to be imposed upon them, or the wisdom of allowing a free press. Franklin's tendency to speak in terms of the rights of Englishmen when he did speak of rights accords with the thought that in reality rights are only legal or constitutional privileges that codify time-honored counsels of prudence.

But about 1768, as Franklin began to lose hope in the reform of the British Empire and the good sense of its leaders, his thinking about rights seems to have changed. At the very least he decided now that it was important to take a firm stand for American interests and to *assert* American rights in a categorical way, even if this provoked British anger.[46] It seems clear, however, that Franklin also viewed himself as taking a firm stand for justice. Even if most so-called rights were in his mind only prudent policies, beneath all particular rules of prudence there lay a principle that for Franklin was inviolable: it is not right that certain citizens be treated merely as tools for the use of others. In 1767 he bitterly suggested that Britain regarded its colonists as slaves; that year he asked in a letter to the *London Chronicle,* "Is there any difference as to justice between our treatment of the Colonists, and the tyranny of the Carthaginians over their conquered Sardinians, when they obliged them to take all their corn from them, and at whatever price they pleased to set upon it?"[47] In the same spirit Franklin appealed to the "natural right" of "a man's making the best profit he can of the natural produce of his lands, provided he does not thereby injure the State in general," and the right to emigrate "from any Part of his King's Dominions into those of any other Prince where he can be happier," for to prevent such movement is clearly to use one person for the benefit (or imagined benefit) of others.[48]

Franklin never explicitly sorted out the precise difference among natural rights based on universal justice (such as the right to the fruits of one's own labor), legal rights or privileges based on principles of prudence (such as the right to trial by jury), and erroneous assertions of right (such as Parliament's claimed right to legislate for the colonies). But his general thought is evident: the test of a government's right is whether it is acting for the good of the people; the test of a right asserted by any of the people is whether what they claim is consistent with the good of the whole nation. When part of a country is exploiting another in pursuit of its own interests, justice has clearly broken down, and after about 1768, Franklin was willing to say, natural rights are being violated.

Because Franklin was so inclined to identify what is useful with what is good and what is good with what is right, cases of exploitation pose a most interesting problem for his moral understanding. If it really were the case that Britain was systematically exploiting America and prospering as a result, if the welfare of the British and that of the Americans really were in conflict, what grounds does Franklin's philosophy provide for saying that the British *should* limit their own good for the sake of the Americans? He has a clear concept of fairness:

> No one doubts the Advantage of a strict Union between the Mother Country and the Colonies, if it may be obtain'd and preserv'd on equitable Terms. In every fair Connection each Party should find its own Interest.[49]

But he never argues that anyone should do what is fair simply because it is fair. His argument is invariably that the fair policy is also the best policy for everyone concerned, and that it is for *this* reason that we should do it.

> The ordaining of laws in favor of one part of the nation, to the prejudice and oppression of another, is certainly the most erroneous and mistaken policy. An *equal* dispensation of protection, rights, privileges, and advantages, is what every part is entitled to, and ought to enjoy; it being a matter of no moment to the state, whether a subject grows rich and flourishing on the Thames or the Ohio, in Edinburgh or Dublin.

But immediately the appeal to mutual interests comes back in: inequitable measures, he argues,

> never fail to create great and violent jealousies and animosities between the people favored and the people oppressed; whence a total separation of affection, interests, political obligations, and all manner of connexions, necessarily ensue, by which the whole state is weakened, and perhaps ruined forever.[50]

What is fair is best for everyone in the long run, but what makes it good is in large part the fact that it is *perceived* as fair and hence is conducive to friendship or concord within the political community. Franklin gives great weight to people's passionate beliefs about justice and to their resentment at what they believe to be injustice, just as he does to their beliefs about rights. What he does not ever do is assess those beliefs on their own terms. He does not explain what would be wrong with real exploitation *apart* from the usually bad consequences of the resentment it provokes; he certainly does not prove that it is never possible to exploit others and get away with it. His arguments for the goodness of justice always implicitly assume that such exploitation is impossible, yet his smoldering anger at the British suggests a suspicion, at least, that they were getting away with just that.

In his more reflective moments Franklin always transcended this anger and returned to the thought that unjust policies are self-destructive for the whole and not truly good for anyone. This is roughly and generally true, but is it ever completely true, for instance in war, in taxation, or even in trade policies? Franklin's difficulty in remaining with the thought that justice is the good of all and injustice is the true good of no one may reflect the limits of the truth he was trying to maintain. His philosophy is admirably adept at finding the common good wherever it exists, but it is ill equipped to speak coherently about the irreducible conflicts of interest between citizens and peoples that also exist or to explain why it is just for some to limit their pursuit of a real good so that others may thrive.

Just as striking as Franklin's indignation at British imperial policies is the moral language he often used to describe American loyalty. Writing about the Seven Years' War, he explained British and American participation in the war in terms of shared self-interest even as he denied that the Americans were moved by self-interest at all.

> It will not be a conquest for them, nor gratify any vain ambition of theirs. It will be a conquest for the whole; and all our people will, in the increase of trade, and the ease of taxes, find the advantage of it. . . . [I]f ever there was a *national war*, this is truly such a one: a war in which the interest of the whole nation is directly and fundamentally concerned. Those who would be thought deeply skilled in human nature, affect to discover self-interested views everywhere at the bottom of the fairest, the most generous conduct.[51]

He went so far as to present the colonists' participation as self-sacrifice.

> The inhabitants of them are, in common with the other subjects of Great Britain, anxious for the glory of her crown, the extent of her power and commerce, the welfare and future repose of the whole British people. They could not therefore but take a large share in the affronts offered to Britain, and have been animated with a truly British *spirit* to exert themselves beyond their strength, and *against their evident interest.*[52]

Why did Franklin, whose exhortations always consist in appeals to enlightened self-interest, resort to the language of altruism? Is it because his pride had been provoked by British charges of American shirking? Is it because foolish narrowness is so common that he thought any display of enlightened self-interest should be encouraged with all the praise he could heap on it, even if undeserved? Or is there, deep beneath all his arguments that morality consists in enlightened prudence, a lingering belief that the highest thing of all is generous self-sacrifice?

Representation and Federalism

If Franklin came around only cautiously and late to the language of natural rights, he was always comfortable talking in terms of traditional English liberties and thinking about how to extend them equitably to the whole empire. No other American patriot gave this problem the attention that Franklin did; no other champion of the British Empire realized better how critically important it was. Given how few took the problem seriously, it is no discredit to Franklin that his efforts to solve it made so little headway. But, we may ask, were those efforts really coherent? We have seen the problems with the Albany Plan of Union, which might have deflected a collision between the colonies and Parliament, although it never addressed the question of their precise relation. In the two decades that intervened between that plan's rejection and the Revolution, the question of parliamentary power came increasingly to the fore and became impossible to evade. Did Franklin ever devise a practicable and principled solution to the constitutional problems of the empire, or did he only offer a series of makeshift proposals that failed to get to the bottom of them?

Franklin's fundamental argument was that Americans were entitled to the same "English liberty" as their forefathers, the liberty of having neither laws nor taxes imposed upon them without the approval of a legislature that represented them. Franklin never argued that political representation had to be based upon universal suffrage, which the Englishmen of his day were far from enjoying, nor did he worry, as Hamilton and Madison did, about the problem of permanent minorities, who even with the vote might be inadequately represented and protected. He did insist that a legitimate legislature had to be answerable in at least a minimal way to the people for whom it was legislating: the idea that Americans enjoyed "virtual representation" through members of Parliament whom they did not choose but who claimed to act on behalf of the whole empire was to him an absurdity.

Franklin argued that the basic principle of English liberties was defined in a 1762 statute enfranchising the county of Durham. The preamble to this law stated that the people of Durham, being subject to the same taxes as other counties, were "therefore concerned *equally* with others the Inhabitants of this Kingdom to have Knights and Burgesses in Parliament of THEIR OWN ELECTION to represent *the condition of their* COUNTRY."[53] As Franklin understood it, the Durham statute did not mean that members of Parliament had a duty to behave as a microcosm of their districts, following the wishes of the majority of their constituents. It did mean, first and most simply, that each part of the kingdom should have members in Parliament who came from there and were capable of "representing" or conveying to the other members the particular conditions and needs of that part. This the representatives of one part of the kingdom could not adequately do for another part. Second, the representatives were expected to act collectively on behalf of the whole people, of which they were members. Franklin remarked,

> The laws made here to tax the Americans affect them as a distinct body, in which the law makers are in no manner whatever, comprehended; whereas the laws made to tax Great-Britain, affect alike

> every member who gives his concurrence to such law. And hence arises the essential difference between *real* and *virtual* representation, so much agitated.[54]

Or as Locke puts it in the *Second Treatise of Government,* it is an essential safeguard of liberty that the legislative power consist, wholly or at least in predominant part, "in Assemblies which are variable, whose Members upon the Dissolution of the Assembly, are Subjects under the common Laws of their Country, equally with the Rest." Otherwise, there is a danger that "they will think themselves to have a distinct Interest from the rest of the Community; and so will be apt to increase their own Riches and Power, by taking what they think fit" from their subjects. "For a Man's *Property* is not at all secure, though there be good and equitable Laws to set the bounds of it, between him and his fellow Subjects, if he who commands those Subjects, have Power to take from any private Man, what part he pleases of his *Property,* and use and dispose it as he thinks good."[55] Following Locke, Franklin insisted that for one people to legislate on behalf of another without their consent is the height of oppression.

Franklin's chief efforts in the two decades after his arrival in London in 1757 were bent upon winning for American colonial legislatures, and for a continental legislature if it could be established, recognition as equals to the British Parliament, united only by their common allegiance to the king. Franklin claimed that this was indeed the original arrangement under which the colonies had been founded. In 1766 he wrote that the colonies had been granted charters from the king in a process in which Parliament had had no part, and that the colonial assemblies were the only bodies authorized to legislate for them.[56] It is certainly true that after the Seven Years' War Parliament was asserting powers to impose internal taxes on the colonies and to direct their internal affairs in a way that it had not done before, but Franklin also knew that for over a century Parliament had directed imperial trade and defense without challenge. Undaunted, he argued that ever since the overthrow of Charles I, Parliament had been acting the usurper.

> At present the Colonies consent and Submit to it for the regulation of General Commerce: But a Submission to Acts of Parlia-

> ment was no part of their original Constitution. Our former Kings Governed their Colonies, as they Governed their Dominions in France, without the Participation of British Parliaments. The Parliament of England never presum'd to interfere with that prerogative till the Time of the Great Rebellion, when they usurp'd the Government of all the King's other Dominions.[57]

Or as he put it the next year, in an effort to stiffen the colonists' spines against their habitual deference to Parliament,

> That the Colonies originally were constituted distinct States, and intended to be continued such, is clear to me from a thorough Consideration of their original Charters, and the whole Conduct of the Crown and Nation towards them until the Restoration. Since that Period, the Parliament here has usurp'd an Authority of making Laws for them, which before it had not. We have for some time submitted to that Usurpation, partly thro' Ignorance and Inattention, and partly from our Weakness and Inability to contend. I hope when our Rights are better understood here, we shall, by a prudent and proper Conduct be able to obtain from the Equity of this Nation a Restoration of them. And in the mean time I could wish that such Expressions as, *The supreme Authority of Parliament; The Subordinacy of our Assemblies to the Parliament* and the like . . . were no more seen in our publick Pieces.

Franklin thus concedes that his theory of parliamentary power is new to most American ears; to Parliament itself it will appear as something far worse.

> This kind of Doctrine the Lords and Commons here would deem little less than Treason against what they think their Share of the Sovereignty over the Colonies. To me those Bodies seem to have been long encroaching on the Rights of their and our Sovereign, assuming too much of his Authority, and betraying his Interests. By our Constitutions he is, with [his] Plantation Parliaments, the sole Legislator of his American Subjects, and in that Capacity is and ought to be free to exercise his own Judgment unrestrain'd and unlimited by his Parliament here.[58]

This claim puts Franklin in a most curious position. If rights are something that only fully exist when they are believed in and asserted, can there really be a usurpation that has been noticed by neither the usurpers nor the subjects they represent nor the subjects at whose expense they have expanded their power nor even the prince upon whom they have encroached? Since the British constitution is an unwritten and gradually unfolding institution, could Franklin consistently approve one aspect of Parliament's gradually increasing power—the limitation on unilateral legislation by the king—and condemn another aspect of that change—Parliament's growing authority over the empire? What theory do we have here of constitutional legitimacy and development? And even if such a theory could be made coherent, was Franklin not taking a highly unrealistic view of the British constitution for the mid-eighteenth century, just as a modern-day jurist would who demanded that we return to a strict-constructionist reading of the United States Constitution and nullify all the federal legislation that has used the commerce clause to encroach upon the rightful powers of the states?

By this time, the king of England really exercised little authority apart from that of Parliament, and it would have required a small revolution to have effected the change that Franklin called for. Even the king himself had no interest in trying to do so. This became clear in 1773, when the Massachusetts House of Representatives went over Parliament's head and protested to the king against Parliament's new policy of paying governors' and judges' salaries directly, thereby undercutting the power of colonial assemblies. The king condemned the petition and affirmed Parliament's absolute authority over the colonies as inseparable from his own, quoting the Declaratory Act, which claimed for Parliament the authority to legislate for the colonies "in all cases whatsoever."[59] Reporting this result to the Massachusetts assembly, Franklin conceded that it would have been hard indeed for the king to have done otherwise.

> When one considers the King's Situation, surrounded by Ministers, Councellors, and Judges learned in the Law, who are all of this Opinion; and reflect how necessary it is for him to be well with his Parliament, from whose yearly Grants his Fleets and Armies are to be supported, and the Deficiencies of his Civil List supplied, it is not to be wondered at that he should be firm in an Opinion establish'd as far as an Act of Parliament could establish it . . . and which is so generally thought right by his Lords and Commons,

> that any Act of his, countenancing the contrary, would hazard his embroiling himself with those Powerful Bodies.[60]

If Franklin could not get Parliament to see the British constitution as he did, he hoped it might be persuaded to adopt policies of prudent, generous forbearance that would have the same effect. He thought the chief problem would be overcome if Britain would simply repeal its taxes on the colonies.

> [I]t would be much better for Britain to give them up, on condition of the colonies undertaking to enforce and collect such, as are thought fit to be continued, by laws of their own, and officers of their own appointment, for the public uses of their respective governments. This would alone destroy those seeds of disunion, and both countries might thence much longer continue to grow great together.[61]

Franklin never addressed in a systematic way the empire's need for fair unified policies on trade and foreign relations and how such policies might be arrived at by disparate peoples with separate legislatures, united only under the king. Nor did he ever propose a good way to end the escalating collisions between royal governors and popular assemblies in America. He had come to recognize the great vices of the system of royally appointed governors, with their lofty connections, modest talents, and fortune-hunting habits. In calling for "officers of their own appointment," was he suggesting that American governors should be popularly elected in America? But without the power to appoint governors, what power would be left to the king except a bare, unenforceable veto over colonial legislation? We are compelled to wonder whether a sentimental attachment to the king was not beginning to collide in Franklin's mind with a growing insistence on responsive, responsible democratic government.

At one point Franklin acknowledged the awkwardness of his vision of the empire as a union of separate peoples with wholly separate legislatures. If Parliament, he said,

> should urge the *Inconvenience* of an Empire's being divided into so many separate States, and from thence conclude that we are not so divided; I would answer, that an Inconvenience proves nothing but itself. England and Scotland were once separate States, under the same King. The Inconvenience found in their being separate

> States, did not prove that the Parliament of England had a Right to govern Scotland. A formal Union was thought necessary, and England was an hundred Years soliciting it, before she could bring it about. If Great Britain now thinks such an Union necessary with us, let her propose her Terms, and we may consider of them.[62]

Was this the solution? Franklin certainly entertained the idea that Americans should be granted their own representatives in Parliament, as the citizens of the Isle of Wight, Cornwall, Wales, Cheshire, Durham, and Scotland had all over time been given. At the time of the Albany convention, he was intrigued by this possibility, but by 1766 he had seen the unlikelihood of any such scheme's succeeding.

> My private Opinion concerning a union in Parliament between the two Countries, is, that it would be best for the Whole. But I think it will never be done. . . . The Parliament here do at present think too highly of themselves to admit Representatives from us if we should ask it; and when they will be desirous of granting it, we shall think too highly of ourselves to accept of it.[63]

By 1775 Franklin had ceased to see a joint British-American parliament as desirable.

> [W]hen I consider the extream Corruption prevalent among all Orders of Men in this old rotten State, and the glorious Publick Virtue so predominant in our rising Country, I cannot but apprehend more Mischief than Benefit from a closer Union.[64]

But this step from enlightened imperialism to American exceptionalism was one that Franklin took only with the greatest reluctance. Even without a plan for a principled, coherent reform of the empire's constitution, Franklin tried until the last to bring about a reconciliation and to prevent war. Even as late as 1775, it seemed he might succeed. In that year William Pitt, now Earl of Chatham, the great military hero of the Seven Years' War, came out of retirement to confer with Franklin and to put before the House of Lords a series of proposals that would have removed all the chief sources of American resentment, including the British troops in Boston, the taxes that had been imposed without colonial consent, and the internal interventions of Parliament in American colonial affairs. But his proposal was summarily rejected, as Franklin's Albany Plan of Union had been twenty-one years ealier. Had there been more such wise men as Chatham and Edmund Burke in its midst, Parliament might have exercised the forbearance that would have rendered both a formal union and a formal renunciation of power over imperial affairs unnecessary, and the American colonies might long have remained in the affectionate dependence that Canada accepted until well into the twentieth century. Whether this would have been a good thing for America or for the cause of liberty is another question. But surely Franklin was right to try to solve as best as he could the crisis confronting him. No one can be expected to do more.

Democratic Diplomacy

Within weeks of his last fruitless attempt at reconciliation, Franklin was back in Philadelphia, a quiet but determined advocate of independence from the empire that he now saw held no future for freedom-loving Americans. During the year that it took his countrymen to accept the inevitability of this outcome, Franklin served as president of the Pennsylvania Assembly, delegate to the Second Continental Congress, Postmaster General, and ambassador at large wherever a negotiator was needed. In the autumn of 1776 he set sail again, as the senior member of America's first official delegation to France. In London he had learned the severe limits of bare reason's persuasive power when opposed by prejudice, ambition, and privilege. In Paris he would discover again the immense power that reason and charm could have under only slightly more favorable circumstances. France was, of course, eager to clip the wings of her old rival England, but the military prospects of the United States were dubious and France's coffers exhausted from previous wars. Franklin still was able to cajole from Louis XVI and his foreign minister, the Comte de Vergennes, a steady stream of gifts and loans that kept the Continental Congress afloat even while engulfing the French monarchy in a financial crisis that a decade later would precipitate the French Revolution. Now that Franklin stood on a more independent footing, he was able to negotiate skillfully with the British as well, helping to win for the United States a favorable peace treaty at war's end. In these ways his services to the American cause were as indispensable as Washington's, and almost as great. What were the principles of Franklin's diplomacy? How did they reflect his unique outlook on life, and how did he adapt age-old practices of secretive, duplicitous diplomacy to the new conditions of an open liberal democracy?

In the gracious world of Parisian society Franklin would be at his best. Here the bitter sarcasm of his London years would lift like a morning fog and the radiance of his genial wit would sparkle again on everyone, especially the ladies. For Franklin was always adept at finding common ground with anyone great or humble, so long as their arrogance did not offend his American pride by claiming the right to rule him. The more ordinary sorts of pride, and especially the vanity of a French court, Franklin was only too happy to oblige with his deft flattery and charm. But before his departure for Paris, Franklin took on the arduous task of traveling overland to Quebec in winter in an unsuccessful attempt to persuade its inhabitants to join the revolution, and the even more disagreeable task of negotiating one last time with Lord Richard Howe, who came to New York as admiral of a British fleet with an offer to forgive the rebellious Americans and accept their surrender.

With tightly controlled outrage Franklin replied to Howe that "it must give your Lordship Pain to be sent so far on so hopeless a Business." He proceeded to offer a penetrating reflection on the effect that cruelty has on the soul of its perpetrators, with bleak implications for the possibility of national reconciliation once atrocities and even ordinary injustices have gone very far.

> Directing Pardons to be offered the Colonies, who are the very Parties injured, expresses indeed that Opinion of our Ignorance, Baseness, and Insensibility which your uninform'd and proud Nation has long been pleased to entertain of us; but it can have no other Effect than that of increasing our Resentment. It is impossible we should think of Submission to a Government, that has with the most wanton Barbarity and Cruelty, burnt our defenceless Towns in the midst of Winter, excited the Savages to massacre our Farmers, and our Slaves to murder their Masters, and is even now bringing foreign Mercenaries to deluge our Settlements with

> Blood. These atrocious Injuries have extinguished every remaining Spark of Affection for that Parent Country we once held so dear: But were it possible for *us* to forget and forgive them, it is not possible for *you* (I mean the British Nation) to forgive the People you have so heavily injured; you can never confide again in those as Fellow Subjects, and permit them to enjoy equal Freedom, to whom you know you have given such just causes of lasting Enmity. And this must impel you, were we again under your Government, to endeavour the breaking our Spirit by the severest Tyranny, and obstructing by every means in your Power our growing Strength and Prosperity.[65]

Each of the signers of the Declaration of Independence doubtless had his own thoughts on what it was that made a group of individuals "one people," entitled to assume the separate station of a nation among equals. To Franklin, a people were a people if they felt themselves to be one, and their shared oppression was no small part of what made the Americans feel themselves distinct from the British. In the same letter Franklin mourned the breaking of "that fine and noble China Vase the British Empire," but irreparably broken it was; and if trust were to be reestablished between the American and British peoples, it could only be as two separate nations, who would expect of each other no obedience and no special protection, but who might still find an extensive common good as trading partners.

Accepting the necessity of this war must have cost Franklin a great deal, so deeply did he love both the British Empire and peace. He never doubted the legitimacy of such a war of self-defense as the Americans fought, though of course on the part of Britain he considered the war both "unjust and unwise." Indeed, he wrote, "of all the Wars in my time, this on the part of England appears to me the wickedest, having no Cause but Malice against Liberty, and the Jealousy of Commerce."[66] Yet Franklin's thinking on war and peace, or at least the emphasis of his thinking, seems to have shifted over time. He always treated both pacifism and aggressive militarism as foolish, but in the 1750s and early 1760s his quarrel was mainly with the former. He spoke of the need for vigilance against the French and Spanish, the folly of American Quakers in relying on divine aid rather than self-help, and the "sordid Views" of British merchants and bankers who, as creditors of the French government, "are striving to diminish the Importance of every conquest we make," so as to persuade the British to make "peace at any price" with France.[67] In his 1760 pamphlet "The Interest of Great Britain Considered, with Regard to her Colonies, and the Acquisition of Canada and Guadaloupe," Franklin argued vigorously for British conquest and retention of Canada, maintaining a right to acquire what national security demands. After peace was concluded with France in 1763, and the main prospect of war for America came to be the fraternal conflict with Britain, Franklin's reflections on war grew darker: he was unwilling to buy peace at the price of American liberty, but he was profoundly dismayed by the approach of a war that he never thought necessary and always considered harmful to both sides.

By the 1780s, Franklin was maintaining that all wars are unnecessary. Two excerpts from letters written in 1783 are typical:

> At length we are in peace, God be praised, and long, very long, may it continue. All Wars are Follies, very expensive, and very mischievous ones. When will Mankind be convinced of this, and agree to settle their Differences by Arbitration? Were they to do it, even by the Cast of a Dye, it would be better than by Fighting and destroying one another.

> I join with you most cordially in rejoicing at the return of Peace. I hope it will be lasting, and that Mankind will at length, as they call themselves reasonable Creatures, have Reason and Sense enough to settle their Differences without cutting Throats; for, in my Opinion *there never was a good War, or a bad Peace.*[68]

Most wars, he maintains, are the result of foolish pride or of short-sighted greed—short-sighted because trade is always worth more when it is free, and even land can be more cheaply purchased than conquered.[69] We need not dwell upon the question of what international relations would look like if every saber-rattling claim upon another nation's territory resulted in a lottery that might award the "disputed" land to either side; in speaking of the casting of a die Franklin is only using a figure of speech. Nor does he seriously mean that all wars are foolish on both sides. The irrationality he abhors is not the recourse to war of those who fight in defense of homeland or liberty; to the contrary, he declares that "[t]hose who would give up essential Liberty, to purchase a little temporary Safety, deserve neither Liberty nor Safety." And he explains that, although "nobody more sincerely wishes perpetual Peace among Men than I do," still "there is a prior Wish, that they would be equitable and just, otherwise such Peace is not possible, and indeed wicked Men have no right to expect it."[70] His condemnation of war is only a condemnation of aggressors too proud and ambitious to seek peace on equitable terms. And yet it is significant that Franklin decries such passions as an irrationality that should and can be overcome, rather than viewing them as a central and permanent feature of human nature. It goes without saying that he does not fear that anything of importance would be lost in a state of perpetual peace, in which men would never be required to muster the courage and sacrifice that war calls forth.

As the fledgling republic's first and most celebrated diplomat, Franklin showed no penchant for an activist foreign policy, at least where Europe was concerned. He was at first disinclined to seek political or military alliances for the United States at all, writing in 1777, "I have never yet changed the Opinion I gave in Congress, that a Virgin State should preserve the Virgin Character, and not go about suitering for Alliances, but wait with decent Dignity for the application of others." He felt keenly the indignity and therefore the imprudence of sending ambassadors to courts to seek an audience where they were not welcome, and the danger of suggesting an American willingness to make diplomatic concessions merely in order to gain recognition. True, America was in dire need of funds during the Revolutionary War, and Franklin willingly bent his enormous talents to finding them, but this penury was largely the fault of her own quarrelsome, narrow-minded state governments. Franklin shared with Washington and Adams a desire to see America rely more upon itself and a distrust of entangling alliances that would draw the new nation into the corrupt politics of old Europe.[71] Like Adams, he preferred treaties of friendship and free trade that could easily be multiplied and extended over time "to any or every other nation."[72] Earlier in 1776 Franklin and Adams had helped prepare a model treaty along liberal lines, which became the basis for the commercial treaty with France two years later and with other nations subsequently. But had Franklin guided American foreign policy at a much later time, when Europe and its machinations had ceased to hold any threat, his sense of the importance of national self-reliance and of dignity in international relations would still have given his policies enormous caution. He always spoke of liberty as something that one must sometimes wrest from others and always build for oneself, rather than as a gift that can be conferred. Human pride makes even true teachings about liberty a difficult gift to give: recall Richard Saunders' lesson that the only advice we gladly embrace is the advice we give ourselves. But with steady, inspiring examples and patient reasoning, much may be accomplished.

This appreciation for the power of dignity was part of what gave Franklin's realism a depth and subtlety that was rare in the American diplomatic service. In France Franklin had to work with colleagues, including Adams and Arthur Lee, who more often than not impeded his delicate negotiations with their suspicious cavils and blunt demands. To them it was axiomatic that every nation acted out of self-interest and none could be trusted. As Franklin put it in a letter to Congress explaining the differences that had strained his relations with Adams and had ultimately provoked the Comte de Vergennes to refuse to have any further dealings with Adams,

> He thinks as he tells me himself, that America has been too free in Expressions of Gratitude to France; for that she is more oblig'd to us than we to her; and that we should show Spirit in our Applications. I apprehend that he mistakes his Ground, and that this Court is to be treated with Decency & Delicacy. The King, a young and virtuous Prince, has, I am persuaded, a Pleasure in reflecting on the generous Benevolence of the Action, in assisting an oppressed People, and proposes it as a Part of the Glory of his Reign. I think it right to encrease this Pleasure by our thankful Acknowledgements, and that such an Expression of Gratitude is not only our Duty, but our Interest.[73]

Franklin's always keen appreciation for the mixed character of human motives gave him a fuller perspective and made him alive as well to the variety of ways in which that mixture could express itself in different nations. Of aristocratic France he wrote,

> This is really a generous nation, fond of glory, and particularly of protecting the oppressed. Trade is not the admiration of their noblesse, who always govern here. Telling them, their *commerce* will be advantaged by our success, and that it is in their *interest* to help us, seems as much as to say, "Help us, and we shall not be obliged to you." Such indiscreet and improper language has been sometimes held here by some of our people, and produced no good effects.

In the same letter Franklin expresses the characteristic idea that the surest way to get the help we need "is vigorously to help ourselves." But he adds a new thought, about the reasons that may lie behind people's wariness of helping the improvident: not that their good deeds will go unreturned, but rather that they will be ineffective. "People fear assisting the Negligent, the Indolent, and the Careless, lest the Aids they afford should be lost."[74]

Franklin's regard for French honor was but one part of a general policy of seizing every opportunity to win goodwill for the United States. It was no different from the care he had always taken to win goodwill for himself. In international affairs hard power is important; but for a nation that has too little of that, a reputation for principle, loyalty, and gratitude is indispensable.

> A few Years of Peace, well improved, will restore and encrease our Strength; but our future Safety will depend on our Union and our Virtue. Britain will be long watching for Advantages, to recover what she has lost. If we do not convince the World, that we are a Nation to be depended on for Fidelity in Treaties; if we appear negligent in paying our Debts, and ungrateful to those who have served and befriended us; our Reputation, and all the Strength it is capable of procuring, will be lost, and fresh Attacks upon us will be encouraged and promoted by better Prospects of Success.[75]

In Franklin's reflections on international generosity, gratitude, friendship, and interest, we see the suppleness of his philosophy of enlightened self-interest. He knew France considered it in her interest to help the Americans,[76] but he also saw in France's generosity an expression of real goodwill and a pleasure in being beneficent. He was ready, as always, to acknowledge kindness from whatever source it might come and to gratify others' vanity by putting the most generous construction possible on their good deeds, especially when those deeds showed an unusual freedom from narrow, short-sighted contentiousness. But he also expressed a deep sense of obligation to the French. This appears most strikingly in a discussion Franklin had in 1872 with the British representative Thomas Grenville, who argued that America owed France nothing because France's aid had been in her own interest.

> I gave him a little more of my Sentiments on the general Subject of Benefits, Obligations and Gratitude. I said I thought People had often imperfect Notions of their Duty on those Points, and that a State of Obligation was to many so uneasy a State, that they became ingenious in finding out Reasons and Arguments to prove they had been laid under no Obligation at all, or that they had discharged it; and that they too easily satisfied themselves with such Arguments.

Franklin goes on to insist that even when one has repaid a loan to a friend, he has not discharged his obligation, for he owes him still the debt of kindness that calls for a similar loan if the friend should be in similar need, and yet a further debt of kindness due to the fact that the first loan was spontaneously given and not the response to a previous favor. Then he concludes,

> I told him I was so strongly impress'd with the kind Assistance afforded us by France in our Distress, and the generous and noble manner in which it was granted, without exacting or stipulating for a single Privilege or particular Advantage to herself, in our Commerce or otherwise, that I could never suffer myself to think of such Reasonings for lessening the Obligation, and I hoped, and indeed did not doubt but my Country-men were all of the same Sentiments. Thus he gained nothing of the point he came to push.[77]

And of course this last line brings everything back to hard-nosed prudence: Franklin's warm protestations of gratitude were in the service of cementing the French alliance and keeping a dangerous enemy from exploiting any crack in it. Is Franklin's oft-expressed sense of obligation towards France nothing more, then, than shrewd prudence?

Certainly there is no just cause to think that Franklin's gratitude ever led him into imprudence. As Jefferson said of Franklin, defending him against the charge of excessive gratitude and hence excessive subservience to France,

> He possessed the confidence of that government in the highest degree, insomuch, that it may truly be said, that they were more under his influence, than he was under theirs. . . . Mutual confidence produces, of course, mutual influence, and this was all which subsisted between Dr. Franklin and the government of France. . . . The fact is, that his temper was so amiable and conciliatory, his conduct so rational, never urging impossibilities, or even things unreasonably inconvenient to them, in short, so moderate and attentive to their difficulties, as well as our own, that what his enemies called subserviency, I saw was only that reasonable disposition, which, sensible that advantages are not all to be on one side, yielding what is just and liberal, is the more certain of obtaining liberality and justice.[78]

Franklin's approach was so effective because his realism was capacious enough to take account not only of the prudential calculations but also of the moral spirit of his French counterparts. Whether his warm feelings of gratitude cohered perfectly with his philosophy of enlightened self-interest and whether a France that had digested all his reasonings about enlightened self-interest would have behaved in so generous a way are harder questions to answer.

One way Franklin sought to show American good faith and win goodwill was by conducting his negotiations in as simple and open a manner as possible. When, at the beginning of his mission to Paris, he was warned by the paranoid but often perceptive Arthur Lee that his private secretary was a spy, and was informed by a compatriot living in Paris that he was in fact surrounded by spies, he responded,

> I have long observ'd one Rule which prevents any Inconveniences from such Practices. It is simply this, to be concerned in no Affairs I should blush to have made publick, and to do nothing but what spies may see and welcome. When a Man's Actions are just and honorable, the more they are known, the more his Reputation is increas'd and establish'd. If I was sure therefore that my Valet de Place was a Spy, as he probably is, I think I should probably not discharge him for that, if in other Respects I lik'd him.[79]

In his conduct of the embassy at Paris we have a useful gloss on Franklin's teaching that honesty is the best policy. Franklin was convinced that almost always it was the best: that a reputation for truthfulness, even in a diplomat, was far more valuable than people tended to think, that frank and friendly statements of what one wanted were usually the shortest and surest route to getting it, and that, in any case, a society as open as America's would be especially inept at schemes of duplicity.[80]

But if honesty was a much-underrated asset, it was no categorical imperative. There was nothing wrong with giving the wrong impression now and then, as Franklin did when he maneuvered France into open support for America in part by holding out the threat that without it the former colonies might soon return to the British fold, even though they had no intention of doing so. Ironically, it was precisely Franklin's policy of open diplomacy and indifference to spies that made this false threat easier to apply. As Franklin suspected, his discussions at the end of 1777 with a British agent, Paul Wentworth, were all reported to Vergennes, and the false hopes of reconciliation he allowed the British to entertain had precisely their desired effect, clinching the treaty of friendship with France. At the same time, leaked information of his intensive negotiations for a French alliance kept the British on guard against an imminent French attack on England and prevented them from devoting all their resources to the American war.[81] At the end of the war it was France that Franklin allowed to be deceived, as he led his colleagues in negotiating a separate peace with Britain despite having promised to consult with France in all things.[82] The treaty with Britain, in setting the United States' western boundary at the Mississippi and giving her full navigation rights on the river, at Franklin's insistence, was more advantageous for the United States than France would have wished and was disadvantageous to France's ally Spain. Only the deep reservoir of trust Franklin had built up with Vergennes and a most forthright plea for forgiveness afterward prevented this breach of promise from erupting into a new diplomatic crisis.[83]

What should we make of Franklin's combination of honesty and shrewd maneuvering? It is, at the least, ironic that this crafty man who had such a love of concealment should also have been unusually alive to the uses of truthfulness. Is it also a sign of a deep dishonesty or cynicism, and did Franklin ultimately view honesty, like humility, as a quality one should cultivate in appearance but not in reality? Our answer to this must depend on our answer to the question of how much it mattered to Franklin that his ultimate purposes were honest, which is to say, capable of being seen by the world and judged as honorable. I believe his political writings, taken as a whole, show that it mattered enormously to him that the cause he was advancing was just, that it was the cause of freedom, and that it could be—and he hoped ultimately would be—embraced as the cause of all mankind.

Upon arrival at his home in Passy, outside Paris, Franklin had set up a small printing press, with which to assist his diplomatic efforts on all fronts. On it he produced passports for his countrymen, amusing bagatelles for his French lady friends, and information to win a broader European public to America's cause. He saw to it that all the important documents of the Revolution were translated and disseminated in France, confident as he was that the cause of America needed only to be known to be embraced. "All Europe is for us," he wrote in 1777.

> Our Articles of Confederation being by our means translated and published here have given an Appearance of Consistence and Firmness to the American States and Government, that begins to make them considerable.
>
> The separate Constitutions of the several States are also translating and publishing here, which afford abundance of Speculation to the Politicians of Europe. And it is a very general Opinion that if we succeed in establishing our Liberties, we shall as soon as Peace is restored receive an immense Addition of Numbers and Wealth from Europe. . . . Tyranny is so generally established in the rest of the World that the Prospect of an Asylum in America for those who love Liberty gives general Joy, and our Cause is esteem'd the Cause of all Mankind. Slaves naturally become base as well as wretched. We are fighting for the Dignity and Happiness of Human Nature. Glorious it is for the Americans to be call'd by Providence to this Post of Honor. Cursed and Detested will every-one be that deserts or betrays it.[84]

Such a reputation could not but bring allies in the long run and a great increase in strength after the peace; such an awareness of that reputation as Franklin endeavored to spread among Americans back home could not but increase their determination immediately, and hence their actual strength in the field. But beyond these eminently sober considerations we see here something further: an appeal, at least, to a sense of mission that transcends revolutionary America's immediate self-interest and perhaps its self-interest altogether, an appeal to the messianic hope that America, as the favored agent of a wise providence, might usher in a new era of international liberty and peace.

The suggestion that Franklin was in fact embarking, however gingerly, on a far-reaching project to transform international relations is supported by further evidence from this period. In February 1776 Franklin was the first in the Continental Congress to propose a policy of free trade with all nations, and he was a leader in developing Congress's plan, adopted that September, to devise model articles for treaties of commerce and amity with European courts. These articles included the principle that goods carried on neutral ships in wartime could not be seized as contraband, and a strictly limited list of goods that could ever be counted as contraband, including neither food nor naval stores. Such policies were of course all in the interest of America and against that of Britain, the largest naval power of the day; Franklin was also convinced, however, that they would be for the good of people everywhere. To Edmund Burke he wrote, "Since the foolish part of Mankind will make Wars from time to time with each other . . . it certainly becomes the wiser Part, who cannot prevent those Wars, to alleviate as much as possible the Calamities attending them."[85] During the Revolutionary War he urged both sides to refrain from attacking a scientific expedition of Captain Cook's and a humanitarian shipment of food to relieve famine in the West Indies.[86] In 1780 he warmly embraced the proposal of small neutral states in Europe to extend neutral rights in wartime, and he ordered American ships to comply:

> All the neutral states of Europe seem at present disposed to change what had never before been deemed the law of Nations, to wit, that an Enemy's Property may be taken wherever found, and to establish a Rule that free Ships Shall make free Goods. The rule is in itself so reasonable, and of nature so beneficial to mankind that I cannot but wish it may become general. And I make no doubt but

> that the Congress will agree to it in as full an extent as France and Spain.[87]

A few days later he added,

> I wish they would extend it still farther, and ordain that unarm'd Trading Ships, as well as Fishermen and Farmers, should be respected, as working for the common Benefit of Mankind, and never be interrupted in their Operations even by national Enemies: but let those only fight with one another whose Trade it is, and who are armed and paid for the Purpose.[88]

To both Britain and France he proposed terms of peace that included complete free trade, the suppression of piracy and privateering, and an end to the impressment of seamen and the molestation of noncombatants in any future war with any party.[89] But significantly, Franklin looked only to voluntary treaties and not to international courts or third-party arbitration to enforce the new law of nations, observing that every nation that might pose as a neutral mediator invariably also had its own interests that would tend to skew its judgments.[90]

His hopes for a new era in international relations are shown also in other terms he sought in the treaty of peace with Britain. He argued that Britain should go beyond narrow self-interest and try to recover America's true friendship with generous concessions. In addition to his nonnegotiable demands, which included the full recognition of American independence, secure boundaries, the removal of all British troops, and fishing rights off the Canadian coast—all of which were accepted—he urged Britain to accept war guilt, pay reparations for American towns and property destroyed, and cede Canada to the United States—all of which were summarily rejected. These terms were of course all in America's interest, but Franklin's appeal for true reconciliation between the former belligerents showed a hope, at least, that in future nations might conduct international affairs in a new spirit of humane self-restraint.

In his efforts to rewrite the norms of belligerency and international trade, Franklin anticipated efforts that advocates of peace would still be working to implement two centuries later. But boldest of all was his publication, using his Passy printing press, of Pierre-André Gargaz's 1782 pamphlet *A Project of Uni-*

versal and Perpetual Peace and his proposal that Europe should unite as America had done. To a French friend he wrote,

> I send you enclos'd the propos'd new Federal Constitution for those States. I was engag'd 4 Months of the last Summer in the Convention that form'd it. It is now sent by Congress to the several States for their Confirmation. If it succeeds, I do not see why you might not in Europe carry the Project of good Henry the 4th into Execution, by forming a Federal Union and One Grand Republick of all the different States and Kingdoms by means of a like Convention; for we had many Interests to reconcile.[91]

These proposals for an international order, however visionary they must have seemed at the time, were not the stray musings of an old man but a necessary consequence of the logic of Franklin's philosophy, and they are as true and revealing an exemplar of the modern spirit as his most closed-fisted proverbs of cautious thrift. To a large extent the move to universal philanthropy made so early by Franklin and later by all liberal internationalists is simply a necessary playing-out of the logic of national interest. For the growth of global economic interdependence and modern armament prevents all nations from being fully secure so long as any are oppressive tyrannies or simply benighted imperialists, seeking conquest and glory rather than commerce and peace. And while Franklin was intrigued by the physiocrats' hope that enlightenment and free trade alone would pacify the world, he was too much of a realist not to see that the need for security itself drove nations into expansionist policies. As a proud British American in the late 1750s and early 1760s, he himself had embraced such policies. The same security concerns that had led him to call first for continental union and later for a solid British-American front against the threat of France made him always an enthusiastic proponent of continental expansion. At a minimum, he thought, security demanded regime change in Canada; and in 1774 he called for the repeal of Britain's Quebec Act, which failed to extend English liberties to that newly acquired territory or to disestablish the Catholic church. He later explained that, "loving Liberty ourselves, we wish'd it to be extended among all Mankind, and to have no Foundation for future Slavery laid in America."[92] His real goal regarding Canada was to absorb it, together with the rest of North America, into the United States. Yet even that degree of unity did not seem sufficient to ensure peace. In 1783 he proposed a "family compact" between the United States, Britain, and France. He would like to have gone further, but he was realist enough to see that Europe alone would take at least "one hundred and fifty or two hundred years" to unite and would do that only under the pressure of some outside threat, and he was patriot enough to see the advantages of isolationism for the virtuous young American republic.[93] Yet at heart he was never a nationalist, and he was never content to accept the wars that national divisions inevitably bring.

And so Franklin was left with an unsolved conundrum. He sought to keep his feet firmly planted in a prudent pursuit of American national interest, yet his faith in enlightened self-interest was a hope that the most prudent policies could also be, in every case, generous and humane ones. He thought he had found a union of the two in his personal life; in international relations the problem was harder. If it was best for America to remain disentangled from Europe, determining its own interest at every juncture and letting its foreign policies be dictated by no one else, would not the same autonomy also be best for each European country? One may well wonder whether the risks attendant on any effort to transform politics by surrendering national sovereignty are ever wholly prudent for each nation taken by itself; this is a problem that Kant wrestled with endlessly. Thus, it is tempting to conclude that prudence itself must be reconceived, that we each must learn to identify our good with the good of all humanity and nothing less: only in a cosmopolitan union of all peoples can Franklin's wished for union of virtue and prudence be fully realized. But would the convergence even then be unproblematic? Or may it be that something rather different from the logic of national security was really a crucial force in Franklin's move to liberal internationalism? May it be that the human spirit is incapable of remaining firmly on the low ground of prudent national interest and that an irrepressible longing to find meaning by dedicating ourselves to a cause nobler than our own advantage lay behind Franklin's belief in America's cause as "the cause of all Mankind," and in the eventual condition of mankind as one of true harmony?[94]

But it is time to turn from these wishes and speculations to Franklin's participation in the convention that achieved the more urgent and attainable union of the American states, the crowning office of his long career in public service.

The Constitutional Convention

Franklin had shown an interest in constitution making from at least the time of the Albany Convention in 1754. James Madison credited him with drafting the plan that served as the basis for the Articles of Confederation, and he had taken an active part in designing the Pennsylvania constitution of 1776.[95] At the federal Constitutional Convention, the 81-year-old Franklin's very presence lent the weight of his influence to the proceedings and helped assure the plan's subsequent ratification. He urged from the outset that the delegates all regard themselves as representatives of the whole rather than of the separate states, and during tense negotiations, his humor and gentle admonitions helped bring the fractious delegates together into difficult but necessary compromises. His charming speech at the close of the convention, urging all to mistrust their own judgment a little, defer to the wisdom of the majority on the matters that still troubled them, and give the constitution their unqualified support, ensured that it would be unanimously endorsed by the states represented and signed by all of the delegates except three. Yet Franklin contributed little of substance to the constitution itself. Indeed, of all the signers, he was perhaps least in agreement with the structure the constitution gave to the federal government.

Scholars have tended to see the constitutional views Franklin advanced at the convention as an idiosyncratic assortment of impractical ideas, sometimes crediting this to his being an old man in decline. As much as his fellow delegates were glad that the charming elder statesman was among them, no doubt some of them saw his ideas in the same way. After Franklin had made a long speech against attaching salaries to the highest offices, Madison observed, "No debate ensued, and the proposition was postponed for the consideration of the members. It was treated with great respect, but rather for the author of it, than from any apparent conviction of its expediency or practicability."[96] Certainly Madison, Hamilton, and a number of others probed constitutional problems more deeply than did Franklin, and the constitution they gave us was better than the one we would have if Franklin's ideas had prevailed. But what has perhaps not been sufficiently appreciated is the unity of Franklin's ideas and the way in which his disagreements with Madison are all of a piece, shedding light on an interesting divergence in their fundamental outlooks.

Franklin's 1775 draft for the Articles of Confederation shows that he shared at that time the prevalent colonial vision of a loose confederation or "League of Friendship" between the states, with the central government regulating external relations but otherwise leaving the states free and sovereign. His plan included a weak executive council that would preside over meetings and carry out the decisions of Congress, and a system of finance that depended entirely on voluntary requisitions. In the Albany Plan of Union he had been bolder, stipulating that the president and grand council might "lay and levy such General Duties, Imposts, or Taxes, as to them shall appear most equal and Just."[97] Perhaps Franklin's subsequent experience with the British Parliament, which was only too ready to dip its fingers into American pockets, made him wary of any such central power. At the same time, in defense of colonial liberties, he had become committed to the claim that the old system of requisitions or requests from the king, to which the colonial legislatures had responded by voluntarily voting funds for his use, had worked perfectly.[98] Franklin found it hard to acknowledge just how disastrous the system of requisitions under the Continental Congress had been, and in 1787 he was still expecting the federal government to be funded by requisitions rather than by taxes imposed directly by the federal government.

Franklin did have one suggestion that would have improved the requisition system, and it was a matter on which he had strong opinions. Congress, he always thought, should represent the people and their contributions to the whole, not the states; delegates should be apportioned by population and by actual funds contributed, with decisions taken by a majority of the delegates. He was deeply dismayed when in 1776 Congress adopted the opposite plan. "Let the smaller Colonies give equal Money and Men, and then have an equal Vote," he protested. "But if they have an equal Vote, without bearing equal Burthens, a Confederation upon such iniquitous Principles, will never last long."[99] Franklin was tempted to urge Pennsylvania to have no part in such an inequitable union, and he even drafted a petition calling on the state to withdraw from it. As on other occasions, however, having discharged his spleen on paper, he recovered his customary equanimity and never sent the missive to its intended recipients. Yet curiously, in this as in other cases, neither did he dispose of it, as if he wished both his fiery, eloquent indignation and his self-control to be someday seen.[100] In the Constitutional Convention Franklin acknowledged that for the foreseeable future congressmen would view themselves as representatives of their states and not of the whole, but he urged that "in all Appropriations and Dispositions of Money to be drawn out of the General Treasury, and in all Laws for the supplying of the Treasury, the Delegates of the several States shall have Suffrage *in proportion to the Sums their respective States do actually contribute to that Treasury, from their Taxes or internal Exises.*"[101]

Franklin's desire for unity and his democratic spirit led him to prefer a simple governmental structure, including a unicameral legislature elected equitably by the people on a broad franchise and a weak executive without veto power. These elements had all been included in the 1776 Pennsylvania constitution, no doubt largely in deference to his wishes. When the question was put at the Constitutional Convention whether the national legislature should have two branches, it was, according to Madison, "agreed to without debate or dissent, except that of Pennsylvania, given probably from complaisance to Docr. Franklin who was understood to be partial to a single House of Legislation."[102] Instead of a system modeled upon Britain's mixed regime, with its royal executive, its aristocratic House of Lords, and its House of Commons representing the people, Franklin wished for a thoroughgoing democracy.[103] He saw as much potential paralysis and mischief in a two-headed legislature as in a cart with a horse at each end, or in the two-headed snake that had recently been caught near Philadelphia and that he displayed for the delegates in a jar.[104] But knowing that he would be overruled, he made little resistance.

Franklin took a stronger and altogether successful stand against those in the convention who wanted to allow the national legislature to put more restrictions on the franchise than the states did. He praised the patriotism of ordinary sailors in the Revolutionary War, many of whom might, by such restrictions, be deprived of the vote. Madison reports,

> Doctr Franklin expressed his dislike for every thing that tended to debase the spirit of the common people. If honesty was often the companion of wealth, and poverty was exposed to peculiar temptation, it was not the less true that the possession of property increased the desire of more property—Some of the greatest rogues he was ever acquainted with, were the richest rogues.[105]

Franklin's thoughts on executive power were shaped by his experiences with the king of England and with the underqualified courtiers who, too often, had been appointed as colonial governors. Rather than the single strong leader he had proposed in the Albany plan, he had come to prefer a plural executive or at least a president with a strong executive council to assist him and limit his prerogative. Where Madison saw the former plan as maximizing responsibility, Franklin now saw it as likely to lead to monarchy. He opposed giving the president even a limited veto over legislation, recounting the colonial governors' habit of vetoing essential legislation in order to extort for themselves higher salaries, exempt their property from taxation, and win other unjust privileges.[106] His focus was much less on providing checks on the use of power and balances among ambitious men in different branches of government than on limiting governmental power and augmenting the sovereignty of the people.

Perhaps the most interesting intervention Franklin made at the Constitutional Convention is his speech on salaries, which takes these thoughts a step further. His concern about the pernicious influence of money in politics went back at least to his days in London. At the close of his long sojourn there, after Lord Chatham's valiant and gracious effort to reconcile Britain and her colonies had been so contemptuously rejected by the House of Lords, Franklin reflected,

> To hear so many of these *Hereditary* Legislators declaiming so vehemently against, not the Adopting merely, but even the *Consid-*

> *eration* of a Proposal so important in its Nature, offered by a Person of so Weighty a Character . . . ; to perceive the total Ignorance of the Subject in some, the Prejudice and Passion of others, and the willful Perversion of Plain Truth in several of the Ministers; and upon the whole to see it so ignominiously rejected by so great a Majority, and so hastily too, in Breach of all Decency and prudent Regard to the Character and Dignity of their Body as a third Part of the National Legislature, gave me an exceeding mean Opinion of their Abilities, and made their Claim of Sovereignty over three Millions of virtuous sensible People in America, seem the greatest of Absurdities, since they appear'd to have scarce Discretion enough to govern a Herd of Swine. Hereditary Legislators! Thought I. There would be more Propriety, because less Hazard of Mischief, in having (as in some University of Germany,) Hereditary Professors of Mathematicks! But this was a hasty Reflection: For the *elected* House of Commons is no better, nor ever will be while the Electors receive Money for their Votes, and pay Money where with Ministers may bribe their Representatives when chosen.[107]

During the Constitutional Convention Franklin drew together a lifetime of thinking about the peculiar combination of passions that he believed to be the bane of republican political life.

> Sir, there are two passions which have a powerful influence on the affairs of men. These are ambition and avarice; the love of power, and the love of money. Separately each of these has great force in prompting men to action; but when united in view of the same object, they have in many minds the most violent effects. Place before the eyes of such men a post of *honour* that shall at the same time be a place of *profit,* and they will move heaven and earth to obtain it. The vast number of such places it is that renders the British Government so tempestuous. The struggles for them are the true sources of all those factions which are perpetually dividing the Nation, distracting its councils, hurrying sometimes into fruitless & mischievous wars, and often compelling a submission to dishonorable terms of peace.
>
> And of what kind are the men that will strive for this profitable pre-eminence, through all the bustle of cabal, the heat of contention, the infinite mutual abuse of parties, tearing to pieces the best of characters? It will not be the wise and moderate, the lovers of peace and good order, the men fittest for the trust. It will be the bold and the violent, the men of strong passions and indefatigable activity in their selfish pursuits.[108]

Even moderate salaries, once established, will be under constant pressure for augmentation, Franklin continues. The natural tendency of mankind is always to drift into royal government, and in the salaries paid to officials are the seeds of monarchy and an invitation to the endless wranglings that Franklin had witnessed between peoples and their kings or governors, the former striving to keep their taxes low, the latter constantly endeavoring to extract more money, with which to extend their power and obtain yet more money, and all too often succeeding. Franklin argues that in both England and France, local, unpaid offices of great trust and responsibility "are executed and well executed, and usually by some of the principle Gentlemen of the Country."[109]

Franklin was surely right that politics often becomes more turbulent as the stakes grow higher, but it is curious that he failed to recognize that in England and France it was precisely the aristocracy he opposed that ensured a supply of principled and leisured gentlemen to fill these unpaid positions of honor. In the 1776 Pennsylvania constitution Franklin showed a more realistic appreciation of a democracy's need for at least moderate salaries in order to put all offices within the reach of the majority, who must earn their own living: this consideration was surely what caused his fellow delegates at the Constitutional Convention to reject his proposal to ban all executive salaries. Why, then, did Franklin go so far? From Madison's perspective, he put too much weight on the issue of money and too little on the proper curbs for excessive ambition and greed: checks and balances in the governmental structure and regular elections to hold the chief executive responsible for his actions and his appointments. There is something about the whole idea of checks and balances and even that of keeping leaders on a short leash that did not sit right with Franklin.

From long personal experience of the contests between assemblies and governors in Pennsylvania, Franklin had come to see adversarial politics as dysfunctional and irrational.[110] He was persuaded that when leaders judged fairly, they would always find their "*true* INTEREST . . . to consist in just, equitable, and generous Measures, and in securing the Affections of their People."[111] So convinced was he of the true rewards of serving well that when men in power acted against the people's best interest, Franklin looked for some particular source of corruption. He thought he had found it in Britain in the noxious mixture of power with money. In contrast, Madison and the majority of delegates at the convention argued that most political men will act out of greed and self-aggrandizement as a matter of course, unless restrained by a watchful electorate and by the checks provided by other ambitious men in other branches of government. Madison saw politics as essentially a realm of competition—competition between interest groups and between leaders motivated by combinations of self-interest, honor, and patriotism, but rarely more by patriotism than by self-interest. Franklin, precisely because he pondered the nature of human happiness more deeply and saw better the blindness that underlies most seeming conflicts of interest, expected more of people in politics. Surprised and almost indignant at the petty narrowness he found, he fell prey to the same lack of realism that infected his scheme for a party of virtue.[112]

While Franklin's constitutional thinking illuminates, by way of contrast, the very different Madisonian thinking that prevailed, his greatest contribution to the convention was not as a constitutional thinker but as a diplomat, urging compromise. As he put it at the time, "when a broad table is to be made, and the edges of planks do not fit, the artist takes a little from both, and makes a good joint."[113] Despite his own strong preference for representation by population in both House and Senate, it was Franklin who proposed the great compromise that eventually broke the convention's logjam, providing for representation by state in the Senate, representation by population in the House, and a rule that appropriations bills must arise in the latter. His diplomacy was equally in evidence at the close of the convention, in his charming tale of the French lady who thought she was always in the right, and in his humble willingness to set aside all his own reservations as quite likely mistaken.

> In these sentiments, sir, I agree to this Constitution with all its Faults, if they are such; because I think a general government necessary for us, and there is no form of government but what may be a blessing to the people if well administered, and believe farther that this is likely to be well administered for a course of years, and can only end in Despotism, as other forms have done before it,

> when the people shall become so corrupted as to need despotic Government, being incapable of any other.[114]

He goes on to praise the constitution they have produced as quite likely the best possible, warning the delegates that if they all go home and vent their various objections to it, they might well bring it down.

> Much of the strength & efficiency of any government in procuring and securing the happiness to the people, depends on opinion, on the general opinion of the goodness of the Government, as well as of the wisdom and integrity of its Governors. I hope therefore that for our own sakes as part of the people, and for the sake of posterity, we shall act heartily and unanimously in recommending this Constitution (if approved by Congress & confirmed by the Conventions) wherever our influence may extend, and turn our future thoughts & endeavors to the means of having it well administered.[115]

And, we might add, Franklin urged that after winning ratification, any who wished to do so should seek to improve the constitution by proposing amendments. As pleased as Franklin was with the result, he lost no time in attempting to bring one improvement that he had come to consider fundamental: the extension to slaves of the freedom now secured for all white Americans. It was to be his last important political undertaking in a lifetime of useful projects.

Immigration, Race, and Slavery

By this point in his life Franklin was a most cosmopolitan soul, equally at home in Philadelphia, London, Edinburgh, and Paris and strikingly open to what might be learned from Native Americans, Africans, and Muslims. But it had taken him time to get there. He began life thinking of himself as an Englishman, a member of the finest race on earth, who happened to live in America. He looked down on the German and Dutch settlers who were then pouring through Philadelphia into the Pennsylvania countryside, and he reacted with bitter surprise when he began to realize that his fellow Englishmen across the water looked down on him.

What were his complaints about the new immigrants? Was it anything more than love of his own? In 1751 he lamented,

> [W]hy should the *Palatine Boors* be suffered to swarm into our Settlements, and by herding together establish their Language and Manners to the Exclusion of ours? Why should Pennsylvania, founded by the English, become a Colony of *Aliens,* who will shortly be so numerous as to Germanize us instead of our Anglifying them, and will never adopt our Language or Customs, any more than they can acquire our Complexion?[116]

Another complaint made that same year is a little more substantive, if ultimately no more sensible in light of his free-market economic theories.

> [T]he Dutch under-live, and are thereby enabled to under-work and under-sell the English; who are thereby extreamly incommoded, and consequently disgusted, so that there can be no cordial Affection or Unity between the two Nations.[117]

But he proceeds to voice a more serious concern about immigration and liberty.

> Those who come hither are generally of the most ignorant Stupid Sort of their own Nation, and as Ignorance is often attended with Credulity when Knavery would mislead it, and with Suspicion when Honesty would set it right; and as few of the English understand the German Language, and so cannot address them either from the Press or Pulpit, 'tis almost impossible to remove any prejudices they once entertain. . . . Not being used to Liberty, they know not how to make a modest use of it. . . . these seem to think themselves not free, till they can feel their liberty in abusing and insulting their Teachers.[118]

To overcome credulity and suspicion, so conducive to demagoguery and so problematic for freedom, a people must acquire new habits of learning and critical thought. For a time Franklin published a German newspaper in Philadelphia, but the real solution he saw was to teach the immigrants English, expose them to liberal education, and include them in the common public discourse of the colony. Among his many projects, he served as trustee for an English school for German children, and among the reasons he advanced for establishing an academy in Philadelphia was the consideration that "those who of late years come to settle among us, are chiefly foreigners, unacquainted with our language, laws and customs."[119] Education would prepare men from both communities in Pennsylvania for positions of public trust, which Franklin agreed should be reserved for those who had learned English.[120] If Franklin judged the Germans rather too harshly, he did not regard them or anyone else as incapable of acquiring the necessary tools for freedom.

Nor, in the end, did he make any objections to the free movement of peoples from one nation to another. In fact, when Britain tried to prevent its peasants from abandoning their fields and emigrating to America, he wrote,

> God has given to the Beasts of the Forest and to the Birds of the Air a Right when their Subsistence fails in one Country, to migrate into another, where they can get a more comfortable Living; and shall Man be denyed a Privilege enjoyed by Brutes, merely to gratify a few avaricious Landlords?[121]

But if there is a right to emigrate, is there a corresponding right to immigrate to any country one chooses? Franklin did not say, but he did recognize a duty in wise governments to educate those it admits, so as to ensure that their free choices do not result in less liberty for the world.

With time, Franklin also overcame prejudices he had held against other races. After visiting a school for free African American children in Philadelphia in 1763, he wrote,

> I was on the whole much pleas'd, and from what I then saw, have conceiv'd a higher Opinion of the natural Capacities of the black Race, than I had ever before entertained. Their Apprehension seems as quick, their Memory as strong, and their Docility in every respect equal to that of white Children. You will wonder perhaps that I should ever doubt it, and I will not undertake to justify all my Prejudices, nor to account for them.[122]

Likewise, Franklin's dismissive comment on "ignorant Savages" in 1751 gave way in subsequent decades to far more respectful accounts of Indians' natural and naturally satisfying way of life. He praised the North American natives for their freedom from "artificial wants," their civility, their fine oratory, and for keeping order in a way that required no prisons or other harsh punishments. With evident amusement, he recounted the story of one tribe's polite but firm refusal of an offer to educate some of their youth at Williamsburg, because others who had been so "educated" had come back "neither fit for Hunters, Warriors, or counselors; they were totally good for nothing."[123]

It is sometimes difficult to determine where Franklin's genuine admiration for simpler peoples leaves off and his rhetoric begins, since he is all too happy to use them as a battering-ram with which to assault the smug self-satisfaction of purportedly civilized Christians whose treatment of one another too often descends into the worst kinds of barbarism. In "Narrative of the Late Massacres in Lancaster County" he excoriates the frontier vigilantes known as the "Paxton Boys" for the injustice of avenging the attacks of certain Indians by the cold-blooded murder of others, including some children from other tribes who were under the protection of the white settlers: "We pretend to be Christians, and from the superior Light we enjoy, ought to exceed Heathens, Turks, Saracens, Moors, Negroes and Indians, in the Knowledge and Practice of what is right." He goes on to adduce numerous stories of enlightened humanism and true (i.e., humane) religion among all these peoples, in contrast to the savagery of the so-called Christians in Pennsylvania. In one story, an African named Cudjoe has taken in a sick English sailor. When a Dutch ship raids his tribe and carries off some of its members as slaves, he finds at his door an angry gang of tribesmen who want to avenge the crime of the Dutch by killing the Englishman.

> *Nay,* said Cudjoe; *the White Men that carried away your Brothers are bad Men, kill them when you can catch them; but this White Man is a good Man, and you must not kill him.*—But he is a White Man, they cried; the White Men are all bad; we will kill them all.—*Nay,* says he, *you must not kill a Man, that has done no Harm, only for being white. This man is my Friend, my House is his Fort, and I am his Soldier. I must fight for him. You must kill me, before you can kill him.—What good man will ever come again under my Roof, if I let my Floor be stained with a good Man's Blood!*—The Negroes seeing his resolution, and being convinced by his Discourse that they were wrong, went away ashamed.[124]

Franklin recounts the story of an Indian who is puzzled by the institution of the church, where whites allegedly go to learn good things. "If they met so often to learn *good things,* they would certainly have learnt some before this time. But they are still ignorant." For example, they still show no hospitality to Indians, as Indians do to them; this is proof that "they have not yet learnt those little Good Things that we need no Meetings to be instructed in, because our Mothers taught them to us when we were Children."[125] On the whole Franklin's observations on simpler peoples show keen curiosity and interesting reflections on the distance we have come from the most natural state, but they do not show any doubts as to whether we could or would do better to return to that state. Although he admired many things about the Indians, Franklin's preference for advanced civilization was strengthened by his growing horror at savagery and war. His comments on Indian brutality and his portrayal of a drunken Indian brawl at Carlisle in the *Autobiography* make clear that ultimately he was no romantic idealizer of the noble savage.[126]

Observations Franklin made about other peoples in his latter years show the same freedom from racial prejudice as his stories of Cudjoe and others and the same confidence that the principles of enlightened, forward-looking British Americans like himself are absolutely the right principles, whether they are in fact better observed in the Anglo-American world or elsewhere. Nowhere is there any shadow of suspicion that the Western outlook is defective, limited, arbitrary, or in need of supplement from any other tradition.

The most marked change in Franklin's thinking about race and ethnicity came in his views of American slavery. As a young man he accepted the institution without much thought. His newspaper often ran advertisements offering slaves for sale or rewards for the recovery of those who had run away. He even owned Negro slaves himself. Having found them unprofitable, he had by 1750 resolved to divest himself once and for all of "negro servants," but the scarcity of free labor and the pressure to accept slaves as payment for debts kept the occasional slave in his possession for many years thereafter, despite his resolution to the contrary. Eventually the moral evils of slavery came to eclipse in his mind the economic ones, and in the last years of his life he accepted the presidency of the Pennsylvania Society for the Abolition of Slavery.[127]

Franklin's first recorded remarks on the moral effects of slavery appear in his 1751 study of population growth.

> The Negroes brought into the English Sugar Islands, have greatly diminish'd the Whites there; the Poor are by this Means depriv'd of Employment, while a few Families acquire vast Estates; which they spend on Foreign Luxuries, and educating their Children in the Habit of those Luxuries; the same Income is needed for the Support of one that might have maintain'd 100. The Whites who have Slaves, not labouring, are enfeebled, and therefore not so generally prolific; the Slaves being work'd too hard, and ill fed, their Constitutions are broken, and the Deaths among them are more than the Births; so that a continual Supply is needed from Africa. The Northern Colonies having few Slaves increase in Whites. Slaves also pejorate the Families that use them; the white Children become proud, disgusted with Labour, and being educated in Idleness, are rendered unfit to get a Living by Industry.[128]

In his irate patriotism of 1770 Franklin made one awkward attempt to defend the American practice of slavery as at least no worse than the Scottish treatment of coal miners and the British treatment of impressed sailors and of the working poor when they are forbidden to negotiate wages with their employers and to emigrate to other countries. In "A Dialogue on Slavery," he blames the English for the slave trade: "You bring the Slaves to us, and tempt us to purchase them." If it is wrong to buy such stolen human beings, surely it is just as wrong to steal them in the first place. He stresses how few Americans own slaves and how innocent of the evil are all the others. He even blames the harshness of American slave laws in large part on the temper of the slaves themselves: "In proportion to the greater Ignorance or Wickedness of the People to be governed, Laws must be more Severe." While observing that some of the slaves are mild-tempered, he maintains that "the Majority are of a plotting Disposition, dark, sullen, malicious, revengeful and cruel in the highest Degree." Franklin's only irreproachable argument in this piece is his complaint that when colonial legislatures attempted to curtail the slave trade, their laws were overruled by Parliament as prejudicial to the interests of the British traffickers. Perhaps in this essay Franklin's polemical skills got the better of his calm judgment, as they did in others of his writings during this bitter period. At any rate, the essay's worst arguments were never seen again, while its best were repeated with increasing forcefulness.[129]

Two years later, Franklin called publicly for the abolition of the slave trade and the gradual enfranchisement of all slaves in America, acknowledging that responsibility for these evils was indeed shared in some degree by everyone who enjoyed the fruits of slave labor. He decried the constant death of slaves both en route to America and in bondage there, especially in the sugar plantations of the Caribbean.

> Can sweetening our tea, &c. with sugar, be a circumstance of such absolute necessity? Can the petty pleasure thence arising to the taste, compensate for so much misery produced among our fellow creatures, and such a constant butchery of the human species by this pestilential detestable traffic in the bodies and souls of men?[130]

As appalled as Franklin came to be by slavery, he still was willing to joke about it, as he was about everything. In an essay warning would-be aristocratic emigrants to America about what they would face there, he says that Americans "are pleas'd with the observation of a Negro, and frequently mention it, that Boccarorra (meaning the Whiteman) make de black man workee, make de Horse workee, make de Ox workee, make ebery ting workee; only de Hog. He, de Hog, no workee; he eat, he drink, he walk about, he go to sleep when he please, *he libb like a Gentleman*."[131] In America, Franklin insinuates, the stock of the honest workingman is ever on the ascendancy and the days of gentleman-hogs and slaveowners are numbered. His last public writing and his last hoax, penned after an unsuccessful petition to Congress to end slavery, pours further ridicule on slaveowners and their self-serving sophistries. It purports to be the speech of the North African Muslim Sidi Mehemet Ibrahim in 1687, explaining why the abolition of white Christian slavery in North Africa is economically impossible and would indeed be a disservice to the Christians.

> "[I]f we set our slaves free, what is to be done with them? Few of them will return to their countries, they know too well the greater hardships they must there be subject to; they will not embrace our

holy religion; they will not adopt our manners; our people will not pollute themselves by intermarrying with them. Must we maintain them as beggars in our streets, or suffer our properties to be the prey of their pillage; For men long accustomed to slavery, will not work for a Livelihood when not compelled."[132]

For all the scorn Franklin heaps upon such arguments, he also acknowledges a substantial grain of truth to them, but it is a truth that increases rather than lessens our burden of responsibility:

> Slavery is such an atrocious debasement of human nature, that its very extirpation, if not performed with solicitous care, may sometimes open a source of serious evils.
>
> The unhappy man, who has long been treated as a brute animal, too frequently sinks beneath the common standard of the human species. The galling chains, that bind his body, do also fetter his intellectual faculties, and impair the social affections of his heart. . . . [R]eason and conscience have but little influence over his conduct, because he is chiefly governed by the passion of fear. He is poor and friendless; perhaps worn out by extreme labour, age, and disease.
>
> Under such circumstances, freedom may often prove a misfortune to himself, and prejudicial to society.
>
> Attention to emancipated black people, it is therefore to be hoped, will become a branch of our national policy.[133]

The plan Franklin lays out for the assistance of freedmen is an ambitious one, including advice, mentoring, education, apprenticeships, employment training, and job placement—but, it goes without saying, no cash assistance. Franklin's reflections on the duties society owes to those it has once exploited stand as an important supplement to his early embrace of free market economics and his warnings about the dangers of charity. The danger is not with charity as such but with charity so thoughtless and careless that it fails to plumb the depths of the problem it is intended to address. For all his insistence on the importance of standing on one's own feet, Franklin was not naïve about the immense amount of learning and habituation that it often takes to get there.

CHAPTER 5

THE ULTIMATE QUESTIONS

Franklin's political project rested on a faith in the power of reason to grasp moral truths and to guide human society. This man who, in Turgot's famous phrase, snatched lightning bolts from heaven and scepters from tyrants was confident that people could live more happily when not overawed, either by hereditary powers that claimed divine authority or by the priests and dogmas that traditionally supported and were supported by them. Yet Franklin was also in his own way a friend to religion as well as to religious freedom, one who saw faith as an often useful and sometimes essential aid to civic virtue. How could he be confident that his spirited promotion of reason and religious skepticism would not undermine the piety that society needed? How, indeed, could he be certain that his own sunny irreverence would not someday bring upon him the wrath of a long-suffering but terrible God? In concluding our study of Franklin's political thought, we will examine the grounding of his rationalist claims and his views on civil religion, religious freedom, and the truth about religion. We will also examine his thoughts on human mortality and the yearning for eternity, a yearning that poses serious challenges to liberal democracy and that has led more than one critic to judge Franklin's project as shallow and corrosive of what is highest in the human soul.

Enlightenment and the Adequacy of Reason

In the writings we have examined there have been two major and sometimes conflicting strands to Franklin's thinking about human reason. In his comments on economics, the science of politics, and the natural sciences, Franklin showed enormous confidence in the power of reason and experimentation to bring us ever more precise and more useful information. He trusted improvements in technology eventually to overcome hunger, disease, and perhaps mortality itself. He trusted critical learned discourse progressively to dispel error and to bring understanding to an ever-expanding circle of educated people. And he believed that schools could teach ordinary people how to think usefully for themselves and that the combination of education and a free press could provide sufficiently accurate knowledge of public affairs for a democracy to manage them well.

Yet Franklin was given almost as often to reflect on the limits of reason. As we have seen, his writings are filled with humorous reflections on the difficulty of following reason and the ease with which it can be fobbed off with flimsy sophistries that ought to convince no one. His story of the breakdown of his vegetarianism and his dialogue with the gout are two of his more memorable tributes to the power of pleasure to bend reason to its designs. His instructions on learning to swim and his admonitions against anger acknowledge similar powers in fear and rage. Every comment he makes in praise of good habits is also an indictment of the weakness of reason in the face of momentary inclinations. All of this should be sobering enough, but Franklin also expresses doubts about the reliability of human reason even when it is not misled by passion. So impressed was he at times with the irrationality of human beings that he once remarked, in exasperation at his stubborn coachmen,

> They . . . made me, as upon a 100 other Occasions, almost wish that Mankind had never been endow'd with a reasoning Faculty, since they know so little how to make use of it, and so often mislead themselves by it; and that they had been furnish'd with a good sensible Instinct instead of it.[1]

In his speech at the close of the Constitutional Convention, Franklin suggests that a great part of folly lies in dogmatic certainty and that a great part of wisdom lies in modest skepticism about one's own judgment. And the more fundamental the question, the more Franklin was inclined to doubt mankind's capacity to answer it. He dismissed metaphysical questions not because they failed to engage him—to the contrary, he says he was extremely interested in them as a young man—but because he was disgusted at the seeming impossibility of making solid progress in them.

In one of the darkest passages Franklin ever wrote, a 1782 letter to Joseph Priestley, he holds to his old faith in the convergence of reason with virtue and virtue with the common good of humanity, but he despairs of human beings' capacity to live together in a reasonable way.

> I have always great pleasure in hearing from you, in learning that you are well, and that you continue your Experiments. I should rejoice much, if I could once more recover the leisure to search with you into the Works of Nature; I mean the *inanimate,* not the *animate* or moral part of them, the more I discover'd of the former, the more I admir'd them; the more I know of the latter, the more I am disgusted with them. Men I find to be a Sort of Beings very badly constructed, as they are generally more easily provok'd than reconcil'd, more easily disposed to do Mischief to each other than to make Reparation, much more easily deceiv'd than undeceiv'd, and having more Pride and even Pleasure in killing than in begetting one another.

Franklin goes on to tell an old West Indian tale of an angel sent to this world on business for the first time. Lighting in the middle of a sea battle, he reproaches his guide with having taken him to hell instead of earth. "'No Sir,' says the Guide, 'I have made no mistake; this is really the Earth, and these are men. Devils never treat one another in this cruel manner; they have more Sense, and more of what Men (vainly) call *Humanity.*'"[2]

How serious a shadow do these indictments cast over Franklin's faith in reason? Was he mistaken in his hopes that society could thrive without a deep-rooted and politically enforced belief in divine sanctions for morality? Was he justified in his confidence that we have no need of revelation to find the truth about ourselves or of divine forgiveness and redemption to find the wholeness and deep contentment that we all restlessly seek and rarely find?

THE CIVIC BENEFITS OF RELIGION

Franklin never showed the least suspicion that scripture has important lessons to teach to which reason lacks direct access. Nor did he seem to find anything deeply mysterious in life—in the human capacity for love or for evil, in the longing for eternity or in the sense that this world is not our true home—which might have caused him to look beyond ordinary experience and reasoning for a deeper explanation. The truth about morality and happiness seemed to him so clear that revelation could only be useful as a supplemental support to reason itself. Such a support he thought important for many people, including his daughter Sarah, whom he enjoined to "go constantly to church whoever preaches." But to those better blessed by nature, such as the sweet and clever young Polly Stevenson, who was almost more than a daughter to him, he had different advice. "As those Beings who have good sensible Instinct, have no need of Reason, so those who have Reason to regulate their Actions, have no Occasion for Enthusiasm."[3] And Franklin was certain that if there was a God, He must judge things the same way Franklin himself did, honoring virtue as the perfection of humanity, honoring reason as the core of virtue, and demanding nothing unreasonable. Heaven, if it existed, must be accessible to all who practice the virtue that is within the reach of all mankind. According to the *Almanack,*

> To lead a virtuous Life, my Friends, and get to Heaven in Season,
> You've just so much more Need of *Faith,* as you have less of *Reason.*[4]

Franklin was persuaded that faith is important, but important only because the human belief in heaven and hell strengthens virtuous resolutions and not because faith elicits any miraculous divine intervention, either in the soul of the believer or in his circumstances. There are two levels to this thought. Franklin observed and compared the lives of the devout with those of skeptics, and he saw no evidence that God in fact favors those who pray and rely upon him with better fortunes or better characters than those who use their heads and apply themselves. The truth seemed to him rather the contrary. And he did not think any intelligent God *would* act this way. He would never crave devotion; he would never be such a bad manager as to reward indolent, useless behavior. Typical of Franklin's comments on faith and self-help is his quip to his brother, then serving in the force sent to reduce Cape Breton Island: "If you do not succeed, I fear I shall have but an indifferent opinion of Presbyterian prayers in such cases, as long as I live. Indeed, in attacking strong towns I should have more dependence on *works,* than on *faith.*" In the same vein he wrote to Deborah after a narrow escape from shipwreck, "were I a Roman Catholic, perhaps I should on this occasion vow to build a chapel to some saint; but as I am not, if I were to vow at all, it would be to build a *lighthouse.*"[5]

In his 1735 essay "A Dialogue Between Two Presbyterians," Franklin spells out more of his thinking about faith. Granting his religious audience's premises as to the authority of scripture, Franklin uses the Sermon on the Mount to prove that good deeds and not beliefs are what God judges us by:

> [H]e tells the Hearers plainly, that their saying to him, *Lord, Lord,* (that is, professing themselves his Disciples or *Christians*) should give them no Title to Salvation, but their *Doing* the Will of his Father, and that tho' they have prophesied in his Name, yet he will declare to them, as Neglecters of Morality, that he never knew them. . . . And I should as soon expect, that my bare Believing Mr. Grew to be an excellent Teacher of the Mathematics, would make me a Mathematician, as that Believing in Christ would of it self make a Man a Christian."

He adduces Jesus' saying, "I come to call not the righteous but sinners," as evidence that salvation is possible for good and wise people without faith. More radically, he questions whether there can be any merit in faith by questioning whether there can be any choice in it. "A virtuous heretic shall be saved before a wicked Christian: for there is no such thing as voluntary Error."[6] Hence a God who rewarded faith and punished unbelief would be the worst kind of arbitrary despot. This argument Franklin develops in a letter to his parents.

> I imagine a Man must have a good deal of Vanity who believes, and a good deal of Boldness who affirms, that all the Doctrines he holds, are true; and all he rejects, are false. . . . I think Opinions should be judg'd of by their Influences and Effects; and if a Man

> holds none that tend to make him less Virtuous or more vicious, it may be concluded he holds none that are dangerous; which I hope is the Case with me. I am sorry you should have any Uneasiness on my Account, and if it were a thing possible for one to alter his Opinions in order to please others, I know none whom I ought more willingly to oblige in that respect than your selves: But since it is no more in a Man's Power *to think* than *to look* like another, methinks that all that should be expected from me is to keep my Mind open to Conviction, to hear patiently and examine attentively whatever is offered me for that end; and if after all I continue in the same Errors, I believe your usual Charity will induce you rather to pity and excuse than blame me.[7]

But there is something slippery here. Franklin somehow suggests that perhaps he does deserves credit for eschewing the pernicious, stubborn opinion that he is in possession of infallible truth. And he almost says, but decidedly pulls back from saying, what he in fact will say in a bitter letter to his son, that children deserve blame if they neglect the duty of nature to defer to the judgments of their parents. He manages always to keep himself on the moral side of both of these questions, but not without some straining of logic. Perhaps one might say that Franklin defends the innocence of all sincere belief while insisting on a principle of loyalty in action, but such a line will not hold, if it is true that virtue is knowledge. That is why, as he says here, error reasonably elicits pity.

While it made no sense to Franklin that God would expect belief in a revelation that lacks rational proof of its veracity or that God would punish people for any belief or disbelief at all, he was inclined to think that the holy scriptures of every religion contain considerable moral truth, and to that extent deserve respect. In the passage of his autobiography in which he explains his rejection of the doctrine of the "Dissertation on Liberty and Necessity" and his newfound conviction that virtue and vice are of utmost importance to happiness, he also reports his renewed respect for religion, as a support to actions that are "beneficial to us, in their own Natures, all the Circumstances of things considered."[8] He asserts that the essence of all religions is the teaching that there is a God who created us and will reward virtue and punish vice "either here or hereafter" and says that on that basis he "respected them all." Persuaded that even "the worst had some good Effects," he tried to "avoid all Discourse that might tend to lessen the good Opinion another might have of his own Religion"; and whenever anyone came soliciting contributions for the construction of a new house of worship in Philadelphia, "my Mite for such purpose, whatever might be the Sect, was never refused."[9] Although he soon ceased to attend any of them, he counted many of their ministers among his friends. At Franklin's funeral all the clergymen of Philadelphia, Catholic, Protestant, and Jewish, marched together in somber procession to pay their last respects to the man who was in so many ways their benefactor.

And Franklin did practice, or at least publicly praise, circumspection in speech as well as generosity to religion. In a 1730 letter to his own newspaper, signed "PHILOCLERUS," he urged himself to consider

> That Wise Men have in all Ages thought Government necessary for the Good of Mankind; and, that wise Governments have always thought Religion necessary for the well ordering and well-being of Society, and accordingly have ever been careful to encourage and protect the Ministers of it, paying them the highest publick Honours, that their Doctrines might thereby meet with the greater Respect among the common People; And that if there were no Truth in Religion, or the Salvation of Men's Souls not worth regarding, yet, in consideration of the inestimable Service done to Mankind by the Clergy, as they are the Teachers and Supporters of Virtue and Morality, without which no Society could long subsist, prudent Men should be very cautious how they say or write any thing that might bring them into Contempt, and thereby weaken their Hands and render their Labours ineffectual.[10]

But of course there is irony in this rebuke: Franklin is slapping his own wrist after the fact for publishing a wicked parody of the clergy, a story of four ministers, meeting "to consult on proper Measures to prevent the *Growth of Atheism,*" who are frightened almost out of their wits to discover that supernatural spirits actually exist.[11] Franklin seems a little too ready to enjoy the best of all worlds—the fun of ridiculing piety, the respectability of giving a high-minded defense of religion the last word, and the brisk newspaper sales that daring humor and lively controversy always ensure.

Three decades later Franklin had grown circumspect enough to rebuke another freethinker with perfect sobriety. Scolding an unnamed correspondent for even considering the publication of a Deistic essay, he writes,

> By the Arguments it contains against the Doctrine of a particular Providence, tho' you allow a general Providence, you strike at the Foundation of all Religion: For without the Belief of a Providence that takes Cognizance of, guards and guides and may favour particular Persons, there is no Motive to worship a Deity, to fear its Displeasure, or to pray for its Protection. . . . You yourself may find it easy to live a virtuous Life without the Assistance afforded by Religion; you having a clear Perception of the Advantages of Virtue and the Disadvantages of Vice, and possessing a Strength of Resolution sufficient to allow you to resist common Temptations. But think how great a Proportion of Mankind consists of weak and ignorant Men and Women, and of inexperienc'd and inconsiderate Youth of both Sexes, who have need of the Motives of Religion to restrain them from Vice, to support their Virtue, and retain them in the Practice of it till it becomes *habitual*, which is the great Point for its Security.[12]

We are reminded of the Farewell Address of Franklin's fellow Freemason George Washington, with its warning that "Whatever may be conceded to the influence of refined education on minds of peculiar structure, reason and experience both forbid us to expect that national morality can prevail in exclusion of religious principle."[13] The somber Washington was nowhere more in earnest than here, but with Franklin we cannot be sure. Certainly Franklin never went so far as to call for public multidenominational support for religion as Washington did. He was less worried than Washington by the materialistic tendencies of rationalism, and he was more inclined to trust enlightenment to support morals adequately. For all his talk about the utility of religion, his actions at times seem to suggest a surprising indifference to it—indifference as to whether religion should thrive or wither away, indifference as to whether it was indeed true or false.

The Defects of Christianity

Franklin's paradoxical mixture of warm support and surprising coolness towards religion is nowhere more striking than in the *Autobiography*'s account of his acquaintance with the master orator and evangelist George Whitefield, who for a time had all the colonies whipped into a froth of religious fervor. Franklin befriended Whitefield and was intrigued by him. He was fascinated by "the extraordinary Influence of his Oratory on his Hearers, and how much they admir'd and respected him, notwithstanding his common Abuse of them, by assuring them they were naturally *half Beasts and half Devils*."[14] Franklin was fascinated by the change that came over Philadelphia as its residents fell under Whitefield's influence. He was fascinated by the range of Whitefield's voice, which he measured at one of his open air sermons by retiring backwards until he could no longer discern his words, and then calculating how many men could stand within a semicircle of such a radius, concluding that the accounts in ancient histories of generals haranguing whole armies were quite credible. He was even fascinated by the power of Whitefield's oratory on himself. Once Whitefield was soliciting donations for a charitable scheme that Franklin thought imprudent and tried to persuade the preacher to abandon, but in vain.

> I happened soon after to attend one of his Sermons, in the Course of which I perceived he intended to finish with a Collection, and I silently resolved he should get nothing from me. I had in my Pocket a Handful of Copper Money, three or four silver Dollars, and five Pistoles in Gold. As he proceeded I began to soften, and concluded to give the Coppers. Another Stroke of his Oratory made me asham'd of that, and determin'd me to give the Silver; and he finish'd so admirably, that I empty'd my Pocked wholly in the Collector's Dish, Gold and all.[15]

But of course Franklin soon recovered his sanity and laughed at himself.

The only thing about Whitefield that did not interest Franklin was his central subject.

> His Delivery . . . was so improv'd by frequent Repetitions, that every Accent, every Emphasis, every Modulation of Voice, was so perfectly well turn'd and well plac'd, that without being interested in the Subject, one could not help being pleas'd with the Discourse, a Pleasure of much the same kind with that receiv'd from an excellent Piece of Music.[16]

Was Franklin simply cold to every concern that was not practical and worldly? It would not be fair to say so. From his earliest writings in the Silence Dogood papers, it is evident that he in fact gave long and careful thought to the subject of Whitefield's sermons. Through this examination he grew convinced that the teachings of traditional religion, especially Calvinist Christianity, reveal a faulty understanding of human nature and human motivations. This judgment was at the root of his confidence that the Christian faith is not essential for living well and indeed that it is in need of serious supplementation to provide a good foundation for citizenship and self-government. With reform it could be made useful, but Franklin could not take seriously the idea that traditional Christianity might be true. As it gave but middling guidance for this life, how could one put any stock in the fabulous claims it made about the next?

We have seen Franklin's criticisms of the Christian understanding of human nature in many scattered particulars, but it may be useful to summarize them. The church makes people credulous and easy prey for ambitious hypocrites. It makes them quarrelsome by encouraging disputes about abstruse questions, disputes that are useless because they make no difference to the way anyone lives and because no one has sufficient evidence from which to answer them. As Poor Richard says,

> Men differ daily, about things which are subject to sense, is it likely then they should agree about things invisible?

> Many a long dispute among Divines may be thus abridg'd, It is so: It is not so. It is so; It is not so.

With such questions it was impossible to get any traction and a waste of time to try; Franklin regretted the time he spent as a boy reading books of polemic theology when so many more useful studies might have been acquired.[17]

He found Christianity misguided also in making unreasonable demands for purity and self-denial and impossible demands for humility. The maiden lady Franklin found in a London garret might teach beneficial lessons about frugality, but she accomplished nothing more, and she never did succeed in purging herself of pride. To live is to be in action, and it made no sense to Franklin that God would have given us such capacities for pleasurable activity if he meant us to use none of them and to make self-denial and devotion our only study. Does the ascetic's hair shirt do anyone any good? Does God need the maiden lady's endless prayers in order to be beneficent? And Franklin suggests that such people not only enjoy life too little but also demand too little of themselves. "Serving God is Doing Good to Man, but Praying is thought an easier Service, and therefore more generally chosen."[18] And surely a perfect God would be too self-sufficient to need our devotion. The one endeavor to worship God that Franklin seems to have made begins with this reflection: after surveying the grandeur of the universe, he writes,

> When I think thus, I imagine it a great vanity in me to suppose, that the *Supremely Perfect,* does in the least regard such an inconsiderable nothing as man. More especially, since it is impossible for me to have any positive clear Idea of that which is infinite and incomprehensible, I cannot conceive otherwise, than that He, *the Infinite Father,* expects or requires no Worship or Praise from us, but that he is even INFINITELY ABOVE IT.[19]

Franklin found Christianity still more deficient in its understanding of human failings and of the proper response to them. Christianity teaches that all human beings are corrupted with original sin and that God regards this evil with righteous anger. At times Franklin makes the conventional but still powerful argument against the doctrine of original sin that "to suppose a Man liable to Punishment upon account of the Guilt of another, is unreasonable; and actually to punish him for it, is unjust and cruel."[20] At other times he goes further and argues that anger is irrational and that a wise God could have no need of bloody sacrifices, suggesting that he would regard the failings of his creatures not with rage but with the gentle understanding and calm equanimity of Franklin himself at his best. Christianity teaches that people can escape sin only through prayer and divine grace. Franklin, believing that error comes from carelessness, ignorance, and bad habits, devises a method to overcome it and, by demonstrating the efficacy of that method in his own life, provides intriguing evidence for the truth of his own account of the soul.

Franklin also criticizes the Christian teaching that we should ask God for good things, as if a benevolent father would not give those few things that we truly need unasked. He criticizes Christian charity for breeding weakness and dependency. Franklin's reflections on the problem of beneficence and charity show that his view of human nature is not simply more sunny than the Christian view, and that in a way he thinks the reformation of failed lives even harder to achieve than Christians do. They believe that the poor need charity and grace; Franklin thinks they need two things that require more human effort, education and hard work to overcome entrenched bad habits. Christianity teaches that the poor will always be with us, evidently always in large numbers; Franklin's study of political economy leads him to conclude that this need not be the case if we can devise economic policies that provide the right opportunities and incentives. Here again, the success of his methods offers some evidence for his underlying claims about human nature.

Even on the matter of how to deliver effective admonitions, Franklin thought that traditional Christianity had something to learn from his subtle psychology. He spiced his teachings with humor; he showed a neglected army chaplain how to get better attendance at chapel by dispensing the rum after prayers; he even improved upon the Bible with two edifying forgeries of his own devising. Clearly he thought the stern tone of the Old Testament might profitably be supplemented with a gentle tale about brotherly love:

> 1. In those days there was no Worker of Iron in all the Land, And the Merchants of Midian passed by with their Camels, bearing Spices, and Myrrh, and Balm, and Wares of Iron. And Reuben bought an Ax from the Ishmaelite Merchants, which he prized highly, for there were none in his Father's house. . And Simeon said unto Reuben his Brother, lend me I pray thee, thine Ax: But he refused, and would not. 3. And Levi also said unto him, My

> Brother, lend me thine Ax. And he refused him also. 4. Then came Judah unto Reuben and entreated him, saying, Lo, thou lovest me, and I have always loved thee do not refuse me the use of thine Ax, for I desire it earnestly. 5. But Reuben turned from him, and refused him Likewise. 6. Now it came to pass that Reuben hewed Timber on the Bank of the River, and the Ax fell therein, and he could by no means find it. 7. But Simeon, Levi and Judah, had sent a Messenger after the Ishmaelites with money and had bought for each of them an Ax also. 8. Then came Reuben unto Simeon, and said unto him, Lo, I have lost mine Ax, and my work is unfinished, lend me thine I pray thee. 9. And Simeon answered, saying, Thou wouldst not lend me thine Ax, therefore I will not lend thee mine. 10. Then went he unto Levi, and said unto him, My Brother, thou knowest my Loss and my Necessity; lend me, I pray thee, thine Ax. 11. And Levi reproached him, saying, Thou wouldst not lend me thine when I desired it, but I will be better than thee, and will lend thee mine. 12. And Reuben was grieved at the Rebuke of Levi; and being ashamed, turned from him, and took not the Ax; but sought his Brother Judah. 13. And as he drew near, Judah beheld his Countenance as it were confused with Grief and shame; and he prevented him, saying, My Brother, I know thy Loss, but why should it grieve thee? Lo, have I not an Ax that will serve both thee and me? Take it I pray thee, and use it as thine own. 14. And Reuben fell on his Neck, and kissed him with Tears, saying, Thy Kindness is great, but thy Goodness in forgiving me is greater. Lo thou art indeed a Brother, and whilst I live will I surely love thee. 15. And Judah said, let us also love our other Brethren; Behold, are we not all of one Blood. 16. And Joseph saw these Things, and reported them to his Father Jacob. 17. And Jacob said, Reuben did wrong but he repented, Simeon also did wrong, and Levi was not altogether blameless. 18. But the Heart of Judah is princely. Judah hath the Soul of a King. His Fathers Children shall bow down before him, and he shall rule over his Brethren, nor shall the Sceptre depart from his house, nor a Lawgiver from between his Feet, until Shiloh come.[21]

Does not the Bible err, Franklin asks in effect, when it thinks it can make us good and happy while mortifying our pride? It is this critique—it is Franklin's judgment that through long and successful experience he had come to understand the human soul even better than the Bible did—that assured him that reason, not revelation, is the surer guide to life and that we need not fear the vengeful God of traditional Christianity. Never for a moment did he doubt that if there is a God, He must be at least as wise and at least as reasonable as Franklin himself was.[22]

Toleration and Religious Freedom

Franklin thus judged religion to be in need of reform, and he was convinced that the best way to promote progress in religion, just as in commerce and in science, is to free it from governmental interference and to expose it to the salutary challenge of fresh ideas. Religious toleration is the theme of his second biblical forgery, "A Parable Against Persecution." In this story Abraham offers a stranger hospitality for the night, only to discover that the man is an idolater.

> 1. And it came to pass after these Things, that Abraham sat in the Door of his Tent, about the going down of the Sun. 2. And behold a Man, bowed with Age, came from the Way of the Wilderness, leaning on a Staff. 3. And Abraham arose and met him, and said unto him, Turn in, I pray thee, and wash thy Feet, and tarry all Night, and thou shalt arise early on the Morrow, and go on thy Way. 4. And the Man said, Nay, for I will abide under this Tree. 5. But Abraham pressed him greatly; so he turned, and they went into the Tent; and Abraham baked unleavened Bread, and they did eat. 6. And when Abraham saw that the Man blessed not God, he said unto him, Wherefore dost thou not worship the most high God, Creator of Heaven and Earth? 7. And the Man answered and said, I do not worship the God thou speakest of; neither do I call upon his Name; for I have made to myself a God, which abideth always in mine house, and provideth me with all Things. 8. And Abraham's Zeal was kindled against the Man; and he arose, and fell upon him, and drove him forth with Blows into the Wilderness. 9. And at Midnight God called unto Abraham, saying, Abraham, where is the Stranger? 10. And Abraham answered and said, Lord, he would not worship thee, neither would he call upon thy Name; therefore have I driven him out from before my Face into the Wilderness. 11. And God said, Have I born with him these hundred ninety and eight Years, and nourished him, and cloathed him, notwithstanding his Rebellion against me, and couldst not thou, that art thyself a Sinner, bear with him one Night?[23]

In characteristic fashion, Franklin embraced religious toleration because he considered it salutary and because he considered it only reasonable in light of our ignorance of ultimate truths; he did not champion religious freedom as a natural right. Nor did he think all religions had an equal claim on our respect. His promotion of toleration was not an effort to protect the sanctity of religion from governmental interference but rather an active effort to reform and improve the churches he found in America, making them more conducive to civic virtue and harmony and less divisive. Thus, his most sustained effort on behalf of toleration was a vehement attempt to persuade the Presbyterian church to change its internal rules governing heresy and orthodoxy. Franklin had been raised in the Calvinist Presbyterian church of New England, which for a long time he felt a vague sense of duty to attend. In Philadelphia he attended services only fitfully, but in 1735 he became a warm supporter of a new clergyman, Samuel Hemphill, whose sermons eschewed doctrinal disputes and focused on practical morality. Hemphill soon fell afoul of the Presbyterian Synod, which charged him with heresy. Franklin sprang to his defense, writing and printing in his newspaper a number of long essays in defense of doctrinal toleration within the church, essays which betrayed a rare degree of passion and even bitterness. When Hemphill was convicted by the synod and left Philadelphia, Franklin severed his ties with the Presbyterian church forever, but he never ceased to work for toleration both between and within all religions.

His case for toleration rested on the assertion that at the heart of every religion lay the same few fundamental teachings. Franklin expounded this idea in a letter to Madame Brillon, whom he had earlier attempted in vain to seduce and whom he was now attempting (again in vain) to persuade to accept his Protestant grandson as husband for her Catholic daughter. Franklin argued that the difference in religion was immaterial.

> In each religion there are some essential things, and others which are only forms and fashions; as a piece of sugar which can be wrapped up in brown or white or blue paper, and tied with flaxen or wool string, red or yellow; it is always the sugar which is the essential thing.

The essence of religion, Franklin avers, lies in belief in the existence of a providential God who is to be served by doing good to men and the existence of an afterlife of rewards and punishments. "These essentials one finds in your religion and in ours," he concludes, asserting, "the differences are but paper and string."[24] He expresses the same thought in the *Autobiography*, but there he presents the varied wrappings as less innocuous, telling us that for the essential moral teachings that every sect shares "I respected them all, but with different degrees of respect as I found them more or less mix'd with other Articles which without any Tendency to inspire, promote, or confirm Morality, serv'd principally to divide us and make one unfriendly to one another."[25]

But if the essence of every religion is the same, that fact has been insufficiently recognized by practitioners of the religions themselves, with the result that they have not properly appreciated the reasonableness of toleration. John Locke hints as much while overtly insisting that toleration is an expression of the true spirit of Christianity; Franklin more boldly points out that in actuality it has taken many centuries (if not, indeed, the wisdom of a skeptical Locke) for the church even to begin to adopt this virtue.

> If we look back into history for the character of present sects in Christianity, we shall find few that have not in their turns been persecutors, and complainers of persecution. The primitive Christians thought persecution extremely wrong in the Pagans, but practiced it on one another. The first Protestants of the Church of England blamed persecution in the Roman Church, but practiced it against the Puritans. . . . To account for this we should remember, that the doctrine of *toleration* was not then known, or had not prevailed in the world. Persecution was therefore not so much the fault of the sect as of the times. . . . By degrees more moderate *and more modest* sentiments have taken place in the christian world; and among Protestants particularly all disclaim persecution, none vindicate it, and few practice it. We should then cease to reproach each other with what was done by our ancestors, but judge of the present character of sects or churches by their *present conduct* only.[26]

There is indeed a hint here, made more explicit elsewhere, that perhaps the essential commonality of all religions is more an edifying fiction and hopeful prediction than a present truth. Franklin is also suggesting that religions, invariably beginning in a state of imperfection, need to embrace the same spirit of progress that benefits all human endeavors. He criticizes Whitefield for publishing his sermons and thereby giving handles to his enemies. "Unguarded Expressions and even erroneous Opinions delivered in Preaching might have been afterwards explain'd, or qualify'd by supposing others that might have accompany'd them; or they might have been deny'd, but *litera scripta manet*." He adds that a preacher can leave behind a "more important sect" if he writes nothing and allows his followers latitude to refine his teachings and "to feign for him as great a Variety of Excellencies, as their enthusiastic Admiration might wish him to have possessed"—a reflection that has obvious applicability to the founders of more than one religion.[27]

For the same reason, Franklin criticizes the Quakers for publishing and locking themselves into the foolish doctrine of pacifism; in contrast, he praises the Dunkers, the only sect he has encountered that is so modest in its claims to truth and so open to progress that it has declined to publish any of its doctrines,

> every other Sect supposing itself in Possession of all Truth, and that those who differ are so far in the Wrong: Like a Man travelling in foggy Weather: Those at some Distance before him on the Road he sees wrapt up in the Fog, as well as those behind him, and also the People in the Fields on each side; but near him all appears clear. Tho' in truth he is as much in the Fog as any of them.[28]

But if all religions are in the fog, what are we to conclude? The 1781 letter to Madame Brillon might suggest that the fog of incorrect doctrine surrounds the true insights that all religions share, such as the existence of an afterlife. But how is the existence of an afterlife any more clear and certain than the predestination of the elect? Are we truly on solid ground here, and truly out of the fog? Or are the only solid truths in religious teachings the moral truths that all may grasp directly, and are Franklin's "essential" doctrines true only to the extent that they are truly useful? In the end it seems that Franklin's project of reform was less one of returning all faiths to their original, shared core of solid truth than one of reinventing religion in a more useful form.[29] This improved religion he wished to steer everyone towards is generally known as deism, although in his most public writing, his *Autobiography,* Franklin does not call it by that name, for among orthodox believers deism was in bad odor. Instead, he reserves the term *deism* for its most austere form, the denial of providence, which he once embraced and now disowns as pernicious. At the same time, he slyly assimilates into his account of the essential faith of "everyone" his new, morally edifying providential deism, knowing full well that not everyone will agree.[30]

In another part of the essay "On Toleration in Old and New England," Franklin follows Locke's example to show how churches might profitably be induced to reinterpret their own teachings and practices in light of a new and better understanding of morals and politics. He describes the early laws in New England that required freeholders to support Presbyterian schools and ministers, and then the subsequent change by which other Protestant Christians were allowed to direct their tithes to schools and ministers of their own denomination but were still required by law to contribute them.

> It seems that the legislature considered the *end* of the tax was, to secure and improve the morals of the people, and promote their happiness, by supporting among them the public worship of God and the preaching of the gospel; that where particular people fancied a particular mode, that mode might probably therefore be of most use to those people; and that if the good was done, it was not so material in what mode or by whom it was done.[31]

Franklin suggests that the legislators regarded religion as nothing but a means to morals and happiness, and that any religion would do; he says nothing of the salvation of souls and the glorification of God that the early Puritan leaders in fact held up as the highest purpose of all legislation.[32] In reforming religion as in reforming morals, Franklin's usual approach is to encourage in others both a spirit of progress and the belief that their good ideas are really their own, even when they have been planted by the benevolent Franklin.

As churches begin to view themselves as bastions of peace and good morals, the next step in Franklin's project is to wean them away from the view that they need any governmental support to fulfill their mission. Even nonsectarian support for religion is pernicious, he argues, in coddling lazy and incompetent clerics. The more citizens are left free to vote with their feet, as Franklin has done, to attend or not attend worship as they choose and to give their tithes to any minister or none, the more the clergy will strive to make themselves truly useful, on the model of the practical and popular Samuel Hemphill.

> When a religion is good, I conceive that it will support itself; and when it cannot support itself, and God does not take care to support, so that its Professors are oblig'd to call for the help of a Civil Power, it is a sign, I apprehend, of its being a bad one.[33]

Religious liberty thus improves religion by making it more energetic, more pragmatic, and more peaceful. Each sect competes to show the social benefits of religion and to help its parishioners experience those benefits in their lives. Gradually attention shifts away from abstruse doctrinal questions; mystifying confessions of faith are simplified; prayers are brought up to date; and long, uncomfortable, dull services give way to short, uplifting, and encouraging ones.[34] Each sect defends toleration because it finds itself in a minority and feels itself vulnerable without the protection of religious freedom, and defending toleration gives it an additional reason to refrain from maligning other sects and to focus its attention on matters of moral agreement rather than of doctrinal division. In a 1782 pamphlet Franklin advises Europeans who might wish to immigrate that in the United States,

> serious Religion, under its various Denominations, is not only tolerated, but respected and practiced. Atheism is unknown there, Infidelity rare and secret; so that Persons may live to a great Age in that Country, without having their Piety shocked by meeting with either an Atheist or an Infidel. And the Divine Being seems to have manifested his Approbation of the mutual Forbearance and Kindness with which the different Sects treat each other, by the remarkable Prosperity with which He has been pleased to favour the whole Country.[35]

Franklin opposed not only financial support for religion but also all religious tests for public office. He recounts how he failed to prevent a clause from being included in the 1776 Pennsylvania constitution requiring members of the Assembly to declare that the whole of the Old Testament was given by divine inspiration, but he did manage to have included a provision that no further or more extended Profession of Faith should ever be enacted.[36] Unlike Locke, who excludes from the protection of religious liberty both atheists, whose oaths cannot be trusted, and Muslims (and by implication also Roman Catholics), whose beliefs require loyalty to a foreign power, Franklin saw no need to exclude even polytheists and atheists from public office. But also unlike Locke, Franklin was ready to go quite far in accommodating religious belief, even at significant cost to civil society: he favored exemption from military service for Quakers, not merely as a legislative indulgence but as a right enshrined in the Pennsylvania constitution.

Franklin's view of religion was nothing if not sanguine. He was confident that faith was by and large a good thing and that generous and tolerant treatment of all the sects would make it better. He was confident that neither irrational Quakers nor papists nor infidels posed any significant danger to republican liberty, and was seemingly unafraid that a widespread loss of faith would pose any threat to liberty. But where did he himself finally come down? Moral observations and arguments had freed him from fear of an angry God, but did he believe in a providential God of a more rationalist stamp? Was he certain that America would always have churches to support civic virtue because as a believing deist he was certain that God favored his country and would keep it faithful to the essential truth? Or was he indifferent to the churches' fate because as a convinced atheist he judged that either piety improved by toleration or pure rationalism was a good enough basis for civic virtue? And what were the grounds of his judgment?

The Existence of God

It is hard to know what Franklin really thought about religious questions because he was so given to concealment, both by temperament and by principle. His written statements make it clear that if he were an atheist, he would have considered it most imprudent to admit it. Franklin's clearest if not his frankest statement about his own beliefs comes in the *Autobiography,* where he says that whatever ideas he may have entertained in his reckless youth, he never doubted certain fundamental things:

> I never doubted, for instance, the Existance of the Deity, that he made the World, and govern'd it by his Providence; that the most acceptable Service of God was the doing Good to Man; that our Souls are immortal; and that all Crime will be punished and Virtue rewarded either here or hereafter.[37]

But this statement is useless for our purposes, however useful it may have been for Franklin's, since in composing the "Dissertation on Liberty and Necessity" Franklin did openly doubt the immortality of the soul and the existence of heaven and hell.[38] Although he later regretted the publication of that essay, he evidently never rued the writing of it. While in the *Autobiography* he deplores the social effects of teaching that God, if he exists, does not enforce justice and takes no care for individuals, he condemns this austere deism with the weak indictment that "this Doctrine tho' it might be true, was not very useful." In his later essay "On the Providence of God," he again questions whether God in any way rules the world.[39] Moreover, Franklin's list of fundamental tenets is followed by a comment that "these I esteem'd the Essentials of every religion," and that he was making it a principle "to avoid all Discourse that might lessen the good Opinion another might have of his own" religion. Are these doctrines Franklin's beliefs at all, or are they simply what he calls them in a 1731 page of notes to himself, "Doctrine to be Preach'd"?

Equally suspect is the confession of faith Franklin wrote at the end of his life to the Presbyterian minister and president of Yale College, Ezra Stiles. After expressing surprising surprise that anyone should ever inquire about his religious beliefs, Franklin gives out as his own the usual litany of edifying deist doctrines, but he throws into the mix an even more glaring contradiction than the one in his autobiographical account. He is certain, he writes, that "the Soul of Man is immortal, and will be treated with Justice in another Life respecting its Conduct in this." But he adds that "I have no Doubt" of God's continuing benevolence in the afterlife, "though without the smallest Conceit of meriting such Goodness."[40]

If Franklin was too cautious to commit his true beliefs to paper, did he reveal them more fully in unguarded conversation? Testimony by two who knew him during his years in France suggests that Franklin was known at that time as a virtual atheist. John Adams records in his diary that when asked by a Frenchman whether he was surprised that Franklin never attended religious services, he replied, "No, because Mr. Franklin has no— I was going to say, what I did not say, and will not say here. I stopped short and laughed." The Abbé Flamarens wrote, "Our free thinkers have adroitly sounded him on his religion, and they maintain that they have discovered he is one of their own, that is, that he has none at all."[41] But if he was indeed a virtual atheist, how should we understand this "virtual"? From the perspective of a serious man of faith there is little to choose between the impious half-believer and the unbeliever: both are abominable. But from the perspective of Socrates, the difference between one who wholly rejects the existence of a providential god and one who harbors secret hopes of his existence is fundamental.

Many stories might be told about Franklin's outrageous impiety, but for the present question, they are all irrelevant. The real question is not whether Franklin had any fear of the vengeful God of Abraham; clearly he had none. Nor is it whether he was a perfect atheist in the sense of being a materialist. Franklin, like the vast majority of eighteenth-century Enlightenment skeptics, clearly believed in some kind of divine creator. In the years before Darwin proposed his theory of evolution, the idea that the marvelous order of nature could have come about by sheer chance was generally thought implausible. The real question is whether Franklin's faith went any further. In returning to a belief in virtue and vice as a young man, did he also return to faith in a providential God, or did he think that God, after devising the world and winding it up like a clock, simply left it to play out as it might? This is the crucial divide that Franklin finesses with such superb and devious skill, always praising God's wisdom and the splendid design of his creation while never quite being clear about providence. But it is this question that the cagy Socrates would no doubt especially wish to press upon the cagy Franklin, should he make his acquaintance. At stake is whether Franklin was wholly reconciled to life without divine protection and fully resigned to the thought that this life is all that there is, or whether he let himself entertain hopes, however slight and however surreptitious, of a God who loved and would protect him and perhaps would not let his soul be extinguished after all.

Evidence that Franklin was an austere deist in the sense of denying providence comes mainly by inference from arguments he made at various points and never retracted. In his 1728 "Articles of Belief and Acts of Religion" he argues that a perfect God must be "infinitely above" concern with petty human matters—too regal, too tranquil and self-contained ever to crave our applause or to stoop to the unpleasant and interminable business of swatting human flies or chastising petty misdemeanors.[42] Furthermore, in his London essay on liberty and necessity he argues that all is fated and all human action is governed by pleasure and pain, and in later years he calls virtue wisdom and vice folly, either of which claim leads to the same inference, that any divine imposition of retributive punishments would be irrational. The reasons he gives for retreating from the austere deism of his London years include no arguments for retreating from his belief in the fundamental irrationality of condign rewards and punishments, and he does continue to call anger insane.

A further, intriguing piece of evidence comes in Franklin's use of the term *Providence* in the *Autobiography.* Describing the founding of the Philadelphia Academy, he tells us that just as the school was outgrowing its original building, "Providence threw into our way a large house ready built."[43] But reading carefully, we see that this "Providence" was really only the human providence of a shrewd and prudent man, our own Franklin, who served on the boards of both the academy and the civic hall, which had fallen into disuse, and he was able to strike a deal. Might "Providence" in Franklin's mind be nothing more than this, the good fortune that people think God is bringing to reward them for their virtue but that in fact reliably comes to those who exercise self-control and think ahead?

But we must be content with such hints as these, and there are others on the other side. It is curious that in his many reflections in later years on the question of whether a providential God exists Franklin never connects the question to his more fundamental arguments about the loftiness of God's concerns or the irrationality of retribution. What is even more curious is that Franklin seems to have tried to preach the edifying belief in providence even to himself. It is time we examined his strange "Articles of Belief and Acts of Religion," which were written in 1728, about the time he repudiated his essay on liberty and necessity, and which were purportedly devised to guide him in his own private worship.[44]

Franklin begins his credo with the reflections we have quoted on the perfection and loftiness of the creator of the universe, a being too magnificent to regard in the least "such an inconsiderable Nothing as Man." But he finds in himself a persistent inclination and, he therefore infers, a duty "to pay Divine Regards to SOMETHING." He then proceeds with amazing casualness to posit for himself just the sort of God he is inclined to worship and finds most useful to believe in for the support of his moral resolutions: a little god of the solar system, benevolent and wise, but sharing enough in human passions and concerns that "he is not above caring for us, being pleas'd with our Praise, and offended when we slight Him," a god who takes pleasure in the happiness and therefore the virtue of his little creatures and who is eager to have such a one as Ben Franklin for his especial friend. Franklin writes prayers and hymns to his demigod, who, he posits, is one of many such little gods. He praises his god's wisdom and, with astonishing carelessness, even attributes to his wise devising "the wondrous Laws" by which the planets move. He goes so far as to prescribe for himself the facial expression he should wear during worship, a "Countenance that expresses filial Respect, mixt with a kind of Smiling, that signifies inward Joy, and Satisfaction, and Admiration." It is all too much, and perhaps deliberately too much. Is it indeed another of Franklin's outrageous jokes?[45]

Perhaps, but Franklin is just the sort of person who might well think that if there could possibly be such a god, and if it is useful to worship him, why not? We are far indeed from the high stakes and grim terror of Pascal's wager—and equally far from the profound desire to get to the bottom of the inclination to worship that fueled the searchings of Socrates. There is something in Franklin so self-contented that he just might think his smiling satisfaction would satisfy a god, if not the God. And the god Franklin conjures up is admirably suited to be a friend to Franklin: they have all the same virtues, and all the same pleasures. This god is author and owner of the solar system as Franklin is of his little print shop; he is the center of a circle of admirers whom he is delighted to help, just as Franklin is center of the Junto, of the Fire Company, and increasingly of the wider circle of Philadelphia and colonial life. And the exercise of trying to honor this god is of a piece with all of Franklin's projects. In all of them we see the same single-minded stress on what is useful, the same hopefulness, the same absence of fear and awe. That this piece, if comic, might be unintentionally so is suggested by the fact that Franklin's odd creed is followed by what seems a most diligent and earnest compilation of edifying writings that he proposes to read from each day to put himself in a mood to do good. The prayers he includes make no requests for the gifts of fortune (friends don't ask friends for things they can get for themselves), but they do include the request to "preserve me from Atheism," and prominent among the readings he prescribes himself are arguments for the existence of God. We may postulate that at this stage of his life Franklin was inclined to an austere deism but thought that a more robust, moral deism might be of more use to him; he worried on some level that enlightened self-interest was perhaps not quite enough to support perfect virtue in every case; he thought that some sense of deep gratitude, obligation, and hope were still needed or would at least be very helpful.

If this is what the "Articles" were, there is no evidence that this exercise in trying to believe what it would be most useful to believe lasted for long. Two years later, Franklin wrote an essay, "On the Providence of God," attempting to prove that God does in fact intervene in human life to answer prayers and assist the virtuous, but he was discontented with the result. The strength of this essay is that it elucidates a certain problem with the hypothesis that a powerful and wise God would have made the universe, designed all the living beings, and then left it to run its course. Does it really make sense, Franklin asks, that "that Being which from its Power is most able to Act, from its Wisdom knows best how to act, and from its Goodness would always certainly act best," would, after one act of creation, "become the most unactive of all beings and remain everlastingly Idle"?[46] Thus Franklin shows how a belief in any god opens the door to a belief in a providential one and how even the most austere deists may be tempted to hope that a wise creator would take some care for the fate of the beings he has so carefully designed. The weakness of the essay is that it can find no grounds on which to nail the question down; it begins from the thoughts about God that "all Mankind in all Ages have agreed in," which certainly carry considerable weight but are not decisive, and so it ends in mere speculation. This exercise seems to have marked the point at which Franklin abandoned as futile all attempts to prove metaphysical truths.[47]

In the following decades Franklin reflected occasionally on the question of providence. He evidently thought he had shown to his own satisfaction that the answer made no practical difference: he was confident he knew the right way to live and confident that God would not demand of him an impossible faith or a degree of purity beyond what he himself considered reasonable. If heaven existed, he was surely as eligible for it as any; but if it did not, he would live so as to have no regrets. But of course no human being who is fully awake can be simply indifferent to the possibility of heaven and providence, and Franklin's comments on this from his middle years are intriguing.

In a 1753 letter to Joseph Huey, in which Franklin renounces any claim to a return for his generous assistance to Huey and urges him instead to "let good Offices go round," Franklin explains that he considers his own good works not as favors conferred but as debts inadequately paid, and that he can never repay God's beneficence. Yet for all that, he is not devoid of hope.

> You will see in this my Notion of Good Works, that I am far from expecting (as you suppose) that I shall merit Heaven by them. . . . I have not the Vanity to think I deserve it, the Folly to expect it, nor the Ambition to desire it; but content myself in submitting to the Will and Disposal of that God who made me, who has hitherto preserv'd and bless'd me, and in whose fatherly Goodness I may well confide, that he will never make me miserable, and that even the Afflictions I may at any time suffer shall tend to my Benefit.[48]

In a 1771 letter to his sister he expresses a similar sense of trust in providence.

> Upon the whole I am much disposed to like the World as I find it, and to doubt my own Judgment as to what would mend it. I see so much Wisdom in what I understand of its Creation and Government, that I suspect equal Wisdom may be in what I do not understand. And thence have perhaps as much Trust in God as the most pious Christian.[49]

Of course, it was to his pious sister that he was writing.

The strongest evidence that Franklin resisted the temptation to believe in providence comes in a letter the honesty of which we have every reason to trust, for its message is one that its recipient, the evangelist George Whitefield, could only be displeased to hear.

> I *see* with you that our affairs are not well managed by our rulers here below; I wish I could *believe* with you, that they are well attended to by those above; I rather suspect, from certain circumstances, that though the general government of the universe is well administered, our particular little affairs are perhaps below notice, and left to take the chance of human prudence or imprudence, as either may happen to be uppermost. It is, however, an uncomfortable thought, and I leave it.[50]

It is significant that Franklin, who had so much to say and so much time to think about God, still felt discomfort in thinking that God might *not* take notice of particular human beings.

And hence we are not altogether unprepared when, after all, the famously irreverent Franklin gives evidence of drifting back into piety in his old age. Of course he may simply have grown more convinced over time that religion is essential for society and that a reputation for piety is a good thing to leave behind, and he was an old master at creating impressions. But his remarks about God in the last decade of his life have a new ring of earnestness that is deepened by a shift in content, for now as never before Franklin links reflections about God with expressions of righteous indignation on the one hand and with a somber awareness of the approach of death on the other. In a 1782 letter to his "old and dear friend" James Hutton, he comments on a recent massacre of peaceful Indians:

> The Dispensations of Providence in the World puzzle my weak Reason. I cannot comprehend why cruel Men should have been permitted thus to destroy their fellow Creatures. Some of the Indians may be suppos'd to have committed sins, but one cannot think the little Children had committed any worthy of Death.

Nor can he understand why George III was allowed to carry out such cruel depredations in America.

> And yet this Man lives, enjoys all the good Things this World can afford, and is surrounded by Flatterers, who keep even his Conscience quiet, by telling him he is the best of Princes! I wonder at this, but I cannot therefore part with the comfortable Belief of a Divine Providence; and the more I see the Impossibility, from the number & extent of his Crimes of giving equivalent Punishment to a wicked Man in this Life, the more I am convinc'd of a future State, in which all that here appears to be wrong shall be set right, all that is crooked made straight. In this Faith let you & I, my dear Friend, comfort ourselves. It is the only Comfort, in the present dark Scene of Things, that is allow'd us.[51]

Two years later he would write, to his close friend William Strahan, of his faith in providence and would again link that faith to his love of justice, in this case the satisfaction of seeing America's just cause prevail.

> But after all my dear Friend, do not imagine that I am vain enough to ascribe our Success to any superiority in any of those Points. I am too well acquainted with all the Springs and Levers of our Machine, not to see that our human means were unequal to our undertaking, and that, if it had not been for the Justice of our Cause, and the consequent Interposition of Providence in which we had Faith we must have been ruined. If I had ever before been an Atheist, I should now have been convinced of the Being and Government of a Deity. It is he who abases the Proud and favours the Humble! May we never forget his Goodness to us, and may our future Conduct manifest our Gratitude.[52]

The following year he would take up the question of his personal mortality, in a speculation that may or may not have been simply playful.

> You see I have some reason to wish that in a future State I may not only be *as well as I was,* but a little better. And I hope it: For I, too,

> with your Poet, *trust in God*. And when I observe, that there is great Frugality as well as Wisdom in his Works, since he has been evidently sparing both of Labour and Materials. . . . I say that when I see nothing annihilated, and not even a Drop of Water wasted, I cannot suspect the Annihilation of Souls, or believe, that he will suffer the daily Waste of Millions of Minds ready made that now exist, and put himself to the continual Trouble of making new ones. Thus finding myself to exist in the World, I believe I shall in some Shape or other always exist.[53]

In a speech in the Constitutional Convention, Franklin connects the concern with death and the concern with justice, hinting that if even a sparrow cannot be extinguished without God's notice, perhaps with his help a human soul may escape extinction altogether, and a just republic might at least never be forgotten.

> I have lived, Sir, a long time; and the longer I live, the more convincing proofs I see of this truth—*that* God *governs in the Affairs of Men*. And if a sparrow cannot fall to the ground without his notice, is it probable that an empire can rise without his aid?[54]

Should the Americans forget God, they will be like the builders of Babel, Franklin warns, and mankind will lose faith in democracy. But with his aid, what may we not hope for?

It is in this context that we should reconsider Franklin's 1790 letter to Ezra Stiles, one of the last he would ever write. Is it perhaps no accident that he expresses such strong faith both in a God who rewards everyone according to his merits and in a heaven that no one deserves? Is it not likely that, suffused with both gratitude and hope, he might have failed to see the contradiction?

These signs of a return to piety are not conclusive, but they are suggestive and intriguing; in a certain way they are even in character. The thoughts Franklin expresses would have been comforting to an old man, especially one who had never held a grudge against God, unlike Aristophanes, Machiavelli, Voltaire, Thomas Paine, and other radical skeptics. Franklin had his quarrels with the established church and especially with its depiction of God as jealous and vengeful, but nowhere did he express the thought that the existence of a providential god as such would be bad news for humanity, as fatal to human dignity.[55] Nor did he ever claim absolute certainty for his religious views. And such a drift back to piety would be perfectly natural: it would be hard to withstand the temptation to hope for an afterlife unless one saw God as hostile, or unless one had spent a lifetime probing and scouring one's moral hopes and confusions and forcefully keeping the fact of death before one's eyes, as Socrates did. If the elder Franklin would seem, from the perspective of the younger Franklin, to have grown a bit soft, who is to say which of the two is really the wiser? Is it the younger, who, finding no way out of his metaphysical conundrums, resolutely and cheerfully turned his mind to the happiness that could be had and the problems that could be solved? Or is it the elder, who would not insist that he knew what he did not know?

We cannot help observing, and perhaps regretting, the easy-goingness of both. In the letter to Stiles, Franklin says that the question of the divinity of Jesus "is a Question I do not dogmatize upon, having never studied it, and I think it needless to busy myself with it now, when I expect soon an Opportunity of knowing the Truth with less Trouble."[56] Would a little more angst not become him better? Our regret is the keener because in this as in so many respects Franklin's influence on the American character was incalculable. Tocqueville observes in Americans a combination of the most cheerful and practical-minded piety with the most striking aversion to metaphysical thought; it is on this last deficiency that he criticizes us most harshly and compares us most unfavorably with great and profound human spirits such as Pascal. For all Franklin's endless curiosity, there is a lack of gravity to his thinking, an absence of the urgent, incessant habit of connecting immediate questions with eternal ones and seeking in every new fact evidence for the truth about where we stand as human beings and what the fate of our souls is. It is the absence of this impulse, which Pascal shared so deeply with Socrates, that leaves Franklin open to his most penetrating critics.

Eros, Death, and Eternity

However we understand the apparent change in Franklin in his closing years, it was not a change that caused him to call into question his life's work or the philosophy that had guided it. Let us, then, step back and assess that character and that philosophy as a whole. What are we to think of his infectious Yankee spirit, so acquisitive and yet so public-spirited, and in everything so eminently practical? How adequate is the guidance offered by his vision of democratic citizenship? Is a life of economic self-sufficiency, community involvement, and collective self-government the right prescription for human happiness? If so, is the inspiring model of Franklin's own life still attainable, a model in which business success is built upon personal bonds of trust, in which a rich social nexus is forged by collective projects to meet vital needs that government leaves unaddressed, and in which thoughtful citizens can take a part in public life without becoming professional politicians? Or do the capitalist spirit, the philanthropy, and the democracy Franklin championed all turn out to have their own trajectories and pull in different directions, the first drawing resources into ever-larger corporations, the second spawning professionalized charities that still need volunteers but that give few of the satisfactions of creative initiative and honor that Franklin's projects brought him, the last growing ever more centralized and bureaucratized, with crucial decisions being made at a level more and more distant from the lives of ordinary citizens?

Franklin's models of economic, civic, and political life surely are in key respects healthier than what tends to replace them. They are by no means simply out of reach, and it is worth a great deal of effort to preserve what we can of them. But the very need for such vigilance to prevent ownership of our lives and communities from slipping out of our hands may be due to another feature inherent in the elements of Franklin's spirit. Perhaps as much as acquisitiveness, philanthropy, and the love of liberty are compatible and even to a degree mutually reinforcing, there is always a tendency, in the absence of great national crises, for economic interests to eclipse the other two, to pull our energies more and more tightly into their orbit, causing us to work longer and longer hours to buy more and more things, to give up on the social nexus sustained by past generations, and, as Tocqueville observes, to withdraw into an ever-narrower circle of private relationships and concerns.

But if the latter tendencies are always present, perhaps Franklin's vision carries with it the seeds of its own decay, and perhaps its higher reaches cannot, on his terms, be sustained. This raises the question of whether the higher reaches of Franklin's vision are insufficiently high and thus whether Tocqueville's Franklinian remedy for "individualism"—voluntary associations and a civil religion of self-interest rightly understood—is less radical than the disease requires. Is there not perhaps some truth to the critique of America made by its most serious opponents, that the practical-minded humanism of men like Franklin leads to a self-indulgence, decadence, and shallowness that fails to address the deepest needs of the human soul?

For example, the nineteenth-century French writer Charles Augustin Sainte-Beuve laments:

> An ideal is lacking in this healthy, upright, able, frugal, laborious nature of Franklin—the fine flower of enthusiasm, tenderness, sacrifice,—all that is the dream, and also the charm and the honour of poetic natures. . . . He brings everything down to arithmetic and strict reality, assigning no part to human imagination.[57]

Sainte-Beuve honors Franklin for his honest uprightness, but D. H. Lawrence finds even in Franklin's principles a smugness and shallowness that seem lethal to everything deep and everything high in the human spirit. In all that he does, Lawrence charges, Franklin is pragmatic and calculating, but there is nothing noble in life that is not utterly uncalculating. Nor does the Nietzschean Lawrence think there is anything noble in life that is not divisive. Lawrence sees in Franklin the ultimate herd animal, a "perfect little wheel within the whole," who has become one with all men "through suppression and elimination of those things which make differences—passions, prides, impulses of the self which cause disparity between one being and another." Of course, says Lawrence, we can get along with everyone if we are always obliging and ready to compromise, yet "how can any man be free without a soul of his own, that he believes in and won't sell at any price? But Benjamin doesn't let me have a soul of my own. He says I am nothing but a servant of mankind—galley-slave I call it—and if I don't get my wages here below . . . why, never mind, I shall get my wages HEREAFTER."[58]

At the heart of Lawrence's critique is the thought that Franklin's philosophy leaves no room for the mystery of the divine, and in particular fails to recognize the inner divinity of each human soul. To Franklin's tidy little credo he counterpoises his own:

> That I am I.
> That my soul is a dark forest.
> That my known self will never be more than a little clearing in the forest.
> That gods, strange gods, come forth from the forest into the clearing of my known self, and then go back.
> That I must have the courage to let them come and go.
> That I will never let mankind put anything over on me, but that I will try always to recognize and submit to the gods in me and the gods in other men and women.[59]

Lawrence finds Franklin a man devoid of inspiration, devoid of poetry, and perhaps most tellingly, devoid of eros. Lawrence quotes with scorn Franklin's definition of chastity in his catalogue of virtues and contrasts it with a definition of his own.

> Franklin: "Rarely use Venery but for Health or Offspring; Never to Dulness, Weakness, or the Injury of your own or another's Peace or Reputation." Lawrence: "Never 'use' venery at all. Follow your passional impulse, if it be answered in the other being; but never have any motive in mind, neither offspring nor health nor even pleasure, nor even service. Only know that venery is one of the great gods. An offering-up of yourself to the very great gods, the dark ones, and nothing else.[60]

In his unerotic stance towards eros, Lawrence charges, Franklin shows that he is deaf to the deepest longing of the heart.

A Christian critique of Franklin might focus on a slightly different aspect of the same problem. It might ask whether Franklin has a full experience and gives an adequate account of the phenomenon of love in all its higher reaches, a phenomenon that according to the believer points to the presence in the world of a mysterious, transcendent God, and the presence in us of a spark of that divine being.

But is any of this quite fair? It is at least paradoxical that a man who was still wooing and charming women into old age should be called unerotic and that a man who sustained such lively and affectionate friendships with so many people across such great expanses of time and space should be considered in any way deficient in the capacity for love. And yet there is a strange coolness to Franklin's very warmth. In his earliest published writings he speaks of the ridiculous figure cut by a man in love; did Franklin ever cut a ridiculous figure on account of love? In his *Autobiography* we see him shedding burdensome friendships with simple relief and forgetting his engagement to Deborah Read with scarcely a scruple. Later he entered into a "serious courtship" with another girl, "in herself very deserving"; but when the girl's hitherto encouraging family made sudden difficulties, perhaps "on a Supposition of our being too far engag'd in Affection to retract," so that Franklin might be expected to marry her without a dowry, Franklin proved their supposition wrong. After marrying Deborah, he left both wife and daughter behind on all his trips abroad, seeing little of Sally after she was thirteen and nothing of Deborah during the last years of her life, despite her reports of declining health and her pleas that he return home. Franklin loved having a domestic circle about him wherever he lived, but it mattered little whether the family was really his own. Even his most ardent and daring love letters to other women are too playful, too artful to be the work of a man truly in love. As one scholar has aptly expressed what many have observed, "Franklin somehow never committed himself wholly in love. A part of him was always holding back and watching the proceedings with irony."[61]

The absence of serious eros in Franklin is connected to his silence on another great theme of poetry, of piety, and of brooding souls like D. H. Lawrence: the theme of death. Eros and death are closely associated in ancient political philosophy, Plato's *Symposium* being the classic statement of the way in which eros is given fire and fuel for flight by the awareness that we must die. In the grip of eros, human beings seek to generate progeny to live on after them, they devote themselves to loved ones, they attempt glorious deeds, or they philosophize, depending on their natures—but always with the same hope of finding some form of self-transcendence that might lift them out of their mundane lives, plodding towards death, and allow them to touch eternity.

The wry Franklin no doubt would find all of this a little amusing—and not without some support from the text of the *Symposium*, which does not take itself quite so seriously as most classicists think. With the exception of suitably sober remembrances of particular friends who have died, Franklin seldom spoke of death without irony, when he spoke of it at all. Characteristic of his rare utterances is a 1734 discussion in the *Pennsylvania Gazette* in which Franklin objects (anonymously, of course) to a gloomy religious meditation he had printed the previous week. He mocks the author of the meditation—and by extension the Bible—for excessive belly-aching:

> I never thought even *Job* in the right, when he repin'd that the Days of a Man are *few* and *full of Trouble;* for certainly both these Things cannot be together just Causes of Complaint; if our Days are full of Trouble, the fewer of 'em the better.

Franklin goes on to compare life to a cake shop, comparing one who broods on the brevity of life and its fleeting pleasures to a child who laments that "the Cakes that we have eaten are no more to be seen; and those which are to come are not yet baked," and that "the present mouthful is chewed but a little while, and then is swallowed down, and comes up no more," concluding "O vain and miserable Cake-shop!"[62]

Likewise characteristic is a 1780 letter to an old friend in which Franklin inquires after other old friends and adds,

> For my own part, I do not find that I grow any older. Being arrived at 70, and considering that by traveling further in the same road I should probably be led to the grave, I stopped short, turned about and walked back again; which having done these four years, you may now call me 66. Advise those old friends of ours to follow my example; keep up your spirits and that will keep up your bodies; you will no more stoop under the weight of age than if you had swallowed a handspike.[63]

Even in describing in the *Autobiography* a near-fatal illness of his own at age 21, Franklin writes as if he gained an ironic distance on death itself as soon as the threat of it receded a little: "I suffered a good deal, gave up the Point in my own mind, and was rather disappointed when I found my Self recovering; regretting in some degree that I must now some time or other have all that disagreeable Work to do over again."[64] Death in Franklin's mind is no picnic, but it seems only a matter of work to come to terms with it. There is no evidence that this early brush with death altered his outlook on life or gave him a new insight that he tried to carry with him. Nor does he view coming to terms with death as anything one needs to do in a time of health, let alone on a daily basis, as Socrates suggests; that is why he would have to face that disagreeable work again. The maiden lady in the garret might indeed not have to do it again, but in Franklin's eyes she must have looked half-dead already. Rather than live each day as if it were his last, Franklin is reported to have declared in old age to Thomas Paine, "[I]t has always been my maxim to live on as if I was to live always. It is with such feeling only that we can be stimulated to the exertions necessary to effect any useful purpose."[65]

What should we think about a vision of citizenship that actively seeks to make human beings forget the crucial fact of our mortality and concentrate only on the problem we can do something about, like street lighting? Is it a sign of healthy toughness that Franklin refuses to dwell on morbid thoughts, or is it the ultimate flight from reality?[66] Whatever else we think of it, we should note that this behavior was not peculiar to Franklin. Turning away from the problem of death and addressing ourselves to soluble problems is of the essence of the Enlightenment, that great project of modern, rationalist political theory that stretches back to Hobbes, Bacon, and Spinoza and that attained its fulfillment in the American founding.

It is this entire project that Lawrence and many others have rebelled against, correctly seeing in Franklin its brightest, purest exemplar, and judging him shallow. If Lawrence had found Franklin simply repugnant, he would never have given him the careful attention that he did; but as a boy he found Franklin seductive, deliberately seductive, and as a man he feared the coming of a world of flattened, snuff-colored little men in the image of Franklin on whom poetry could take no hold.[67] Certainly Franklin's refusal to lose himself either in erotic longing or in musings on death makes him look less deep than Lawrence, but what is there in Lawrence's depths to recommend itself? Lawrence provides no guidance for life. His scorn for peaceful accommodation and his casual embrace of "passional impulses" and of the "dark one," of which one can demand no reasoned justification, are chilling in light of the horrors of the twentieth century. Surely Franklin's spirit of capacious sympathy with humanity, his sober hopefulness, his rationalist calculations as to whether following his impulses is likely to make things better or worse, are all superior to the blind passion of Lawrence's brooding.

Yet depth need not be anti-rational. The hopeful pragmatism that forgets death and embraces material progress is of the essence of modern rationalism, but classical rationalism, rooted in Socratic political philosophy, takes a very different approach. As evidenced by Plato's *Symposium,* classical rationalism gives full and unflinching attention to human mortality and to the soul's yearning for transcendent meaning, which admits of no simple satisfaction or easy resolution. Yet classical rationalism has only cold water to pour on Franklin's hope that a whole society can be made rational and humane through the spread of enlightened self-interest. Plato would have judged the modern Enlightenment project unworkable, arguing that the human soul can never rest satisfied with well-lit streets and well-stocked shops. A political project that seeks to lull us into forgetting the source of our deepest sorrow and our highest yearnings is a project that may seem to succeed for a time, but in the end, nature will return to claim its due. If those yearnings are not given central place in the life of a regime by its thoughtful lawgivers, Plato suggests in the *Laws,* they will someday seize it in an outburst of thoughtless fanaticism.

Of course the possibility remains that Franklin is right and Plato and Socrates are wrong. Beside them Franklin looks both shallow and untheoretical, but his life until almost the end was a model of happy serenity. And who does not shudder at the end? Even Socrates asked his friends to cover his face in his final moments. Franklin's life stands as a compelling piece of evidence for another very old view, that of Aristophanes. The thesis of Aristophanes, made especially clear in his play *The Birds,* is that there is in the healthy human soul no fundamental yearning for God, as Augustine teaches, or for the transcendence of death, as Socrates teaches. Granted, says Aristophanes, it would be splendid to live forever, but we could be almost perfectly content if we could live, say, two or three hundred years. With this thought Franklin heartily concurs. It would be splendid, the old Franklin says at the opening of his autobiography, to live again the same life, especially if he had the liberty to correct its few errata, and it would even be delightful to have the same life all over again, warts and all. But failing both of these, Franklin can be quite content with an old man's recollections. Aristophanes suggests that human beings can learn to laugh at Zeus and be happy; the chuckling Franklin steals Zeus's thunder and is satisfied to find that nothing terrible happens to him. Aristophanes and Franklin both suggest that human strength is something dry and bright and full of laughter; strength consists precisely in learning to do what we can and to treasure what we have and not wallowing in inchoate yearnings. What Lawrence and even Socrates think of as depth may after all be only softness.

Even if, in the end, we decide that Socrates is right and Franklin shallow, we must be grateful to Franklin for the compelling challenge he poses to our assumptions about depth and shallowness. To all who are trying to think the great questions of political philosophy through to the bottom he is an inestimable gift. But he is not equally a gift to those who do not start with those questions. Socrates and Aristophanes, to say nothing of Moses and Mohammed, are united in their insistence on keeping open before us the questions of our place in the great scheme of things and the mortality or immortality of our souls. Franklin encourages us to forget them. Classical rationalism teaches us always to confront its rivals and consider whether they might not after all be right: the contest between reason and revelation is always alive in Socrates' conversations, and Socratic philosophy never for a moment stops struggling to justify its own audacious activity. For Franklin these contests are not compelling, and the superiority of rationalism in its peculiar modern variant is treated as self-evident. Franklin's effect is to induce his readers to forget the old rivalry between rationalism and revelation, and with it the urgent human questions upon which it turned.

Indeed, it is an essential element of the seductive genius of the charming, sinuous Franklin that he so skillfully lulls to sleep all rival ways of seeing the world while he awakens us to view it through his eyes. This peculiar genius was evident from the first appearance of Silence Dogood, too modest to engage in theological speculations with the learned menfolk, too sensible to waste time on such abstruse questions anyhow, too self-possessed and self-aware not to make her late clergyman-husband with his amorous awkwardness look foolish in her shadow.[68] Franklin engaged in a number of bitter feuds in his life, but one senses that they were all out of character, and none ended happily for him. Franklin's true mode was not to challenge enemies to battle but to try to win them over, not to refute rival theories but to let his ideas "shift for themselves." And what victory could be sweeter or more complete than that of seeing a detractor live to be "the last of his sect"?[69] Instead of assailing monkish superstition, Franklin was content to leave it looking old-fashioned and faintly ridiculous. His is the devastating weapon of infectious laughter, which, as Aristophanes showed, can disarm the gods without paying the price of Prometheus. Or so, at least, they both charm us into believing.

All in all, the wily Franklin's legacy is a good one, and his rich thoughts about life are eminently worth hearing. If our quarrel is with modernity and the soulless, humorless spirit of capitalism, we cannot lay the fault at Franklin's door. Franklin himself was a wonderful, deeply wise human being who took the soberly practical Yankee spirit that already existed and turned it into something sparkling and effervescent and inspiring in all sorts of good and healthy ways. He represents the best of America and a human type that the world would have been much poorer never to have seen. But Franklin also points us to problematic aspects of the modern project that require us continually to return to premodern challenges and alternative sources of wisdom. Only with such a return and such a confrontation can we ever hope to become as fully and richly human as Franklin himself was.

NOTES

Regarding sources for writings by Franklin, please see the Note on Sources at the front of this book.

Introduction

1. Franklin to Jane Mecom, 24 December 1767; cf. Franklin to an unnamed recipient, 28 November 1768.

2. The critic who goes the furthest in denying to Franklin any coherent philosophy is Charles Angoff, who writes, "Franklin was very good in organizing post offices and fire departments, but he was completely lost when it came to drafting organic bodies of laws. Basic philosophic ideas were beyond him. . . . Abstract ideas, save those of the corner grocery store, somehow irked him." Angoff, who despises Franklin for "making a religion of Babbitry," charges that even his electrical experiments were vastly overrated and that in all respects he was a mediocrity: *A Literary History of the American People,* 2 vols. (New York: Alfred A. Knopf, 1931) 2:295–310. A similar assessment is given by one of the major editors of Franklin's collected works, Albert Henry Smyth, who writes, "Franklin's mind was attentive to trifles; his philosophy never got beyond the homely maxims of worldly prudence": *American Literature* (Philadelphia: Eldredge and Brothers, 1889), 20. Even the more moderate Michael Zuckerman charges that there is no center at all to Franklin's thought, that he "never found a unifying frame for his career," was "always prepared to proceed in spite of principle," and "experimented playfully" with all his "beliefs and values": "Doing Good While Doing Well: Benevolence and Self-Interest in Franklin's *Autobiography,*" in J. A. Leo Lemay, ed., *Reappraising Benjamin Franklin* (Newark: University of Delaware Press, 1993), 448–49. David Levin, in contrast, writes, "The particular form of Franklin's wit, his decision to portray himself as an inquisitive empiricist, the very success of his effort to exemplify moral values in accounts of practical experience, his doctrine of enlightened self-interest, and the fine simplicity of his exposition—all these combine to make him seem philosophically more naïve, and practically more materialistic, than he is": "Franklin: Experimenter in Life and Art," in Wilbur R. Jacobs, ed., *Benjamin Franklin: Statesman-*

Philosopher or Materialist? (New York: Holt, Reinhart and Winston, 1972), 61. A Franklin biographer, Carl Becker, goes further and argues that Franklin was among the greatest philosophers of his age: *The Heavenly City of the Eighteenth-Century Philosophers* (New Haven: Yale University Press, 1932), 21–22. At the other extreme from Angoff is Paul W. Conner, who argues that Franklin's whole political thought is reducible to a "grand design" for a "New American Order": *Poor Richard's Politicks: Franklin and the New American Order* (New York: Oxford University Press, 1965), x, xi; cf. 14, 96.

3. Benjamin Franklin, *Autobiography,* ed. Leonard Labaree (New Haven: Yale University Press, 1964), 157–58.

4. Ibid., 44.

5. "Silence Dogood," no. 1, 2 April 1722.

6. Ibid., no. 2, 16 April 1722.

7. Ralph Lerner nicely brings out the centrality of the theme of humanity's mixed motives in *The Thinking Revolutionary: Principle and Practice in the New Republic* (Ithaca: Cornell University Press, 1987), 48.

8. "Silence Dogood," no. 8, 9 July 1722, reprinting *Cato's Letters,* no. 38, from *The London Journal,* no. 80, 4 February 1721.

9. "Silence Dogood," no. 2, 16 April 1722.

10. Ibid., no. 9, 23 July 1722. H. W. Brands points out that the immediate provocation for this attack was probably the oppressive censorship that Franklin's brother and his newspaper were then suffering from the Massachusetts colonial government, backed up by the Puritan establishment: *The First American: The Life and Times of Benjamin Franklin* (New York: Random House, 2000), 30.

11. See esp. Niccolò Machiavelli, *Discourses on Livy,* trans. Harvey C. Mansfield and Nathan Tarcov (Chicago: University of Chicago Press, 1996), Book 2, Chapter 2.

12. As Ormond Seavey writes in an unusually perceptive essay on Franklin and his quiet way of undercutting traditional authority, "Somehow nothing the late Reverend Dogood could say of an improving nature will escape being colored, in the reader's mind, by a recollection of this mortifying scene": "Benjamin Franklin and D. H. Lawrence as Conflicting Modes of Consciousness," in Melvin H. Buxbaum, ed., *Critical Essays on Benjamin Franklin* (Boston: G. K. Hall, 1987), 64.

13. "Silence Dogood," no. 10, 13 August 1722.

14. Ibid., no. 11, 20 August 1722.

15. Ralph Waldo Emerson remarks that Franklin's "serene and powerful understanding . . . seemed to be a transmigration of the Genius of

Socrates," but he adds, characteristically, that Franklin's was better and more useful than the original: *The Journals of Ralph Waldo Emerson,* ed. Edward Waldo Emerson and Waldo Emerson Forbes, 10 vols. (Boston: Houghton, Mifflin, 1909), 1:375–76.

16. *Autobiography,* 64–65.

17. Ibid., 115.

18. "On Simplicity," *Pennsylvania Gazette,* 13 April 1732. This essay, like many pieces in the *Gazette* that are almost certainly by Franklin, is not included in the Yale edition of Franklin's papers, but it is reprinted in Benjamin Franklin, *Writings,* ed. J. A. Leo Lemay (New York: Library of America, 1987), 183. Hereafter, *Writings* (Lemay).

19. *Poor Richard Improved,* 1749 and 1753, in *Writings* (Lemay), 1255 and 1277. Cf. "Articles of Belief and Acts of Religion," 20 November 1728, where Franklin calls anger a "momentary madness."

20. *Autobiography,* 88.

Chapter 1 The Economic Basis of Liberty

1. This tension was partly but only partly resolved by resting republican government on the wealthy, slave-owning agrarian class exemplified by the gentleman Ischomachus in Xenophon's *Oeconomicus.* For the ancient aspiration to greater equality, simplicity, and moral purity, see esp. Plato *Laws* 684d–e, 737c–d, 741a–744a.

2. "Advice to a Young Tradesman, Written by an Old One," 21 July 1748, quoted in Max Weber, *The Protestant Ethic and the Spirit of Capitalism* (New York: Charles Scribner's Sons, 1958), 48–50.

3. *Poor Richard,* 1737, quoted by Weber, *Protestant Ethic,* 50. It is significant that Weber leaves out the statement immediately before this passage, warning against miserliness: "The Use of Money is all the Advantage there is in having Money."

4. *Poor Richard,* 1733 and 1736, in Benjamin Franklin, *Writings,* ed. J. A. Leo Lemay (New York: Library of America, 1987), 1187 and 1201.

5. *Poor Richard,* 1745 and 1747, in *Writings* (Lemay), 1235 and 1241.

6. *Poor Richard,* 1736 and 1739, in *Writings* (Lemay), 1200 and 1213.

7. Weber, *Protestant Ethic,* 52.

8. Ibid., 53 and 71.

9. In fact, Weber views the religious meaning as not entirely absent, for he asserts that Franklin "ascribes his recognition of the utility of virtue to a divine revelation" (ibid., 53), although the *Autobiography* does not go nearly that far.

10. Leo Strauss makes this point the basis of a penetrating critique of Weber's thesis in *Natural Right and History* (Chicago: University of Chicago Press, 1953), 60–61n. For a fuller analysis of Weber's misreading of Franklin, see Thomas L. Pangle, *The Spirit of Modern Republicanism: The Moral Vision of the American Founders and the Philosophy of Locke* (Chicago: University of Chicago Press, 1988), 16–21.

11. *Poor Richard,* 1736 and 1734, in *Writings* (Lemay), 1200 and 1193. See also Franklin to William Strahan, 2 June 1750.

12. "A Proposal for Promoting Useful Knowledge among the British Plantations in America," 14 May 1743; "On the Need for an Academy," 24 August 1749.

13. *Autobiography,* 164. Cf. Franklin to Jane Mecom, 30 December 1770: "What in my younger Days enabled me more easily to walk upright, was, that I had a Trade; and that I could live upon a little; and thence (never having had views of making a Fortune) I was free from Avarice, and contented with the plentiful Supplies my business afforded me."

14. *Poor Richard Improved,* 1757, in *Writings* (Lemay), 1292.

15. *Autobiography,* 234; cf. Xenophon *Memorabilia* 2:7. In his journal entry of 25 August 1726, Franklin reports the same effect of idleness upon his own spirits while a passenger at sea: "I rise in the morning and read for an hour or two perhaps, and then reading grows tiresome. Want of exercise occasions want of appetite, so that eating and drinking afford but little pleasure. . . . A contrary wind, I know not how, puts us all out of good humour; we grow sullen, silent, and reserved, and fret at each other upon every little occasion."

16. Franklin to James Logan [1737?].

17. *Autobiography,* 207.

18. *Poor Richard,* 1737, in *Writings* (Lemay), 1205.

19. Franklin to Peter Timothy, 3 November 1772.

20. *Poor Richard Improved,* 1750; *Writings,* 1259.

21. Alexis de Tocqueville, *Democracy in America,* trans. and ed. Harvey C. Mansfield and Delba Winthrop (Chicago: University of Chicago Press, 2000), vol. 1, part 2, chap. 9, p. 273, and chap. 6, p. 233.

22. On mob action, see "Petition to the Pennsylvania Assembly Concerning Fairs," 1731; "A Narrative of the Late Massacres, in Lancaster County, of a Number of Indians, Friends of this Province, by Persons Unknown," 30 January 1764; "On the Tenure of the Manor of East Greenwich," 6 January 1766; to William Franklin, 16 April 1768; to Jean-Baptiste Le Roy, 31 January 1769; to the Printer of the Public Ledger [after 9 March 1774]. On the French Revolution, see Franklin to David Hartley, 4 December 1789; and letters to Benjamin Vaughan,

2 November 1789, to Samuel Moore, 5 November 1789, and to Le Roy, 13 November 1789, in *The Writings of Benjamin Franklin,* ed. Albert Henry Smyth, 10 vols. (New York: Macmillan, 1907), 10:50, 10:63, 10:68. Cf. Jefferson to William Smith, 13 November 1787, in *The Papers of Thomas Jefferson,* ed. Julian P. Boyd et al., 33 vols. to date (Princeton: Princeton University Press, 1950–), 12:356. On hereditary privilege, see esp. Franklin to Sarah Bache, 26 January 1784; cf. Jefferson to John Adams, 28 October 1813, in John Adams and Thomas Jefferson, *The Adams-Jefferson Letters,* ed. Lester J. Cappom, 2 vols. (Chapel Hill: University of North Carolina Press, 1959), 2:388. But Franklin shared with Jefferson a belief in a natural aristocracy of a sort: see Franklin to Joshua Babcock, 1 September 1755.

23. "Revision of the Pennsylvania Declaration of Rights" [between 29 July and 15 August 1776].

24. "Information to Those Who Would Remove to America" [1782], *Writings of Benjamin Franklin* (Smyth) 8:604.

25. Franklin to the Abbés Chalut and Arnaud, 17 April 1787; cf. *Poor Richard,* 1739, in *Writings* (Lemay), 1213: "No longer virtuous no longer free, is a Maxim as true with regard to a private Person as a Common-wealth."

26. *Poor Richard,* 1739, in *Writings* (Lemay) 1211.

27. "The Busy-Body," no. 8, 27 March 1729.

28. *Poor Richard,* 1746, in *Writings* (Lemay) 1238.

29. *Poor Richard,* 1733, 1734, and 1735, in *Writings* (Lemay), 1187, 1193, and 1196; *Poor Richard Improved,* 1751, in *Writings,* 1268.

30. *Poor Richard Improved,* 1758, in *Writings* (Lemay), 1301–2.

31. Franklin to Timothy Folger, 29 September 1769. On frugality and luxury, see also Franklin's two delightful spoofs, "Anthony Afterwit" and "Cecelia Single," 10 and 24 July 1732; Franklin to Samuel Cooper, 27 April 1769; to Sarah Bache, 3 June 1779; to Samuel Cooper, 27 October 1779; and to Madame Brillon, 10 November 1779.

32. *Autobiography,* 145.

33. Xenophon *Memorabilia* 1.5.6.

34. Franklin to Peter Collinson, 9 May 1753.

35. "Remarks Concerning the Savages of North-America," 1784.

36. Franklin to Robert Morris, 25 December 1783; cf. Franklin to William Strahan, 2 June 1750: "I imagine that what we have above what we can use, is not properly *ours.*" See also Franklin to Benjamin Vaughan, 14 March 1785; "Queries and Remarks," 3 November 1789.

37. Franklin to Peter Collinson, 9 May 1753.

38. Franklin to Joshua Babcock, 13 January 1772.

39. John Locke, *Second Treatise of Government,* sec. 41. Locke does argue that the right to acquire is limited by the duty to avoid waste, but this duty is easily satisfied by converting one's excess produce into money (secs. 26–50).

40. Franklin to Joshua Babcock, 13 January 1772.

41. Franklin to Lord Kames, 3 January 1760.

42. *Autobiography,* 257; Franklin to Joseph Priestley, 8 February 1780.

43. "The Nature and Necessity of a Paper-Currency," 3 April 1729.

44. Franklin to Lord Kames, 1 January 1769.

45. "The Nature and Necessity of a Paper-Currency," 3 April 1729.

46. Ibid.

47. For a good account of the physiocrats and their disagreement with mercantilist doctrine, see Drew McCoy, "Benjamin Franklin's Vision of a Republican Political Economy for America," *William and Mary Quarterly,* 3rd ser., 35 (1978): 605–28. McCoy views Franklin as an early and bold opponent of mercantilism; cf. Lewis J. Carey, *Franklin's Economic Views* (Garden City, N.Y.: Doubleday, Doran, 1928), esp. 140, and Vernon Lewis Parrington, "Franklin: An Early Social Scientist," in Walter R. Jacobs, ed., *Benjamin Franklin: Statesman-Philosopher or Materialist?* (New York: Holt, Reinhart and Winston, 1972), 29–30. For an opposing view, see Gerald Stourzh, *Benjamin Franklin and American Foreign Policy,* 2nd ed. (Chicago: University of Chicago Press), 1969), 59–60, 97, 104–10, and Paul W. Conner, *Poor Richard's Politicks: Franklin and His New American Order* (New York: Oxford University Press, 1965), 72–75. Both acknowledge many of Franklin's deviations from classic mercantilist doctrine but still class him with the mercantilists because he shared with them an appreciation for the fundamentally competitive nature of international politics, unlike the rival school of French physiocrats. That Franklin was free of the naïveté of the physiocrats on this point, however, does not make him a mercantilist.

48. "Observations Concerning the Increase of Mankind," 1751. See also "Queries," 18 August 1768.

49. "On a Proposed Act to Prevent Emigration," December 1773. On corruption at the British court and the contrasting virtue in America, see also Franklin to Timothy Folger, 29 September 1769; to Thomas Cushing, 10 October 1774; to Joseph Galloway, 25 February 1775; to Richard Price, 9 October 1780; to Jonathan Shipley 17 March 1783; to William Strahan, 16 February 1784; to Henry Laurens 12 February 1784.

50. Franklin to Joseph Galloway, 25 February 1775; to Joseph Priestley, 7 July 1775.

51. Franklin to Vergennes, 16 March 1783. On the advantages of unrestricted free trade, see also "Resolutions on Trade Submitted to Congress," [21 July] 1775; to Richard Price, 1 February 1785; to John Hunter, 24 November 1786.

52. Franklin's fullest statement on the primacy of security is in his 1760 pamphlet "The Interest of Great Britain Considered." On the Navigation Act, see Franklin to William Franklin, 22 March 1775, and "Intended Vindication and Offer from Congress to Parliament," 21 July 1775.

53. Franklin to Peter Collinson, 30 April 1764; cf. Franklin to David Hume, 27 September 1760; to Jared Eliot, 16 July 1747.

54. Franklin to Pierre Samuel du Pont de Nemours, 28 July 1768.

55. See Chapter 4 below.

56. "The Nature and Necessity of a Paper-Currency," 3 April 1729.

57. "Positions to Be Examined," 4 April 1769.

58. Franklin is sometimes credited with originating the labor theory of value, which he propounds in "The Nature and Necessity of a Paper-Currency," 3 April 1729, and in a letter to Lord Kames of 21 February 1769. He in fact derived it from his reading of Sir William Petty's *Treatise of Taxes and Contributions* (1662). The theory was later discussed and developed by David Hume, Adam Smith, and David Ricardo, whose analysis most influenced Marx.

59. "Positions to Be Examined," 4 April 1769.

60. Franklin to Timothy Folger, 29 September 1769.

61. Franklin to James Lovell, 22 July 1778.

62. 2 October 1780; cf. Franklin to Robert Livingston, 12 August 1782; to Charles Pettit, 10 October 1786.

63. Montesquieu, *The Spirit of the Laws,* ed. and trans. Anne Cohler et al. (1748; Cambridge: Cambridge University Press, 1989), Book 20, Chapters 1–5.

64. Franklin to Benjamin Vaughan, 26 July 1784; see also "The Internal State of America" [c. 1785].

65. "Observations Concerning the Increase of Mankind," 1751.

66. "Miscellaneous Observations," 1732.

67. "Observations Concerning the Increase of Mankind," 1751.

68. "Information to Those Who Would Remove to America" [1782], *Writings of Benjamin Franklin* (Smyth) 8:610–11.

69. "The Interest of Great Britain Considered," 1760.

70. "On the Laboring Poor" [April 1768]; see also "'Arator': On the Price of Corn, and Management of the Poor," 29 November 1766.

71. "On the Laboring Poor" [April 1768].

72. "Some Account of the Pennsylvania Hospital," 28 May 1754; cf. Franklin's *Gazette* extract of 25 August 1743.

73. See esp. Aristotle *Nicomachean Ethics,* 10.6–7.

74. Gordon Wood fails to see both this fundamental kinship with gentlemen and Franklin's irrepressible self-confidence; he presents Franklin's decision to retire from business and even his scientific studies as the acts of a painfully class-conscious social climber: *The Americanization of Benjamin Franklin* (New York: Penguin Books, 2004), 49–61. Conner finds Franklin similarly wracked by class-consciousness in *Poor Richard's Politicks,* 212–17.

75. *Poor Richard Improved,* 1758.

76. The Greek word is *scholē,* from which *scolar* and *school* derive.

77. *Poor Richard,* 1736, 1737, and 1746, in *Writings* (Lemay), 1201, 1205, and 1238.

78. Franklin to Cadwallader Colden, 29 September 1748; cf. Franklin to Colden, 14 September 1752.

79. Franklin to John Perkins, 4 February 1753.

80. Franklin to William Shipley, 27 November 1755; to Lord Kames, 2 June 1765.

81. Franklin to Robert Livingston, 4 March 1782.

82. Consider *Poor Richard Improved,* 1750: "On the 30th of this Month, 1718, Charles XII of Sweden, the modern Alexander, was kill'd before Fredericstadt. He had all the Virtues of a Soldier, but, as is said of the Virtues of Cesar, *they undid his Country:* Nor did they upon the whole afford himself any real Advantage. For after all his Victories and Conquests, he found his Power less than at first, his Money spent, his Funds exhausted, and his Subjects thinn'd extreamly. Yet he still warr'd on, in spite of Reason and Prudence, till a small Bit of Lead, more powerful than they, *persuaded* him to be quiet."

83. Carl Becker, *Benjamin Franklin: A Biographical Sketch* (Ithaca: Cornell University Press, 1946), 36; Franklin to Peter Collinson, 28 March 1747; cf. Franklin to Beccaria, 19 February 1781. Adrienne Koch observes, "Only the proper passion for theoretical understanding can explain Franklin's sustained and highly constructive inquiry into the nature of electrical phenomena—an inquiry which might or might not have had ultimate practical significance": *Power, Morals, and the Founding Fathers: Essays in the Interpretation of the American Enlightenment* (Ithaca: Cornell University Press, 1961), 16. William B. Willcox argues that Franklin's interest in politics was less intense, less promiscuous, and less objective than his interest in nature, citing especially the narrow focus of his political concerns while in London as agent for the colonies:

"Franklin's Last Years in England: The Making of a Rebel," in Melvin H. Buxbaum, ed., *Critical Essays on Benjamin Franklin* (Boston: G. K. Hall, 1987), 102–3.

84. "Dialogue Between Franklin and the Gout," 22 October 1780, *Writings of Benjamin Franklin* (Smyth) 8:154–62; to James Logan, 20 January 1750; to Peter Collinson, 1752; to John Perkins, 13 August 1752. In the latter letter Franklin also reproaches himself for, of all things, his laziness in pursuing those "amusements": "I own I have too strong a penchant to the building of hypotheses; they indulge my natural indolence: I wish I had more of your patience and accuracy in making observations, on which, alone, true Philosophy can be founded."

85. "Remarks on Balloons and New-born Babe," 27 August 1783.

86. See Franklin to James Logan, 20 January 1750. Franklin carries this view of science to comical extremes in his letter to the Royal Academy of Brussels [after 19 May 1780], in which he proposes a prize for the invention of a means to make intestinal gas aromatic, and asks the academy to consider "of how small Importance to Mankind, or to how small a Part of Mankind have been useful those Discoveries in Science that have heretofore made Philosophers famous. Are there twenty Men in Europe at this Day, the happier, or even the easier, for any knowledge they have pick'd out of Aristotle?"

87. Franklin to John Fothergill, 14 March 1764.

88. Franklin to Benjamin Waterhouse, 18 January 1781.

89. Franklin to Cadwallader Colden, 11 October 1750.

90. *The Papers of Thomas Jefferson,* ed. Julian P. Boyd et al., 22 vols. to date (Princeton: Princeton University Press, 1950–), 2:202–3.

91. Edmund S. Morgan, *Benjamin Franklin* (New Haven: Yale University Press, 2002), 45. Of the recent flurry of books on Franklin, this is far and away the best. Although Morgan confines his attention chiefly to Franklin's political projects, he makes the case for Franklin with unusual sympathy and insight into the nerve of Franklin's thought.

92. As Robert Spiller adds, "In the context of pious Victorian moralizing—so foreign to the cool reasoning of Franklin's time—his very whimsies were distorted into parables of opportunistic duty": "Franklin on the Art of Being Human," *Proceedings of the American Philosophical Society,* 100 (1956), 307. For a humorous perspective on how the spirit Franklin inspired can easily turn even the serious activities of leisure into joyless duties, consider the complaint of Mark Twain:

> His simplest acts . . . were contrived with a view to their being held up for the emulation of boys forever—boys who otherwise might have been happy. . . . With a malevolence which is without parallel in history, he would work all day and then sit up nights and let on to be studying algebra

> by the light of a smoldering fire, so that all other boys might have to do that or else have Benjamin Franklin thrown up to them. Not satisfied with these proceedings, he had a fashion of living wholly on bread and water, and studying astronomy at meal time—a thing which has brought affliction to millions of boys since, whose fathers have read Franklin's pernicious biography. (Samuel Clemens, "The Late Benjamin Franklin," in *Tales, Sketches, Speeches, and Essays, 1852–1890* [New York: Library of America, 1967], 425)

93. W. E. B. Du Bois, *The Souls of Black Folk* (1903; New York: Barnes and Noble Classics, 2003), 36 and 64.

Chapter 2 The Virtuous Citizen

1. Thomas Jefferson, *Notes on the State of Virginia* (New York: W. W. Norton, 1954), Query XIX: Manufactures, 164–65.

2. Plato *Phaedrus* 230d.

3. Walter Isaacson, *Benjamin Franklin: An American Life* (New York: Simon and Schuster, 2003), 35; but cf. Franklin to Catherine Greene, 2 March 1789. On Franklin's chosen destination of Philadelphia and the freedom of thought there as compared with seventeenth-century Boston, see E. Digby Baltzell, *Puritan Boston and Quaker Philadelphia: Two Protestant Ethics and the Spirit of Class Authority and Leadership* (New York: Free Press, 1979), chap. 10; and Carl and Jessica Bridenbaugh, *Rebels and Gentlemen: Philadelphia in the Age of Franklin* (New York: Oxford University Press, 1962).

4. Niccolò Machiavelli, *The Prince,* trans. Harvey C. Mansfield (Chicago: University of Chicago Press, 1985), chap. 25.

5. Alexis de Tocqueville, *Democracy in America,* trans. and ed. Harvey C. Mansfield and Delba Winthrop (Chicago: University of Chicago Press, 2000), vol. 2, part 2, chap. 8, p. 501. The editors add, "The name of Benjamin Franklin is so obvious among these 'American moralists' as to obscure all others."

6. Franklin, *Autobiography,* 100; "On Ill-Natured Speaking," 12 July 1733; "Rules for Making Oneself a Disagreeable Companion," 15 November 1750; "Standing Queries for the Junto, 1732; *Autobiography,* 116–17; "The Morals of Chess," 28 January 1779; "The Rise and Present State of Our Misunderstandings," 6 November 1770. Cf. "On Railing and Reviling," 6 January 1768, and "Rules Proper to be Observed in Trade," *Pennsylvania Gazette,* 20 February 1750, in Benjamin Franklin, *Writings,* ed. J. A. Leo Lemay (New York: Library of America, 1987), 345–50.

7. Thomas Hobbes, *Leviathan,* ed. Edwin Curley (Indianapolis: Hackett Publishing, 1994), chap. 15, sec. 17; Franklin, *Autobiography,* 65, 143, 158–60. Cf. John Locke, *Some Thoughts Concerning Educa-*

tion, in *The Educational Writings of John Locke*, ed. James L. Axtell (Cambridge: Cambridge University Press, 1968), sec. 109.

8. "Journal of a Voyage," 22 July 1726; *Poor Richard Improved*, 1757, in *Writings* (Lemay), 1290; cf. Franklin to Peter Collinson, 28 May 1754.

9. "Lying Shopkeepers," *Pennsylvania Gazette*, 19 November 1730, in *Writings* (Lemay), 161; *Poor Richard Improved*, 1758, ibid., 1301; "A Letter from Father Abraham to His Beloved Son" [August 1758].

10. Immanuel Kant, *Groundwork of the Metaphysic of Morals*, trans. H. J. Paton (New York: Harper Torchbooks, 1964), 77–79.

11. *Autobiography*, 150.

12. *Autobiography*, 165–66.

13. Franklin to Madame Brillon: Letter and Printed Bagatelle, 10 November 1779.

14. *Autobiography*, 181. For a sample of Franklin's painstaking agreements with his partners, see "Articles of Agreement with David Hall," 1 January 1748. For his extension of the same principle to imperial politics, see Franklin to Joseph Galloway, 18 February 1774.

15. "A Dissertation on Liberty and Necessity," 1725.

16. *Autobiography*, 64, 113–14.

17. William Wollaston does not follow it either: he asserts that the existence of virtue and vice depend upon that of God and a free will: *The Religion of Nature Delineated* (London: Samuel Palmer, 1724), 7–8.

18. This argument presented a deep challenge to Christian orthodoxy and also, as Kerry S. Walters points out, to those Deists who accepted the mechanistic teachings of modern science but took pride in human freedom: *Benjamin Franklin and His Gods* (Urbana: University of Illinois Press, 1999), 52.

19. As Douglas Anderson argues, however, this argument does not even do full justice to Franklin's motives in writing the essay and dedicating it to James Ralph, let alone to other actions of every period of his life: *The Radical Enlightenments of Benjamin Franklin* (Baltimore: Johns Hopkins University Press, 1997), 34–36.

20. Franklin to Hugh Roberts, 16 September 1758.

21. Although I find attractive the idea that this essay is largely a *reductio ad absurdum*, some evidence against it occurs in a letter probably addressed to Thomas Hopkinson [16 October 1746], in which Franklin says of the study of metaphysics, "the horrible Errors I led myself into when a young Man, by drawing a Chain of plain Consequences as I thought them, from true Principles, have given me a Disgust to what I was once extreamely fond of." In the margin of the manuscript copy he kept of the letter, Franklin wrote "Dissertation on Liberty and

Necessity" (*Papers* 3:88–89). Without presenting the essay as a *reductio ad absurdum,* Donald H. Meyer argues for its playful character in "Franklin's Religion," in Melvin H. Buxbaum, ed., *Critical Essays on Benjamin Franklin* (Boston: G. K. Hall, 1987), 155.

22. And presumably he was not confident he had shown the latter, for I think James Campbell is right that Franklin's real purpose in making the strained argument about the equal happiness of everyone is to remove any need for heaven and hell: *Recovering Benjamin Franklin* (Chicago: Open Court, 1999), 103.

23. *Autobiography,* 114.

24. Franklin to Benjamin Vaughan, 9 November 1779; cf. to Thomas Hopkinson [16 October 1746]. The essay referred to is evidently "On the Providence of God in the Government of the World" [1732], written as a Junto exercise. Franklin's genuine interest in knowing the truth about metaphysical questions, an interest he abandoned only out of a failure to find solid footing there, distinguishes him from the shallower view of many of the later utilitarians, who cannot understand how we lost our way so badly as ever to concern ourselves with such impractical questions.

25. "Men are Naturally Benevolent as Well as Selfish," *Pennsylvania Gazette,* 30 November 1732, in *Writings* (Lemay), 200–201.

26. *Autobiography,* 115, 158. Characteristically, Franklin never takes up this pair of possibilities and pushes both sides to the point where they become problematic, as Socrates does in Plato's *Euthyphro.*

27. This false inference is made by Jerry Weinberger in *Benjamin Franklin Unmasked: On the Unity of His Moral, Religious, and Political Thought* (Lawrence: University Press of Kansas, 2005), 55, with grave consequences for his understanding of Franklin's whole moral philosophy.

28. "Self-Denial Not the Essence of Virtue," 18 February 1735.

29. In his claim that nature gives us an inclination to act in sociable and benevolent ways and makes it satisfying to do so, Franklin of course reproduces an argument that was common to his time and shared by Jefferson and the "moral sense" school of the Scottish Enlightenment. In his murkiness on the question of whether we have duties that go *beyond* what natural compassion and benevolence make truly satisfying and hence prudent, Franklin likewise reproduces the murkiness of those same thinkers.

30. *Autobiography,* 115.

31. Ibid., 66.

32. Ibid., 95.

33. Ibid., 148.

34. On the importance of method in Franklin's philosophy see esp. Ralph Lerner, *The Thinking Revolutionary: Principle and Practice in the New Republic* (Ithaca: Cornell University Press, 1987), 49–50.

35. *Autobiography,* 148.

36. Franklin's success in seeming blandly to adopt the moral wisdom of the ages is seen, for example, in Robert Spiller's assessment that Franklin merely "follows closely, with a general modernization of terms, that discussed by Aristotle in the *Nicomachean Ethics,*" although even Spiller notes the absence of the Christian virtues: "Franklin on the Art of Being Human," *Proceedings of the American Philosophical Society* 100 (1956): 313.

37. "The Antediluvians Were All Very Sober"[c. 1745]; Franklin to the Abbé Morellet [after 5 July 1779].

38. *Autobiography,* 128.

39. "Old Mistresses Apologue" 25 June 1745.

40. Franklin to Madame Helvétius, [c. 1 January 1780]; to Madame Brillon, 10 March 1778.

41. *Autobiography,* 64–65, 116–17, 150–51, 158–59.

42. Ibid., 68–69, 110–11, 126–28, 214.

43. Ibid., 127.

44. The connection between Franklin's equanimity and his curiosity is suggested by David Levin in "Franklin: Experimenter in Life and Art," in Wilbur R. Jacobs, ed., *Benjamin Franklin: Statesman-Philosopher or Materialist?* (New York: Holt, Reinhart and Winston, 1972), 57–58. For examples of Franklin's amicable relations with political rivals and even enemies, see *Autobiography,* 212–13, 239, 247–48. The French friend is Pierre-Samuel Du Pont de Nemours, quoted by Walter Isaacson in *Benjamin Franklin: An American Life,* 327.

45. *Autobiography,* 148, 54.

46. *Poor Richard,* 1739, in *Writings* (Lemay), 1213; *Poor Richard Improved,* 1748, in ibid., 1247.

47. *Autobiography,* 157–58. Weinberger notes the change in *Benjamin Franklin Unmasked,* 34.

48. Franklin to William Nixon, 5 September 1781.

49. Franklin to John Franklin, 8 December 1752; to Jane Mecom, 17 July 1771; to Joseph Huey, 6 June 1753.

50. *Poor Richard Improved,* 1748.

51. *Autobiography,* 160. Cf. Franklin to George Whatley, 23 May 1785, where Franklin makes fun of an epitaph someone has written touting his own indifference to fame: "It is so natural to wish to be well spoken of, whether alive or dead, that I imagine he could not be quite exempt from that Desire; and that at least he wish'd to be thought a

Wit, or he would not have given himself the Trouble of writing so good an Epitaph to leave behind him."

52. *Autobiography,* 103.

53. As a result of this conundrum, Edwards' need for self-respect twists itself into a yearning to surpass all humanity in humility: "I cannot bear the thought of being no more humble than other Christians." But the yearning to excel grows together with and from the same root as pride: "I am greatly afflicted with a proud and self-righteous spirit. . . . I see that serpent rising and putting forth its head continually, every where, all around me": *Personal Narrative,* reprinted in David Levin, ed., *The Puritan in the Enlightenment: Franklin and Edwards* (Chicago: Rand McNally, 1963), 11–12.

54. It is this difference, rooted in Franklin's identification of virtue with enlightened self-interest, that is insufficiently appreciated by those who assimilate Franklin's moral outlook to Puritanism, above all Perry Miller, who writes that Franklin abandoned only the "theological preoccupation" of his New England forbears without "in the slightest ceasing to be a Puritan," retaining the same "disinterested devotion to a noble cause" and showing himself even "more pessimistic about the human species than the rigid Calvinist": "Benjamin Franklin—Jonathan Edwards," in Miller, ed., *Major Writers of America,* 2 vols. (New York: Harcourt, Brace, and World, 1962), 86–88. Likewise David L. Parker exaggerates the importance of Franklin's confessed errata and concludes, "The most important difference between Franklin and his Puritan forbears is not so much in their views of human nature as in their reactions to those views," the Puritans focusing on the next world and Franklin on this: "Sound Believer to Practical Preparationist," in J. A. Leo Lemay, ed., *The Oldest Revolutionary: Essays on Benjamin Franklin* (Philadelphia: University of Pennsylvania Press, 1976), 74. The depth of the difference is perhaps seen best in what John Griffith observes of Franklin's remarkable self-acceptance: "One reads his collected writings from end to end without seeing a trace of serious self-doubt, self-loathing, self-anger, or any other radical form of intrapsychic conflict and anxiety": "The Man Behind the Masks," in ibid., 131.

55. Franklin to William Strahan, 29 November 1769; speech in the Constitutional Convention, 17 September 1787, in Max Farrand, ed., *The Records of the Federal Convention of 1787,* 4 vols. (New Haven: Yale University Press, 1966), 2:641–42; cf. Franklin to Peter Collinson, 14 August 1747.

56. Franklin to John Perkins, 4 February 1753.

57. *Autobiography,* 243–44; cf. Franklin to [Lebègue de Presle], 4 October 1777. See also Franklin's assessments of General John

Loudon, Governor William Shirley, and Ferdinando John Paris in *Autobiography,* 253–54, 263.

58. *Autobiography,* 155–56. For more detailed reflections on how Franklin manages his vast vanity throughout the *Autobiography,* see J. A. Leo Lemay, "The Theme of Vanity in Franklin's *Autobiography,* in J. A. Leo Lemay, ed., *Reappraising Benjamin Franklin* (Newark: University of Delaware Press, 1993), 372–87.

59. Cotton Mather, *Bonifacius, or An Essay upon the Good,* ed. David Levin (1710; Cambridge: Harvard University Press, 1966), 11.

60. Steven Forde makes this point nicely in "Benjamin Franklin's *Autobiography* and the Education of America," *American Political Science Review* 86 no. 2 (1992): 365.

61. *Autobiography,* 44, 75, 143.

62. "On Censure or Backbiting," *Pennsylvania Gazette,* 7 September 1732, in *Writings* (Lemay), 192–95. Although here it suits his purpose to claim that everyone hates backbiting, in a subsequent letter, signed "Alice Addertongue," (12 September 1732) whose gossipy kitchen soirées have drained all attendants from her mother's high-minded parlor soirées, he reveals that he also knows just how delicious it can be to listen to. For a different Franklinian perspective on backbiting, cf. Franklin to Jared Eliot, 12 September 1751.

63. Cf. Cotton Mather, *Bonifacius,* 38.

64. Franklin to Lord Kames, 3 May 1760.

65. "Dialogue Between the Gout and Mr. Franklin," 22 October 1780, *The Writings of Benjamin Franklin,* ed. Albert Henry Smyth, 10 vols. (New York: Macmillan, 1907), 8:154–62.

66. "A Letter from Father Abraham, to His Beloved Son" [August 1758].

67. Ibid.; Franklin to Joseph Priestley, 19 September 1772.

68. Franklin to O[liver] N[eave], [before 1769].

69. A further difference between Franklin and Aristotle is that Aristotle acknowledges a need to clarify what virtue demands, and this need appears more important the more closely one reads the *Nicomachean Ethics.*

70. *Autobiography,* 153.

71. "A Man of Sense," 11 February 1735.

72. Franklin to William Franklin, 16 August 1784. So bitter was Franklin towards William and the other loyalists that in 1782 he threatened to scuttle the whole peace treaty with England rather than allow it to include American compensation for confiscated loyalist property. For a fascinating account of this aspect of the peace negotiations, see Walter Isaacson, *Benjamin Franklin,* 412–15. For an account of William's

perspective and his efforts to undermine the independence movement and help the loyalists, see Sheila L. Skemp, *Benjamin and William Franklin: Father and Son, Patriot and Loyalist* (Boston: St. Martin's Press, 1994), esp. 134–52.

73. "A Man of Sense," 11 February 1735.

74. *Poor Richard,* 1733.

75. *Poor Richard,* 1733, 1734, 1735, and 1736.

76. *Poor Richard Improved,* 1758. It is the intimate connection between Franklin's humor and his serious message that is missed both by commentators like Weber who see in the almanacs only smug moralism and those like Cameron Nickels who find there an ironic undercutting of moralism: "Poor Richard's Almanacs," in J. A. Leo Lemay, ed., *The Oldest Revolutionary,* 77–89. Nickels' error is shared by Gordon Wood and Patrick Sullivan, who, in interpreting "The Way to Wealth," observe the irony but not the importance of the story's end: Wood, *The Americanization of Benjamin Franklin* (New York: Penguin Books, 2004), 84; Sullivan, "Benjamin Franklin, the Inveterate (and Crafty) Public Instructor: Two Levels in 'The Way to Wealth,'" *Early American Literature* 21 (1986–87): 248–59.

77. "Slippery Sidewalks," 11 January 1733.

Chapter 3 Philanthropy and Civil Associations

1. "The Busy-Body," no. 3, 18 February 1729.

2. Ibid.

3. "Journal of a Voyage," 25 August 1726.

4. *Autobiography,* 58. Mather's book, according to the historian Perry Miller, was "possibly the most important work of the early eighteenth century": *From Colony to Province* (Cambridge: Harvard University Press, 1953), 410. For a discussion of the work's religious purpose and the way in which it was taken over and subverted by Franklin, see Robert E. Spiller, "Franklin on the Art of Being Human," *Proceedings of the American Philosophical Society* 100 (1956): 310.

5. Cotton Mather, *Bonifacius, or An Essay upon the Good,* ed. David Levin (1710; Cambridge: Harvard University Press, 1966), esp. 9, 25, 32, 61–68, 132–37.

6. Alexis de Tocqueville, *Democracy in America,* trans. and ed. Harvey C. Mansfield and Delba Winthrop (Chicago: University of Chicago Press, 2000), vol. 1, part 2, chap. 4, p. 180.

7. As Edmund Morgan points out, the dysfunctional passivity of the Pennsylvania and Philadelphia governments in the eighteenth century left Franklin a fallow field for such endeavors: *Benjamin Franklin* (New Haven: Yale Universtiy Press, 2002), 54, 61.

8. Tocqueville, *Democracy in America,* vol. 2, part 2, chap. 5, p. 489.
9. Ibid., chap. 2, pp. 482–83.
10. Ibid., 483–84.
11. Ibid., chap. 4, pp. 486–87.
12. Ibid, chap. 5, pp. 491–92.
13. *Autobiography,* 118.
14. Compare Mather, *Bonifacius,* 66 and 136–37, with Franklin, "Standing Queries for the Junto," 1732, and "Proposals and Queries to be Asked the Junto," 1732.
15. Mather, *Bonifacius,* 68; Franklin, "Rules for a Club," 206–7.
16. *Autobiography,* 130–31.
17. Ibid., 170–71, 173.
18. Ibid., 161–63.
19. Franklin to Peter Collinson, 26 June 1755; to Cadwallader Evans, 7 September 1769; "Reply to Coffee-House Orators" [9 April 1767]; to Henry Laurens, 12 February 1784.
20. Franklin to [Richard Price], 13 June 1782.
21. Tocqueville, *Democracy in America,* vol. 2, part 2, chap. 6, p. 493.
22. "Apology for Printers," 10 June 1731; but cf. *Autobiography,* 165.
23. *Autobiography,* 165.
24. "The Busy-Body," no. 5, 4 March 1729.
25. Franklin to the *Federal Gazette,* 12 September 1789.
26. See, for example, "Cecelia Single," 24 July 1732; "Query to the Casuist: A Case of Conscience" with replies, 26 June and 3 July, 1732.
27. "Extracts from the *Gazette,* 1729," 23 October 1729; "Extracts from the *Gazette,* 1745," 6 June 1745; "Variant Accounts of a Battle," *Pennsylvania Gazette,* 19 December 1734, in Benjamin Franklin, *Writings,* ed. J. A. Leo Lemay (New York: Library of America, 1987), 235–39. Franklin also encouraged the practice of withholding judgment, as when he informed his readers, "The News of the taking of Porto Bello is confirm'd from all Parts, but the Accounts of the Action are so various, that we chuse not to insert any of them, and wait for one that may be depended on": "Extracts from the *Gazette,* 1740," 20 March 1740.
28. *Autobiography,* 173–74. To be more precise, the bill was passed when Franklin himself became an alderman: see *Papers* 4:37–32.
29. *Autobiography,* 174–75.
30. Franklin's first attempt to found an academy in 1743, related in the *Autobiography* (181–82), came to nothing and his proposal of that year does not survive. He tried again with greater success with his "Proposals relating to the Education of Youth in Philadelphia," 13 Septem-

ber 1749 (for which he laid the groundwork on 24 August of that year by reprinting a letter of Pliny the Younger on education) and with his "Idea of the English School," 7 January 1751. For a fuller discussion of Franklin's proposals for the academy and the somewhat different reality that emerged, see Lorraine Smith Pangle and Thomas L. Pangle, *The Learning of Liberty: The Educational Ideas of the American Founders* (Lawrence: University Press of Kansas, 1993), chap. 4.

31. Franklin to Samuel Johnson, 23 August 1750. On Franklin's lack of mathematical training see Franklin to Cadwallader Colden, 12 April 1753. On the public importance of education see also "Paper on the Academy," 31 July 1750, and the opening of "Proposals relating to the Education of Youth in Philadelphia."

32. "Proposals relating to the Education of Youth in Philadelphia."

33. "From Benjamin Franklin: Tract Relative to the English School in Philadelphia," June 1789.

34. Franklin to Samuel Johnson, 24 December 1751. Consider likewise that the formal "Constitutions of the Academy of Philadelphia" [13 November 1749] contains no mention of God.

35. The case for breaking with precedent and emphasizing the study of English is made in the pages of the proposal that are most filled with learned footnotes and references to the practice of antiquity.

36. "Proposals relating to the Education of Youth in Philadelphia," quoting sec. 210 of Locke's *Some Thoughts Concerning Education,* in *The Educational Writings of John Locke,* ed. James L. Axtell (Cambridge: Cambridge University Press, 1968).

37. *Autobiography,* 166–67.

38. "Proposals relating to the Education of Youth in Philadelphia."

39. "Idea of the English School."

40. "Proposals relating to the Education of Youth in Philadelphia." On emulation see also "Idea of the English School"; "College of Philadelphia: Additional Charter [14 May 1755].

41. "Proposals relating to the Education of Youth in Philadelphia."

42. "A Proposal for Promoting Useful Knowledge," 14 May 1743. For a good discussion of Franklin's thoughts on the importance of publicity for science and the place of scientific advancement in a democracy, see James Campbell, *Recovering Benjamin Franklin* (Chicago: Open Court), 83–89.

43. *Autobiography,* 191–92. David Levin nicely brings out the importance of a spirit of open-minded experimentation for Franklin's whole life project in "Franklin: Experimenter in Life and Art," in Wilbur R. Jacobs, ed., *Benjamin Franklin: Statesman-Philosopher or Materialist?* (New York: Holt, Reinhart and Winston, 1972), esp. 56–57.

44. "Queries on a Pennsylvania Militia," 6 March 1734, *Writings,* 224.

45. "Plain Truth," 17 November 1747.

46. Ibid.

47. Ibid.; "Form of Association," 24 November 1747.

48. Thomas Penn to Lynford Lardner, 29 March 1748, quoted in *Papers of Benjamin Franklin* 3:186.

49. Penn to Richard Peters, 30 March and 9 June 1748, quoted in ibid., 186.

50. "Journal of a Voyage," 27 July 1726.

51. "Form of Association," 24 November 1747; "A Dialogue Between X, Y, and Z," 18 December 1755.

52. *Autobiography,* 159–60. On the way Franklin made an asset of his poor abilities as an orator, see also Morgan, *Benjamin Franklin,* 60.

53. *Autobiography,* 163, 126 144.

54. Mather, *Bonifacius,* 32.

55. Ibid., 10–11.

56. *Democracy in America,* vol. 1, part 2, chap. 5, p. 189.

57. *Autobiography,* 67.

58. Ibid., 143.

59. Thomas Jefferson to Robert Walsh, 4 December 1818, in Julian P. Boyd et al., eds., *The Papers of Thomas Jefferson* (Princeton: Princeton University Press, 1950–), 18:169.

60. Richard Peters to the Pennsylvania Proprietors, 29 November 1747, quoted in Franklin, *Papers* 3:216.

61. *Autobiography,* 199–201.

62. Ibid., 216; "Advertisement for Wagons," 26 April 1755.

63. *Autobiography,* 172; cf. Aristotle *Nicomachean Ethics* 9.7; and Franklin to Lord Howe, 20 July 1776, where he writes that America will have a hard time forgiving England for its cruelty, but England will never be able to forgive the people she has so heavily injured and trust them again as subjects.

64. Most radically, Jerry Weinberger in his book *Benjamin Franklin Unmasked: On the Unity of His Moral, Religious, and Political Thought,* the thesis of which is that "the entire moral saga depicted in the *Autobiography*" is a fraud and that Franklin never believed in virtue at all ([Lawrence: University Press of Kansas, 2005], 7, 55, 65, 67, 141–42, 206, 219–20). Of modern writers, only Cecil Curry has taken this thought to its logical conclusion and charged Franklin, preposterously, with treachery to the American cause: *Code Number 72: Ben Franklin: Patriot or Spy?* (Englewood Cliffs, N.J.: Prentice-Hall, 1972).

65. John Griffith gives a good corrective to the tendency to make too

much of Franklin's masks, pointing out that in all his famous posturings, such as the wheelbarrow in Philadelphia and the fur cap in London, "one readily sees the rhetorical motive . . . ; they are rather more obvious than devious." Griffith concludes that in all important respects Franklin seems in fact to have taken Poor Richard's advice: "What you would seem to be, be really": "The Man Behind the Masks," in J. A. Leo Lemay, ed., *The Oldest Revolutionary: Essays on Benjamin Franklin* (Philadelphia: University of Pennsylvania Press, 1976), 135–36. In contrast, Paul Rahe writes that Franklin's "very candor is a disguise for his guile." Yet Rahe suggests that Franklin's motives were in fact profoundly generous, and his guile was used chiefly to teach, following Pope's dictum that "Men should be taught as if you taught them not": *Republics Ancient and Modern: Classical Republicanism and the American Revolution* (Chapel Hill: University of North Carolina Press, 1992), 327, 330. It was the fact of his teaching (or if you will, his seduction of us), and not its substantive content, that Franklin loved to conceal.

66. Franklin to Jane Mecom, 1 March 1776.

67. Franklin to Joseph Galloway, 8 November 1766.

Chapter 4 Thoughts on Government

1. After all, as Franklin has Poor Richard warn him in his last installment, "The first mistake in public business, is the going into it": *Poor Richard Improved,* 1758, in Benjamin Franklin, *Writings,* ed. J. A. Leo Lemay (New York: Library of America, 1987), 1303.

2. The American Commissioners to the Committee of Secret Correspondence, 12 March[–9 April] 1777.

3. For more instances of Franklin's attachment to simplicity, see Paul Conner's chapter on "Republican Simplicity" in *Poor Richard's Politicks: Franklin and His New American Order* (New York: Oxford University Press, 1965).

4. Franklin to James Parker, 20 March 1751.

5. There has been some dispute about the degree of Franklin's responsibility for the final plan. Robert Newbold discusses this and makes the case for Franklin's authorship in *The Albany Congress and Plan of Union* (New York: Vantage Press, 1955), esp. 103–5.

6. "Reasons and Motives for the Albany Plan of Union" [July 1754].

7. *Pennsylvania Gazette,* 9 May 1754, in *Writings* (Lemay), 377.

8. *Autobiography,* 210–11, quoting John Dryden's translation, lines 1–2, of Juvenal's tenth *Satire,* lines 1–3.

9. *A Plan for Settling Two Western Colonies,* 1754. For an excellent account of Franklin's realism in international politics in this period, see

Gerald Stourzh, *Benjamin Franklin and American Foreign Policy,* 2nd ed. (Chicago: University of Chicago Press, 1969), chap. 2.

10. "Reasons and Motives for the Albany Plan of Union."

11. *Autobiography,* 261–62.

12. "Reasons and Motives for the Albany Plan of Union."

13. Ibid.

14. "Causes of the American Discontents before 1768," 5–7 January 1768; to Samuel Cooper, 8 June 1770; Stourzh, *Benjamin Franklin and American Foreign Policy,* 28. Cf. "Marginalia in *An Inquiry,* an Anonymous Pamphlet" [1770]: "the arbitrary Government of a single Person is more eligible than the arbitrary Government of a Body of Men. A single Man may be afraid or asham'd of doing Injustice. A Body is never either one or the other, if it is strong enough. It cannot apprehend Assassination, and by dividing the Shame among them, it is so Little apiece, that no one minds it."

15. Franklin to William Shirley, 4 December 1754. As Gordon Wood points out, in *The Americanization of Benjamin Franklin* ([New York: Penguin Books, 2004], pp. 77–78), it is striking that Franklin would make such complaints to a man who was himself such an appointed governor. Wood suspects that this letter was never sent and perhaps composed only later, during the struggle for independence. Perhaps, but Franklin was given to such boldness, as his leadership in the Pennsylvania Assembly's altercations with Governor Robert Morris and the proprietors throughout the 1750s makes clear.

16. "Causes of the American Discontents before 1768," 5–7 January 1768.

17. "Reasons and Motives for the Albany Plan of Union," 9 February 1789. On the poor prospects for establishing a continental union by any means other than an act of Parliament, see especially Franklin to James Parker, 20 March 1751.

18. Edward Samuel Corwin praises the Albany Plan as Franklin's greatest contribution to American constitutional law: "Franklin and the Constitution," *Proceedings of the American Philosophical Society* 100 (1956): 283. Andrew McLaughlin writes, "The significance of these proposals lies not so much in their suggestions for a method of saving the old empire as in their *indication* of the route that was to be followed in later years": *Constitutional History of the United States* (New York: Appleton-Century, 1935), 20–21.

19. *Autobiography,* 214; cf. 239.

20. For a good account of this struggle and Franklin's errors in pursuing it, see Edmund S. Morgan, *Benjamin Franklin* (New Haven: Yale University Press, 2002), 104–44. For a sample of Franklin's scathingly

logical rebuttals of the proprietors' specious arguments in defense of their claims, see "Pennsylvania Assembly Committee: Report on the Proprietors' Answer," 11 September 1753.

21. See "Revisions of the Pennsylvania Declaration of Rights" [between 29 July and 15 August 1776].

22. Franklin to Sarah Bache, 26 January 1784.

23. "Observations Concerning the Increase of Mankind," 1751; cf. Franklin to Lord Kames, 3 January 1760.

24. See, for example, Franklin's "A Friend to both Countries" [23 January 1766].

25. Franklin to the Printer of the *London Chronicle,* 9 May 1759.

26. "'N. N.' First Reply to Vindex Patriae," 28 December 1765; cf. "The Rise and Present State of Our Misunderstandings," 6–8 November 1770.

27. Franklin to the Printer of the *London Chronicle,* 9 May 1759; "On Railing and Reviling," 6 January 1768; see also Franklin to Lord Kames, 25 February 1767.

28. "'N. N.' First Reply to Vindex Patriae," 28 December 1765.

29. "Reply to Coffee-House Orators," 9 April 1767.

30. "Extract from a Pamphlet," 9 April 1767; cf. Franklin to the Massachusetts House of Representatives Committee of Correspondence, 15 May 1771.

31. "On Railing and Reviling," 6 January 1768.

32. Franklin to Richard Jackson, 14 March 1764.

33. Franklin to Thomas Cushing, 15 February 1774.

34. "Homespun: Further Defense of Indian Corn" [15 January 1766].

35. Franklin to *The Public Ledger* [after 9 March 1774]; "Subjects of Subjects" [January 1768]; to [Joseph Priestley], 7 July 1775. For an excellent summary of the British vices and errors that in Franklin's mind were the chief cause of the Revolution, and of the centrality of pride among them, see Jack P. Greene, "Pride, Prejudice, and Jealousy: Benjamin Franklin's Explanation for the American Revolution," in J. A. Leo Lemay, ed., *Reappraising Benjamin Franklin,* 119–42.

36. "Rules by which a Great Empire May be Reduced to a Small One," 11 September 1773; "An Edict by the King of Prussia," 22 September 1773; for other examples of angry sarcasm see esp. "'Pacifus': Pax Quaeritur Bello," 23 January 1766, and "Petition to the House of Commons," 12 April 1766.

37. Franklin to Richard Jackson, 14 March 1764; to Joseph Galloway, 9 January 1769 and 20 April 1771; John Locke, *Second Treatise of Government,* secs. 95, 112, 116, 118–19, 134, 138–42; 175; David

Hume, "Of the First Principles of Government," in *Essays: Moral, Political and Literary,* edited by Eugene Miller (Indianapolis: Liberty Classics, 1985), 32–36.

38. This ambiguity leaves Franklin open to the charge of those like Esmond Wright who have found in him no concern for right at all: "Neither in America in 1776 nor in Paris after 1776 did he see the issue as one of justice; his concern was not with ends, but with means": *Franklin of Philadelphia* (Cambridge: Harvard University Press, 1986), 351.

39. Franklin to William Shirley, 4 December 1754.

40. "Causes of the American Discontents before 1768," 5–7 January 1768.

41. Ibid. David Morgan, in one of the most unfair or confused interpretations of Franklin, conflates his concern for public opinion with a cynical concern for nothing but "popularity," castigating his efforts to smooth the waters as a dishonorable attempt to "ingratiate himself to people on both sides of the Atlantic," and his advice to make the best of the Stamp Act (as in a letter to John Hughes of 9 August 1765) as a decision "to take as much practical advantage of it as he could": *The Devious Dr. Franklin: Benjamin Franklin's Years in London* (Macon: Mercer University Press, 1996), 97, 103, 105.

42. Franklin to George Whitefield [before 2 September 1769], italics added.

43. Franklin to Thomas Cushing, 4 June 1773. But this remark also contains an interesting note of indignation that Franklin's sophisticated prudence does not fully explain.

44. "Proposals and Queries to be Asked the Junto" [1732].

45. Edmund Morgan, *Benjamin Franklin,* 143.

46. See Franklin to Samuel Cooper, 8 June 1770; to Thomas Cushing, 10 June 1771; to William Franklin, 6 October 1773.

47. "Right, Wrong, and Reasonable," 18 April 1767; "Queries," 16–18 August 1768.

48. "Causes of the American Discontents before 1768," 5–7 January 1768; "On a Proposed Act to Prevent Emigration [December? 1773]; cf. "Subjects of Subjects" [January 1768].

49. Franklin to the Massachusetts House of Representatives, 7 July 1773.

50. "Magnia Brittania: Her Colonies Reduc'd," 1774; cf. Franklin to Peter Collinson, 28 May 1754; "Causes of the American Discontents before 1768," 5–7 January 1768; "Tract Relative to the Affair of Hutchinson's Letters" [1774].

51. "The Interest of Great Britain Considered," 1760; cf. Franklin to

Thomas Cushing, 4 June 1773. Stourzh also notes this contradiction, but understands it solely as a problem of rhetoric: *Benjamin Franklin and American Foreign Policy,* 90–91.

52. "The Interest of Great Britain Considered," 1760, italics added.

53. "Notes on Parliamentary Precedents" [1765–75].

54. "Subjects of Subjects" [January 1768]. On virtual representation see also "'N. N.': First Reply to Vindex Patriae," 28 December 1765.

55. Locke, *Second Treatise of Government,* sec. 138; cf. sec. 143.

56. "'N. N.': On the Tenure of the Manor of East Greenwich," 6 January 1766; cf. "Preface to the Declaration of the Boston Town Meeting [February 1773].

57. Franklin to William Strahan, 29 November 1769.

58. Franklin to Samuel Cooper, 8 June 1770.

59. Lord Dartmouth to Franklin, 2 June 1773.

60. Franklin to the Massachusetts House of Representatives, 7 July 1773.

61. Franklin to the Massachusetts House of Representatives Committee of Correspondence, 15 May 1771.

62. Franklin to Samuel Cooper, 8 June 1770; cf. Franklin to William Franklin, 13 March 1768.

63. Franklin to Cadwalader Evans, 9 May 1766; cf. Franklin to William Shirley, 22 December 1754; to an unknown recipient, 6 January 1766; to Lord Kames, 25 February 1767.

64. Franklin to Joseph Galloway, 25 February 1775; cf. Franklin to Joshua Babcock, 13 January 1772; "Reply to Vindex Patriae on American Representation in Parliament" [29 January 1766].

65. Franklin to Lord Howe, 20 July 1776.

66. Ibid.; to Joseph Priestley, 27 January 1777.

67. "A Description of Those, Who, at Any Rate, Would Have a Peace with France," 24 November [1759]; cf. "On the Means Of Disposing the Enemie to Peace" [13 August 1761].

68. Franklin to Mary Stevenson Hewson, 27 January 1783; to Sir Joseph Banks, 27 July 1783; cf. Franklin to Richard Price, 6 February 1780.

69. Franklin to Joseph Priestley, 27 January 1777; to Charles Pettit, 10 October 1786; to Jane Mecom, 20 September 1787.

70. "Pennsylvania Assembly: Reply to the Governor," 11 November 1755; to James Hutton, 24 March 1778; cf. Franklin to [Charles de Weissenstein], 1 July 1778; to David Hartley, 2 February 1780, where he reiterates the view that "there has hardly ever existed such a Thing as a bad Peace—or a good War," yet adds, "I should think the Destruction of our whole Country, and the Extirpation of our whole People,

preferable to the Infamy of abandoning our Allies"; and to David Hartley, 15 January 1782.

71. Franklin to Arthur Lee, 21 March 1777; to Dumas [22 September 1778]; to John Adams, 2 October 1780; to Francis Dana, 7 April 1781; to Robert Morris, 23 December 1782. See also Paul Wentworth's account of Franklin's reluctance to rely on French aid, quoted in Stourzh, *Benjamin Franklin and American Foreign Policy,* 133–34. The desire to hold aloof from the corrupt diplomacy and wars of Europe was first voiced by Thomas Paine in *Common Sense* (Philadelphia: R. Bell, 1776) and soon reiterated by Adams as well as Franklin. For an account of that corruption, see Samuel Flagg Bemis, in *Diplomacy of the American Revolution* (Bloomington: Indiana University Press, 1965), 13–15. The radical departure of the American plan from customary practice and the risk it entailed for the new nation are noted by Bemis in ibid. (48) and discussed by Felix Gilbert, *To the Farewell Address: Ideas of Early American Foreign Policy* (Princeton: Princeton University Press, 1961), 1–54.

72. Franklin to Thomas Cushing, 27 February 1778.

73. Franklin to Samuel Huntington, 9 August 1780.

74. Franklin to Robert R. Livingston, 4 March 1782; cf. Franklin and Silas Deane to the President of Congress, 8 February 1778. For an analysis of how the considerable generosity of France served her own public relations interests, see Bemis, *Diplomacy of the American Revolution,* 65, 73.

75. Franklin to Charles Thomson, 13 May 1784; cf. Franklin to Samuel Cooper, 26 December 1782; to Samuel Mather, 12 May 1784. It is the convergence of moral and prudential considerations in Franklin's diplomatic thinking, as in his thinking generally, that is given insufficient weight by Felix Gilbert in his influential book *To the Farewell Address,* where he argues that Franklin and the other revolutionary leaders were torn between utopian "idealism" and "realism" about power politics in their foreign policy. At the root of this error is an inclination to identify the most politically important strain of "idealism" in early America with religious separatist and utopian movements and not with the enlightenment philosophy of Locke and Montesquieu, who cede nothing to anyone in their appreciation of the importance of power but who teach that the world can be transformed to make power more benign. The convergence of moral and prudential considerations and the influence of European liberalism are neglected even more by James H. Hutson, who claims that the Founders were governed not at all by "enlightenment" ideals and entirely by mercantilist principles and considerations of power: "Intellectual Foundations of Early American Diplo-

macy," *Diplomatic History* 1 (1977): 1–19. In contrast, Stourzh gives a careful and nuanced account of the convergence and interplay of realism and gratitude in Franklin's attitude towards France in *Benjamin Franklin and American Foreign Policy,* chap. 5, although he is more inclined than I am to regard Franklin's moral expressions as merely rhetorical.

76. At least Vergennes thought helping America to be in France's interest, and in the end he persuaded the king. For an account of his arguments and Turgot's strong reservations, see Bemis, *Diplomacy of the American Revolution,* chap. 2.

77. *Journal of Peace Negotiations,* 9 May–1 July 1782.

78. Jefferson to Robert Walsh, 4 December 1818, in *The Writings of Thomas Jefferson* (Washington, D.C.: Thomas Jefferson Memorial Association, 1905), 15:176. Stourzh gives an excellent account of Franklin's use of goodwill at crucial junctures, in *Benjamin Franklin and American Foreign Policy,* 163–64, 178.

79. Franklin to [Juliana Ritchie], 19 January 1777. For a full account of the astonishing degree to which the American embassy to Paris was riddled with spies, see Stacy Schiff, *A Great Improvisation: Franklin, France, and the Birth of America* (New York: Henry Holt, 2005), chap. 3. For a contrasting view on the importance of secrecy, however, see Franklin to James Lovell, 22 July 1778.

80. For Franklin's statement on the open, forthright character that is best for a diplomat, see Benjamin Vaughan to Lord Shelburne, 28 January 1783, quoted in Stourzh, *Benjamin Franklin and American Foreign Policy,* 236.

81. For good accounts of these dealings, see Walter Isaacson, *Benjamin Franklin: An American Life* (New York: Simon and Schuster, 2003), 344–46, and Schiff, *A Great Improvisation,* 112–32. Bernard Bailyn notes the striking combination of Franklin's seemingly "bland and righteous innocence" in the face of potential spies and the craftiness with which he actually used the impressions that his open dealings were giving each side. He concludes, "Franklin's slack behavior became an adroit maneuver—half contrived, half the lucky product of his casual ways—which strengthened France's support of America while it inhibited Britain's war effort": *Realism and Idealism in American Diplomacy: The Origins* (Princeton: Institute for Advanced Study, 1994), 12–13.

82. That it was Franklin and not his younger colleagues who took the initiative in treating separately with Britain is demonstrated by Bemis in *Diplomacy of the American Revolution,* 206–9.

83. For his masterful handling of this delicate moment, see Franklin

to Vergennes, 17 December 1782. Jonathan R. Dull incisively describes it, "The provisional Anglo-American agreement of 30 November 1782 is a marvel of Jesuitical evasion. As it was conditional on a general agreement, it did not technically violate the terms of either the French alliance or the American peace commissioners' instructions from Congress": "Benjamin Franklin and the Nature of American Diplomacy," in Melvin H. Buxbaum, ed. *Critical Essays on Benjamin Franklin* (Boston: G. K. Hall, 1987), 84. While recent scholars agree in considering Vergennes to have been out-maneuvered by Franklin in these negotiations (consider Schiff, *A Great Improvisation*, 321), Bemis, without slighting Franklin's achievement, takes a different view of Vergennes in *Diplomacy of the American Revolution*, 239–44, 255–56.

84. Franklin to the Committee of Secret Correspondence, 12 March 1777; cf. Franklin to Samuel Cooper, 1 May 1777. Schiff regards the former as just a typical piece of strategic Franklinian exaggeration: *A Great Improvisation*, 64.

85. To Edmund Burke, 15 October 1781.

86. Franklin to All Captains and Commanders of American Armed Ships, 10 March 1779; to Sir Edward Newenham, 12 February 1781; to David Hartley, 8 May 1783.

87. Franklin to John Torris, 30 May 1780; cf. Franklin to the President of Congress, 31 May 1780, in which prudent concerns for avoiding enmity and litigation are stressed. For a history of the gradual acceptance of these principles in Europe, and states' self-interested motives for promoting them, see Bemis, *Diplomacy of the American Revolution*, chap. 10.

88. Franklin to Robert Morris, 3 June 1780; cf. "Franklin's Thoughts on Privateering and the Sugar Islands: Two Essays," 10 July 1782; and Franklin to Benjamin Vaughan, 10 July 1782, where he hopes that once protection for noncombatants is an established principle, "that Encouragement to war which arises from a Spirit of Rapine would be taken away, and Peace therefore more likely to continue & be lasting." Gregg Lint examines the efforts of Franklin and his colleagues to transform international law and some of the reasons for their immediate failure, but without recognizing the power of the new philosophy that put natural right in place of the old natural law—and that underlay the steady acceptance of those American principles in subsequent years: "The American Revolution and the Law of Nations, 1776–1789," *Diplomatic History* 1 (1977): 20–34.

89. Franklin to John Torris, 30 May 1780; to Robert Morris, 3 June 1780; to Charles W. F. Dumas, 5 June 1780; to Richard Oswald, 14 January 1783; to Benjamin Vaughan, 14 March 1785; on his hopes

for world improvement see Franklin to William Vaughan, 9 December 1788.

90. Oswald to Shelburne, 18 May 1782, quoted in Stourzh, *Benjamin Franklin and American Foreign Policy,* 224.

91. Franklin to Rodolphe-Ferdinand Grand, 22 October 1787.

92. Franklin to William Franklin, 22 March 1775. See also the Continental Congress's 1774 "Appeal to the Inhabitants of Quebec," detailing how the Quebec Act failed to guarantee basic liberties, in Charles S. Hyneman, and Donald S. Lutz, eds. *American Political Writings during the Founding Era, 1760–1805,* 2 vols. (Indianapolis: Liberty Press, 1983), 1:231–39. For a contrasting view, see Reginald Coupland, *The Quebec Act: A Study in Statesmanship* (Oxford: Clarendon Press, 1968).

93. Journal of John Baynes, 23 September 1783, in John Bigelow, ed., *The Complete Works of Benjamin Franklin,* Federal Edition, 12 vols. (New York: G. P. Putnam's Sons, 1904), 10:250–51. On 2 October 1783 Baynes reports Franklin's speculation that the exhaustion of European wars may eventually produce the same result (10:253).

94. Franklin to Samuel Cooper, 1 May 1777. Leo Strauss raises this question and implicitly suggests that some such quasi-religious tendency may pervade the whole of the purportedly sober modern project: *The City and Man* (Chicago: University of Chicago Press, 1964), 3–6.

95. Max Farrand, *The Records of the Federal Convention of 1787,* 4 vols. (New Haven: Yale University Press, 1966), 3:540. The 1776 Pennsylvania constitution may be found in Francis Newton Thorpe, ed. *The Federal and State Constitutions, Colonial Charters, and Other Organic Laws of The States, Territories, and Colonies Now or Heretofore Forming the United States of America,* 7 vols. (Washington, D.C., U.S. Government Printing Office, 1909), vol. 5, although no records remain of the proceedings. The only article known for certain to have come from Franklin's pen is Article 36, prohibiting salaries that would make any state office "so profitable as to occasion many to apply for it" (5:3090).

96. Farrand, *Records,* 1:85. See also Farrand's unflattering assessment of Franklin's role, in *The Framing of the Constitution of the United States* (New Haven: Yale University Press, 1913), 199–200; Bernard Fay, *Franklin, Apostle of Modern Times* (Boston: Little, Brown, 1929), 504, which characterizes Franklin as an advocate of "lost causes"; Hastings Lyon, *The Constitution and the Men Who Made It* (Boston: Houghton-Mifflin, 1936), 73, which portrays him as out of step with the times; and David Schoenbrun, *Triumph in Paris: The Exploits of Benjamin Franklin* (New York: Harper and Row, 1976), 394, which claims, "The Constitution was drafted with only minor contributions by . . . the sick

old man." For contrasting assessments, see Irving Brandt, *James Madison: Father of the Constitution* (New York, Bobbs-Merrill, 1950), 159; and William G. Carr, *The Oldest Delegate: Franklin in the Constitutional Convention* (Newark: University of Delaware Press, 1990), 20–22. Carr calculates that of twenty-six proposals offered or supported by Franklin at the convention, sixteen were approved (131).

97. Albany Plan of Union, 1754, *Writings* (Lemay), 380.

98. Farrand, *Records,* 1:200.

99. Recorded by John Adams in *The Adams Papers, Series I: Diaries,* ed. L. H. Butterfield, 4 vols. (Cambridge: Harvard University Press, 1961), 2:245.

100. "Protest Against the First Draft of the Articles of Confederation," 19 August 1776; see also Franklin's unsent letters to William Strahan of 5 July 1775 and to Arthur Lee of 3 April 1778.

101. Farrand, *Records,* 1:507.

102. Ibid., 1:48; cf. Franklin to Louis-Guillaume Le Veillard, 22 April 1788.

103. Charles Beard judged that Franklin had "a more hopeful view of democracy than any other member" of the constitutional convention: *An Economic Interpretation of the Constitution* (New York: Macmillan, 1935), 197.

104. The horse and cart analogy is quoted by Vernon Louis Parrington in "Franklin: An Early Social Scientist," 34. On the snake, see "Queries and Remarks on 'Hints for the Members of Pennsylvania Convention,'" 3 November 1789.

105. Farrand, *Records,* 2:204–5, 249. Clinton Rossiter calls Franklin's victory on this point "one of his finest moments": *1787: The Grand Convention* (New York: Macmillan, 1968), 213.

106. Farrand, *Records,* 2:249, 1:98–99.

107. Franklin to William Franklin, 22 March 1775; note the belief in "voluntary error"—an idea Franklin elsewhere repudiates—creeping into his declamations against the willful perversion of truth. Cf. Franklin to Richard Price, 9 October 1780.

108. Farrand, *Records,* 1:82; cf. Franklin to Jonathan Shipley, 17 March 1783; to Henry Laurens, 12 February 1784; to William Strahan, 16 February and 19 August 1784.

109. Farrand, *Records,* 1:84.

110. For an interesting comment on the madness of the Pennsylvania Assembly's contests with Governor Robert Morris, see Franklin to Peter Collinson, 26 June 1755.

111. "Pennsylvania Assembly Committee: Report on the Proprietors' Answer," 11 September 1753.

112. But cf. this observation on the workings of legislatures in a letter of 26 July 1784 to Benjamin Vaughan: "It is wonderful how preposterously the Affairs of this World are managed. Naturally one would imagine that the Interest of a few Particulars, should give way to general Interest. But Particulars manage their Affairs with so much more Application, Industry and Address, than the Publick do theirs, that general Interest most commonly gives way to particular."

113. Farrand, *Records,* 1:488; cf. 522–23.

114. Ibid., 2:642.

115. Ibid., 2:643.

116. "Observations Concerning the Increase of Mankind," 1755.

117. Franklin to James Parker, 20 March 1751.

118. Franklin to Peter Collinson, 9 May 1753.

119. "On the Need for an Academy," *Pennsylvania Gazette,* 24 August 1749.

120. Franklin to Peter Collinson [1753?]; cf. "Pennsylvania Assembly Committee: Report on Laws," 15 February 1754.

121. "On a Proposed Act to Prevent Emigration," [December?] 1773. For discussion of the forged document purporting to show Franklin's opposition to the immigration of Jews to America, see Edward Samuel Corwin, "Franklin and the Constitution," 286–87.

122. Franklin to John Waring, 17 December 1763.

123. Franklin to James Parker, 20 March 1751; to Peter Collinson, 9 May 1753; "Narrative of the Late Massacre in Lancaster County," [30 January?] 1764; "Remarks Concerning the Savages of North-America," 1784.

124. "Narrative of the Late Massacre in Lancaster County."

125. "Remarks Concerning the Savages of North-America."

126. See, e.g., "Mutiny Act" [15 April 1756]; "Petition to the King in Council [2 February 1759]; Franklin to Jonathan Shipley, 7 July 1775; The American Commissioners to Lord North, 12 December 1777; *Autobiography,* 198–99.

127. Franklin to Abiah Franklin, 12 April 1750. For a good account of Franklin's evolving activities in support of abolition and Negro education, see John C. Van Horne, "Collective Benevolence and the Common Good in Franklin's Philanthropy," in J. A. Leo Lemay, ed., *Reappraising Benjamin Franklin* (Newark: University of Delaware Press, 1993), 433–37. For a darker appraisal, which stresses and I believe seriously exaggerates the dependence of free America on unfree labor, see David Waldstreicher, *Runaway America: Benjamin Franklin, Slavery, and the American Revolution* (New York: Hill and Wang, 2004), esp. xii, 24–26, 181, 202, 218, 229–31. Waldstreicher treats Franklin's

leadership in the abolitionist movement as a self-serving maneuver to align himself with right-thinking opinion, without, however, acknowledging how unpopular this position was among the American political leadership at the close of the eighteenth century.

128. "Observations Concerning the Increase of Mankind," 1755.

129. "A Conversation on Slavery," 26 January 1770. Although in "Observations Concerning the Increase of Mankind" Franklin also blamed the slaves themselves for having "by nature" a thieving disposition, in a 1769 reprint he changed this to the claim that slaves steal "from the nature of slavery" (reprinted in the 1769 London edition of Franklin's *Experiments and Observations On Electricity;* quote is from 200).

130. "The Sommersett Case and the Slave Trade," 18–20 June 1772; cf. Franklin to Anthony Benezet, 22 August 1772.

131. "Information to Those Who Would Remove to America" [1782], *The Writings of Benjamin Franklin,* ed. Albert Henry Smyth, 10 vols. (New York: Macmillan, 1907), 8:606.

132. "Sidi Mehemet Ibrahim on the Slave Trade," 23 March 1790.

133. "An Address to the Public," 9 November 1789, *Writings* (Lemay), 1154–55.

Chapter 5 The Ultimate Questions

1. Franklin to Mary Stevenson, 14 September 1767.

2. Franklin to Joseph Priestley, 7 June 1782; cf. Franklin to Jane Mecom, 30 December 1770; to Joseph Priestley, 8 February 1780.

3. Franklin to Sarah Franklin, 8 November 1764; to Mary Stevenson, 2 September 1769. To this extent Franklin's view resembles that of sophisticated citizens of Antonine Rome, where, according to Edward Gibbon, "The various modes of worship which prevailed . . . were all considered by the people as equally true, by the philosophers as equally false, and by the magistrates as equally useful": *Decline and Fall of the Roman Empire* (Hertfordshire, England: Wordsworth Editions, 2001), 27. Moving forward in time, were Franklin to encounter a twenty-first-century reader's puzzlement over his now-unfamiliar use of the word "enthusiasm" to denote the excessive religious fervor that his rational century so disdained, he would no doubt regale his reader with the story of the clergyman of his day who was praised at his funeral for having "preached in this parish for forty-seven years without a single trace of enthusiasm" (source unknown).

4. *Poor Richard Improved,* 1748, in Benjamin Franklin, *Writings,* ed. J. A. Leo Lemay (New York: Library of America, 1987), 1246.

5. Franklin to John Franklin, [May?] 1745; to Deborah Franklin, 17 July 1757.

6. "A Dialogue Between Two Presbyterians," 10 April 1735.

7. Franklin to Josiah and Abiah Franklin, 13 April 1738; cf. John Locke, *A Letter Concerning Toleration,* trans. William Popple (Indianapolis: Bobbs-Merrill, 1955), 18: "For no man can, if he would, conform his faith to the dictates of another."

8. Franklin, *Autobiography,* 115.

9. Ibid., 146. We may wonder whether Franklin's characterization really fits all religions and even whether it is seriously intended to, but he never restricts it.

10. Letter to the *Pennsylvania Gazette,* 27 April 1730, *Writings* (Lemay), 149.

11. "Letter of the Drum," 23 April 1730, *Writings* (Lemay), 145–48.

12. Franklin to an unidentified correspondent [13 December 1757]; cf. Franklin to Cadwallader Colden, 14 May 1752; *Autobiography,* 74.

13. George Washington, "Farewell Address," in *The Writings of George Washington from the Original Manuscript Sources,* John C. Fitzpatrick, ed., 39 vols. (Washington, D.C.: Government Printing Office, 1931–40), 35:229.

14. *Autobiography,* 175. Noting Franklin's warmth towards such evangelists as Whitefield and Hemphill, and failing to distinguish the moral grounds on which he supported them from the theological grounds on which he never did, Melvin Buxbaum claims that Franklin fell altogether under their influence: *Benjamin Franklin and the Zealous Presbyterians* (University Park: Pennsylvania State University Press, 1975).

15. *Autobiography,* 177.

16. Ibid., 180.

17. *Poor Richard,* 1743, in *Writings* (Lemay), 1228 and 1230; *Autobiography,* 58, 60.

18. *Poor Richard Improved,* 1753, in *Writings* (Lemay), 1278.

19. "Articles of Belief Acts of Religion," 20 November 1728.

20. "A Defence of Mr. Hemphill's Observations," 1735.

21. "A Parable on Brotherly Love," 1755.

22. For an explicit statement of this certainty, see "A Defence of Mr. Hemphill's Observations," 1735, where Franklin argues that this doctrine of original sin and hopeless depravity without God's grace is an absurd notion meant "to fright and scare an unthinking Populace out of their Senses, and inspire them with Terror, to answer the little selfish Ends of the Inventors and Propagators." If anyone should argue that certain passages in scripture teach such a doctrine, he continues, "I would ingeniously confess I did not understand them, sooner than

admit of a Sense contrary to Reason and to the Nature and Perfections of the Almighty God."

23. "A Parable Against Persecution," 1755.

24. Franklin to Madame Brillon [before 20 April 1781].

25. *Autobiography,* 146.

26. "Toleration in Old and New England," 3 June 1772; cf. Locke, *A Letter Concerning Toleration.* As Perry Miller says of the Puritans who established the early settlements in Massachusetts Bay, "They did not want even toleration, let alone liberty: they intended to rule": "Benjamin Franklin–Jonathan Edwards," in Miller, ed., *Major Writers of America,* 2 vols. (New York: Harcourt, Brace, and World, 1962), 84.

27. *Autobiography,* 180.

28. Ibid., 191.

29. Indeed, Franklin was a proponent of bold experimentation in religion, as in everything else. Madison reports that late in life Franklin confided to him "that he should be glad to see an experiment made of a religion that admitted of no pardon for transgressions; the hope of impunity being the great encouragement to them": James Madison, "Detached Memoranda," *William and Mary Quarterly,* 3rd ser., 3 (1946): 538.

30. In understanding Franklin's strategic use of terminology I am indebted to Steven Forde, "Benjamin Franklin's 'Machiavellian' Civic Virtue," in Paul A. Rahe, ed., *Machiavelli's Liberal Republican Legacy* (Cambridge: Cambridge University Press, 2005), 159–60.

31. "Toleration in Old and New England," 3 June 1772.

32. Franklin engages in the same redefinition of religion in "A Defence of Mr. Hemphill's Observations," 1735.

33. Franklin to Richard Price, 9 October 1780.

34. For Franklin's efforts to assist this process of making religion more user-friendly, see his preface to a revised prayer book he helped prepare (*Writings of Benjamin Franklin,* ed. Albert Henry Smyth, 10 vols. [New York: Macmillan, 1907], 6:165–71) and "A New Version of the Lord's Prayer," 1768; see also the discussion of these in Alfred Owen Aldridge, *Benjamin Franklin and Nature's God* (Durham: Duke University Press, 1967), 170–79.

35. "Information for Those Who Would Remove to America" [1782], *Writings of Benjamin Franklin* (Smyth) 8:613–14. On the connection between religious toleration and peace, see also Franklin to Louis-Guillaume Le Veillard, 8 June 1788.

36. Franklin to John Calder, 21 August 1784.

37. *Autobiography,* 146. Statements like these, together with Franklin's general reticence on theological questions and the lively imagina-

tions of early biographers, have produced one strand of scholarship that paints Franklin as a perfectly pious Christian, beginning with Mason Locke Weems, *The Life of Benjamin Franklin* (Hagerstown, Md.: printed by the author, 1818), followed by James Parton, *The Life and Times of Benjamin Franklin,* 2 vols. (Boston: Houghton, Mifflin, 1892), and continued into the twentieth century by James M. Stifler, *The Religion of Benjamin Franklin* (New York: D. Appleton, 1925), and Albert Hyma, *The Religious Views of Benjamin Franklin* (Ann Arbor: George Wahr Publishing, 1958). Although this view has been superseded, its influence may still be seen in Kerry Walters' interpretation in *Benjamin Franklin and His Gods* (Urbana: University of Illinois Press, 1999), 11: "Franklin's religious beliefs continued until his death to waver between Calvinist and enlightenment allegiances."

38. Jerry Weinberger notes the contradiction in *Benjamin Franklin Unmasked: On the Unity of His Moral, Religious, and Political Thought* (Lawrence: University Press of Kansas, 2005), 49.

39. *Autobiography,* 114; "On the Providence of God in the Government of the World" [1732].

40. Franklin to Ezra Stiles, 9 March 1790.

41. John Adams, *The Adams Papers, Series I: Diaries,* ed. L. H. Butterfield, 4 vols. (Cambridge: Harvard University Press, 1961), 2:391; cf. 4:69; the Abbé Flamarens in a letter of 15 January 1777, quoted in Alfred Owen Aldridge, *Franklin and His French Contemporaries* (New York: New York University Press, 1957), 61. But while the atheists believed Franklin was one of them, so did many Catholics, Anglicans, Presbyterians, and even Quakers: see John Adams, "Extract from the Boston Patriot," 15 May 1811, in *The Life and Works of John Adams,* ed. Charles Francis Adams, 10 vols. (Boston: Little, Brown, 1856), 1:66; cf. Franklin, *Autobiography,* 194.

42. "Articles of Belief and Acts of Religion," 20 November 1728; cf. Franklin to John Huey, 6 June 1753.

43. *Autobiography,* 193.

44. "Articles of Belief and Acts of Religion, 20 November 1728.

45. This is the interpretation of Elizabeth E. Dunn, "From a Bold Youth to a Reflective Sage: A Revaluation of Benjamin Franklin's Religion," *Pennsylvania Magazine of History and Biography* 111 (1987): 501–24. Alfred Owen Aldridge, in contrast, takes the polytheistic premise of the "Articles of Belief" perfectly literally and argues that this remained an important strain in Franklin's thought: *Benjamin Franklin and Nature's God,* 29–33. Important passages cited by Aldridge are Franklin to Henry Bouquet, 14 April 1757; to Pierre Samuel du Pont de Nemours, 28 July 1768; to Joseph Priestley, 7 June 1782; to Abbé

Soulavie, 22 September 1782; to Sir Joseph Banks, 21 November 1783. Kerry Walters argues persuasively that most of these passages are playful in tone and show instead a tolerant agnosticism about the nature of the divine. Walters understands the polytheism of the "Articles of Belief" as Franklin's metaphor for the various historical human attempts to imagine and personify a divinity that is in fact one, impersonal, and unknowable: *Benjamin Franklin and His Gods,* 79–81 and 86.

46. "On the Providence of God in the Government of the World" [1732].

47. On this turn, see Franklin to [Thomas Hopkinson ?], 16 October 1746; to Benjamin Vaughan, 9 November 1779.

48. Franklin to Joseph Huey, 6 June 1753.

49. Franklin to Jane Mecom, 17 July 1771.

50. Franklin to George Whitefield [before 2 September 1769]; cf. Franklin to Jean-Baptiste Le Roy, 18 April 1787, where he questions the wisdom of providence but not providence itself; a similar suggestion is made in a letter to Caleb Whitefoord of 19 May 1785.

51. Franklin to James Hutton, 7 July 1782.

52. Franklin to William Strahan, 19 August 1784.

53. Franklin to George Whateley, 23 May 1785; cf. Franklin to Jan Ingenhousz, 28 August 1785. For a contemporaneous expression of doubt on this question, see Franklin to George Washington [1786?] *The Writings of Benjamin Franklin* (Smyth), 9:41.

54. Speech on Prayer, 28 June 1787, Max Farrand, *The Records of the Federal Convention of 1787,* 4 vols. (New Haven: Yale University Press, 1966), 1:451. Philip Dray interprets this speech as a sign of a return to piety, in *Stealing God's Thunder: Benjamin Franklin's Lightning Rod and the Invention of America* (New York: Random House, 2005), 194. But Walter Berns understands the call for prayer as no more than a plea that the delegates "recognize their fallibility": *The Writing of the Constitution of the United States* (Washington, D.C.: AEI, 1985), 33; and Thomas Pangle notes the irony that what Franklin says he especially fears, should the convention end in failure, is that "Mankind may hereafter . . . despair of establishing Government by *human* Wisdom, and leave it to Chance, War and Conquest": Pangle, *The Spirit of Modern Republicanism: The Moral Vision of the American Founders and the Philosophy of Locke* (Chicago: University of Chicago Press, 1988), 80.

55. According to the uncorroborated but plausible recollections of a contemporary, in 1774 "Franklin, with some emotion, declared he never passed a Church, during Public Service, without regretting that he could not join in it honestly and cordially. He thought it a reproach to Philosophy that it had not a Liturgy and that it skulked from the pub-

lic Profession of its Principles": "Extracts from David Williams's *Autobiography,*" reprinted in David Williams, "More Light on Franklin's Religious Ideas," *American Historical Review* 43 (1938): 810. If genuine, this comment is as revealing about Franklin's view of philosophy as it is about his stance towards religion. On the other side, consider the writing that is probably Franklin's most blasphemous, an allegory based on the Book of Job in which God's part is played by a king surrounded by flattering courtiers and the moral is that even "the best of all possible princes" will be a tyrant if his power is unlimited: "The Levée" [1779], *Writings* (Lemay) 933–35. But "The Levée" is uncharacteristic in casting doubt on the goodness of a providential god.

56. Franklin to Ezra Stiles, 9 March 1790.

57. "Franklin, the Most French of Americans," in Wilbur R. Jacobs, ed., *Benjamin Franklin: Statesman-Philosopher or Materialist?* (New York: Holt, Reinhart and Winston, 1972), 64–65. Cf. Charles Angoff's judgment: "Thrift, industry, and determination were essential virtues in the building of a nation, but they were not, then or at any other time in history, of sufficient human dignity to build a life philosophy on. . . . The vulgarity he spread is still with us": *A Literary History of the American People* (New York: Alfred A. Knopf, 1931), 2:210.

58. Lawrence's two essays on Franklin, both entitled "Benjamin Franklin," were first published in the *English Review* 27 (1918): 397–408, and in D. H. Lawrence, *Studies in Classic American Literature* (1923; New York: Viking Press, 1961), 9–21; both are reprinted in Melvin H. Buxbaum, ed., *Critical Essays on Benjamin Franklin* (Boston: G. K. Hall, 1987), 41–60; passages quoted are from 48, 44, and 58.

59. "Benjamin Franklin" (1923), 56. The imaginative variety of interpretations of Franklin's religious thought is nowhere more strikingly displayed than in Kerry Walters' *Benjamin Franklin and His Gods,* whose central thesis is that Franklin *agrees* with this credo and yearns for contact with the divine just as Augustine and Pascal do: see esp. 9–12, and 76.

60. "Benjamin Franklin" (1923), 58.

61. Claude-Anne Lopez, *Mon Cher Papa: Franklin and the Ladies of Paris* (New Haven: Yale University Press, 1990), 19–20.

62. "Parody and Reply to a Religious Meditation," *Pennsylvania Gazette,* 8 August 1734, *Writings* (Lemay), 230–33. This parody is reminiscent of Epicurean rebukes to those who would wish to live forever as gluttons who cannot bear to leave the table when the feast is over: See Lucretius, *On the Nature of Things,* 3.931–77.

63. Franklin to Thomas Bond, 16 March 1780.

64. *Autobiography*, 107.

65. Quoted in John Epps, *Life of John Walker, M.D.* (London: Whittaker, Treacher, 1831), 143–44.

66. William Carlos Williams argues that behind all Franklin's busy practicality ultimately lay fear: "His fingers itched to be meddling, to do the little concrete thing—the barrier against a flood of lightning that would inundate him. Of course he was the most useful, 'the most industrious citizen that Philadelphia or America had ever known.' He was the dyke keeper, keeping out the wilderness with his wits. Fear drove his curiosity": "Franklin and the Rejection of the American Wilderness," in Jacobs, ed., *Benjamin Franklin*, 86–87.

67. Lawrence, "Benjamin Franklin" (1923), 54–55; on the seriousness of Lawrence's quarrel with Franklin see also Ormond Seavey, "Benjamin Franklin and D. H. Lawrence as Conflicting Modes of Consciousness," in Melvin H. Buxbaum, ed., *Critical Essays on Benjamin Franklin* (Boston: G. K. Hall, 1987), 72 and 79 n. 1.

68. I am indebted to Seavey, ibid., and to Ralph Lerner, *The Thinking Revolutionary: Principle and Practice in the New Republic* (Ithaca: Cornell University Press, 1987), 58–59, for demonstrating the centrality to Franklin's whole project of this effort to reorient our way of seeing the world.

69. *Autobiography*, 243–44.

RECOMMENDED READINGS

Conner, Paul W. *Poor Richard's Politicks: Franklin and His New American Order.* New York: Oxford University Press, 1965.

Forde, Steven R. "Benjamin Franklin's *Autobiography* and the Education of America." *American Political Science Review* 86, no. 2 (1992): 357–68.

Franklin, Benjamin. *The Autobiography of Benjamin Franklin.* Edited by Leonard Labaree. New Haven: Yale University Press, 1964.

Franklin, Benjamin. *Writings.* Edited by J. A. Leo Lemay. New York: Library of America, 1987.

Greene, Jack P. "Pride, Prejudice, and Jealousy: Benjamin Franklin's Explanation for the American Revolution." In J. A. Leo Lemay, ed., *Reappraising Benjamin Franklin.* Newark: University of Delaware Press, 1993, 119–42.

Isaacson, Walter. *Benjamin Franklin: An American Life.* New York: Simon and Schuster, 2003.

Lawrence, D. H. "Benjamin Franklin." *English Review* 27 (1918): 397–408.

Lerner, Ralph. "Dr. Janus." In J. A. Leo Lemay, ed., *Reappraising Benjamin Franklin.* Newark: University of Delaware Press, 1993.

Levin, David. "Franklin: Experimenter in Life and Art." In Wilbur R. Jacobs, ed., *Benjamin Franklin: Statesman-Philosopher or Materialist?* New York: Holt, Reinhart and Winston, 1972, 51–62.

McCoy, Drew. "Benjamin Franklin's Vision of a Republican Political Economy for America." *William and Mary Quarterly,* 3rd ser., 35 (1978): 605–28.

Morgan, Edmund S. *Benjamin Franklin.* New Haven: Yale University Press, 2002.

Seavey, Ormond. "Benjamin Franklin and D. H. Lawrence as Conflicting Modes of Consciousness." In Melvin H. Buxbaum, ed., *Critical Essays on Benjamin Franklin.* Boston: G. K. Hall and Co., 1987.

Stourzh, Gerald. *Benjamin Franklin and American Foreign Policy,* 2nd ed. Chicago: University of Chicago Press, 1969.

INDEX